Additional Praise for *Police Heroes*

"Chuck Whitlock has done an excellent job of chronicling the extraordinary service in his book."

—Craig W. Floyd, chairman,
National Law Enforcement Officers Memorial Fund

"The very best of police officers are all heroes—they just don't know it. *Police Heroes* reflects some of the very best."

—Sgt. Amy Ramsay, executive director,
International Association of Women Police

"To a person, the men and women honored in *Police Heroes* would say that their actions weren't heroic but that they were just doing their jobs. These people are everyday heroes. That's the essence of being a police officer—going to work and facing the unknown requires courage every single day."

—Bill Johnson, executive director,
National Association of Police Organizations, Inc.

"Whitlock offers vivid descriptive details."

—*Publishers Weekly*

ALSO BY CHUCK WHITLOCK

★

MediScams

Chuck Whitlock's Scam School

Easy Money

Secrets of Successful Selling

How to Get Rich

Business Management Basics

Chuck Whitlock

★

TRUE STORIES OF COURAGE

POLICE

HEROES

ABOUT AMERICA'S BRAVE MEN,
WOMEN, AND K-9 OFFICERS

★

THOMAS DUNNE BOOKS
St. Martin's Griffin New York

THOMAS DUNNE BOOKS.
An imprint of St. Martin's Press.

www.stmartins.com

Design by Kathryn Parise

The author is grateful to Ronald Shiftan for permission to use his comments about the impact on the Port Authority of New York and New Jersey of the terrorist attack on the World Trade Center.

Credits for the photographs appear on page 251 and constitute a continuation of this copyright page.

Library of Congress Cataloging-in-Publication Data

Whitlock, Charles R.
    Police heroes : true stories of courage about America's brave men, women, and K-9 officers / Chuck Whitlock.—1st ed.
        p. cm.
    Includes bibliographical references (p. 243) and index (p. 255).
    ISBN 0-312-28800-X (hc)
    ISBN 0-312-33097-9 (pbk)
    EAN 978-0312-33097-2
    1. Police—United States. I. Title.

HV7914 .W6113 2002
363.2'092'273—dc21   2002069303

First St. Martin's Griffin Edition: June 2004

10 9 8 7 6 5 4 3 2 1

POLICE HEROES *is dedicated to the heroic law enforcement officers killed at the World Trade Center on September 11, 2001, and to their law enforcement brothers and sisters throughout the United States who display their courage every day.*

✷ Contents ✷

★ Acknowledgments ★

Words cannot express my gratitude to the many fine people who helped make *Police Heroes* a reality.

I'd wanted to write a book about law enforcement heroes for quite some time and agreed to write this book for Thomas Dunne Books, an imprint of St. Martin's Press, in the spring of 2001. Following the terrorist attacks of September 11 and the tragic deaths that resulted, I feel an even greater sense of purpose and responsibility to honor our men and women in blue. As America watched, frightened people fled the crumbling buildings while our police heroes were running in to help rescue other victims. Along with their firefighter brothers, many officers perished after saving hundreds of lives. I am honored and privileged to add their names to the other police heroes featured in this book. Special thanks to Tom Dunne, my publisher, and Peter Wolverton, my editor at Thomas Dunne Books, for giving me extra time to add the police heroes from the World Trade Center disaster.

My deep appreciation goes to Lieutenant Richard T. Long of the Newport Beach Police Department for his expertise, experience, and fine contributions to the book. He has been a valued consultant in this project. A heartfelt thank-you to Gail Wayper for her hard work in helping to research, edit, and compile *Police Heroes*. No matter what the task, she seems to rise to the occasion. Glenna Brock jumped in to help pull together some loose ends as I was finalizing the manuscript; her research skills and stick-to-it nature were a great help. And Candace Whitlock has my admiration and respect for her untiring dedication in helping me produce the best manuscript possible. Peter Miller, my manager and literary agent at PMA, continues to be supportive by keeping the book projects coming at a manageable pace.

Most important, this book could not have been written without the support of public information officers, chiefs of police, sheriffs, and the heroic police officers and their friends, partners, and relatives who candidly shared their experiences, photos, and research materials.

Though my appreciation for the men, women, and K-9s in law enforcement has always been strong, my feelings of admiration have grown tremendously as a result of writing *Police Heroes*. To them I say: The career you've embraced is awe-inspiring; the responsibilities of the work are immense; and the impact you can have on the lives of those you serve is limitless. You're all heroes in my book.

★ Foreword ★

by Lieutenant Richard T. Long
Newport Beach (California) Police Department

On September 11, 2001, America was attacked, and everything in our country was forever changed. On that day, nineteen Al-Qaida terrorists flew three commercial jetliners into the World Trade Center in New York City and the Pentagon in Washington, D.C. United Airlines Flight 93 crashed into a field in Pennsylvania when its passengers decided to fight their hijackers. More than three thousand Americans were killed.

Clearly this was the worst day in the history of American public safety. Never before had so many peace officers and firefighters been lost. Each one of them, in their own way, was an American hero, and each one had a story that would probably not be told. All of a sudden people were reminded about those men and women who took up arms to stand the post, to be on guard. Americans filled the sidewalks and corners to cheer as local police and firefighters drove to and from Ground Zero. American flags waved and placards were held up showing words that expressed a reverence never seen before. Americans rediscovered what was important in America. What a difference this day made in America.

In the past, too many Americans have based their beliefs about law enforcement on what they've read in the newspapers or seen on their televisions. Stories concerning police misconduct or abuse may involve one officer, or even a few, but the stories carry an implication for almost eight hundred thousand law enforcement officers throughout the country. The old "one bad apple can ruin the barrel" adage becomes the police story personified.

Performance is what counts; action is what matters, and actions make the difference. Police officers by their very nature are bold and decisive individuals. They do things for people that people will not do for themselves. They go down dark alleys and through doors that have armed gunmen behind them. With every car stop and every radio call, they face peril. They willingly go in harm's way to serve their fellow citizens, and they do so under difficult and trying circumstances. On September 11, we could say of our nation's law enforcement officers what Sir Winston Churchill once said of the Royal Air Force in the Battle of Britain, "This was truly their finest hour." You'll read about some of these men and women in *Police Heroes*.

Police officers know only too well that the defense of freedom never really ends. In 1776 Thomas Jefferson wrote in our Declaration of Independence, "We hold these truths to be self-evident, that all men are created equal, that they are endowed by their Creator with certain unalienable Rights, that among these are Life, Liberty and the pursuit of Happiness." He set in stone what freedom in America would represent for all future generations. We have learned and relearned many times in our nation's history that freedom is not without price. And as with any indemnity, from time to time the premiums must be paid.

In his wartime address to the American people, President George W. Bush stated, "On September the eleventh, enemies of freedom committed an act of war against our country. . . . The advance of human freedom— the great achievement of our time, and the great hope of every time— now depends on us." He concluded by honoring all peace officers when he said, "Each of us will remember what happened that day, and to whom it happened. We'll remember the moment the news came—where we were and what we were doing. Some will remember an image of a fire, or a story of rescue. Some will carry memories of a face and a voice gone forever. And I will carry this: It is the police shield of a man named George Howard, who died at the World Trade Center trying to save others. It was given to me by his mom, Arlene, as a proud memorial to her son. This is my reminder of lives that ended, and a task that does not end."

This book is about the never-ending task of protecting and serving the citizens of our country. You'll find stories that chronicle our American police service. That service isn't just good—it is truly beyond measure when compared with anything anywhere else in the world. People truly fear their authorities in many places in the world, places where arrests and searches are made without probable cause or without warrant, places where due process does not exist and the ability to challenge or sue the authorities is prohibited. In these places there is no such thing as bail, and people have a word for those who are arrested and never heard from again: they are known as the "disappeared."

In America we have rights, and due process, and the freedom to feel and speak as we choose. We have professional lawyers and judges, along with competent courts and juries that help keep the government and the police in check. We also have these precious freedoms because we have professional law enforcement officers who are willing to make the ultimate sacrifice to protect our rights and freedoms. Measure that against the Third World's brand of law enforcement. Certainly some of our officers have made mistakes or acted in excess. But still, the average American's worst fear about their local police is of suddenly seeing an officer in the rearview mirror and being afraid of getting a speeding ticket.

Police Heroes is about police officers and their great deeds. President Theodore Roosevelt, who also was a former New York City Police Commissioner, said it best when he wrote, "It is not the critic who counts; not the man who points out how the strong man stumbled, or where a doer of deeds could have done them better. The credit belongs to the man who is actually in the arena; whose face is marred by dust and sweat and blood; who strives valiantly; who errs and comes short again and again; who knows the great enthusiasms, the great devotions, and spends himself in a worthy cause; who, at the best, knows in the end the triumph of high achievement; and who, at the worst, if he fails, at least fails while daring greatly, so that his place shall never be with those cold and timid souls who know neither victory nor defeat."

Police Heroes wasn't written because of what happened on September 11. In fact, the author began this project more than two years ago with one simple intention: He wanted to honor the men and women of American law enforcement. Chuck Whitlock is a well-published and accomplished investigative author and television producer, but this was his first foray into writing about police officers. He and his staff researched hundreds of cases involving true heroism by the police. Unfortunately, many never made it into this book because of space limitations. There were simply too many stories for all to be included. The research confirmed that acts of heroism and extraordinary performance by individual officers are so frequent and widespread throughout our country that they almost have become routine. Taken together, these stories affirmed that uncommon valor is very common among our nation's law enforcement officers.

Included in these pages are individual tales of actions above and beyond the call of duty. But these personal accounts actually represent the everyday work of many who would otherwise remain uncelebrated.

Few of the officers involved in these accounts acted completely alone.

Untold and unheralded partners and support personnel helped the officers as if they were on-scene for the call. Remember the dispatchers who
took and broadcast the calls, helping to coordinate the response through
their professional communication centers. Don't forget the records
clerks, or the desk officers, or the jailers, who all take pride in their part at
providing professional law enforcement services for their communities
and beyond. These are their stories too. When a request for information is
made, if the records staff is simply one digit off in their review of criminal
information databases, it could lead to disaster for the officers in the field.
The need for attention to detail includes the support personnel just as
much as the officer on the beat.

In closing, the stories you are about to read involve America's true
heroes. They are stories of law enforcement doing the very best to ensure
the safety of their communities, of officers throughout the United States
rising to the defense of liberty. This book is about those who wear the
shield and carry the sword to protect and serve their country.

Police Heroes honors and celebrates members of the law enforcement community who have distinguished themselves and their departments by acting in a courageous manner under extraordinary circumstances. I hope this book will inspire others to a greater appreciation for the law enforcement community and the awe-inspiring jobs that they do every day.

In mythology, a hero was a man often of divine ancestry who was endowed with great courage and strength. His bold exploits were celebrated, and he was considered a favorite of the gods. Today, the word *hero* is generally used to describe someone who is courageous and may risk or sacrifice his or her life for an unselfish, noble purpose.

No one really knows how he or she will react until personally faced with danger. Would someone who places a greater value on his own life than on someone else's be considered a coward? Given a set of circumstances, a person may weigh the odds and consciously pass on the opportunity to be a hero. Try to imagine that you are the first passenger off a jetliner that just crashed. Fire has swept over the plane. Knowing that the plane is likely to explode, would you stay to help other passengers, or would you run for your life? Whichever choice you make, someone who's not in your shoes at that precise moment shouldn't Monday-morning-quarterback your decision.

A hero to one person may not be considered a hero by someone else. Is a person such as Mother Teresa who devotes her life to care for others a hero? Is Mahatma Gandhi a hero for winning his country's freedom from the British through peaceful resistance? The label *hero* isn't always confined to individuals who are larger than life. How about the single mom who gets up every day and cares for her children, holds down a full-time job, and single-handedly deals with her family's stresses? Isn't she a hero too?

What makes a police officer a hero? Most police officers recognized for their heroism would say that they were simply doing their jobs. These are people just like you and me who fear pain, injury, and death. In many cases, they are ordinary people who did extraordinary acts for selfless reasons, who imagined themselves in the victims' circumstances and responded courageously, even if it meant jeopardizing their own safety and life. They are also well-trained professionals who get caught up in unfolding life-or-death situations and must react quickly on a gut level. These are people on the job who must worry every day about making the right decision in a split second. Police officers dread the thought of killing someone but know that there's a chance they may have to one day. In every incident of heroism, all had their own reasons for acting as they did, but make no mistake, these are not accidental heroes. A law enforcement officer takes an oath to uphold the laws of the land and protect and serve its citizens.

In its broadest sense, the term *police* includes approximately 740,000 sworn law enforcement officers in about eighteen thousand separate police agencies. Dedicated, honest, hard-working police officers are everywhere. The federal government alone has almost sixty police agencies, including the Drug Enforcement Administration (DEA), Federal Bureau of Investigation (FBI), Bureau of Alcohol, Tobacco and Firearms (ATF), Immigration and Naturalization Service (INS), U.S. Postal Inspectors, U.S. Marshals, and Secret Service. Then there are state agencies, such as the state police or highway patrol. County law enforcement includes about thirty-one hundred sheriffs. The fifteen thousand–plus municipal police departments include some as large as New York City's, with about forty thousand regular officers as well as some that have ten or fewer officers. The agencies employ a total of over 850,000 people and have an annual budget of nearly $3 billion.

Many would argue that *every* police officer is a hero. These individuals get up every day, put on their badges and weapons, and place themselves in harm's way. Their families don't know if they are saying good-bye for one shift or forever. These men and women go to work every day never knowing exactly what to expect. Will they save someone's life that day? Will they be faced with a life-threatening experience? Will a simple speeding ticket turn into a high-speed chase or gun battle?

Because I believe that most police officers are indeed heroes, I want to honor all the men and women who choose law enforcement careers. I chose to do that by celebrating the heroism of a handful of their brethren. There are many stories of extreme heroism by police officers throughout the United States. Often these individuals acted with little regard for their own safety. Many have sacrificed their health and well-being; some have even paid the ultimate price by giving their lives. But they are not and will not be forgotten.

Over 62,200 officers are assaulted each year with an average of over twenty-one thousand injuries annually, according to the FBI. Since the first officer was killed in 1792, over fifteen thousand have been killed in the line of duty. According to the National Law Enforcement Officers Memorial Fund, on average, one police officer died every fifty-seven hours during the last ten years; that's approximately 156 deaths per year. But being a police officer is not only one of the most dangerous jobs in America, it's also often thankless. In our day-to-day lives, our personal contact with police officers is probably limited to a traffic stop or parking ticket. Most of us don't consider that a police officer may have saved a life by issuing a ticket to a drunken motorist or responding to a home burglar alarm system.

To all the police officers featured in *Police Heroes,* I hope that I've done justice to your stories of personal courage and your inner strength. It was nearly impossible to select the individuals featured from the many stories submitted to me by law enforcement agencies all over the country, but I decided to focus primarily on the county and municipal officers whom most Americans know because they see them regularly in their communities. Then tragedy struck the heart of Americans everywhere.

Certainly no one can forget the many heroes of September 11, 2001. Until the terrorists struck the World Trade Center that morning, the deadliest day in law enforcement history in the United States had been November 24, 1917, when nine Milwaukee, Wisconsin, police officers were killed in a bomb blast at the Milwaukee South Station, while a tenth officer from the Columbus (Ohio) Police Department was shot and killed. To help put that number in perspective, there were 150 police deaths in 2000, a 12 percent increase from the 137 officers who died in 1999, according to the National Law Enforcement Officers Memorial Fund.

Even before September 11, New York City had lost more officers in the line of duty than any other department in the country. But on that bleak Tuesday at the World Trade Center, twenty-three NYPD officers, thirty-seven Port Authority officers and one K-9 officer, and three Manhattan court officers gave their lives. In addition, the FBI lost one agent, as did the Secret Service. We honor their memories in *Police Heroes*.

To the thousands of officers from every agency not included in this book, I sincerely apologize. There are so many heroes who enthusiastically do their jobs every day that I wish I could honor each and every one of you. If your story of heroism wasn't included, please know that it was due to the space limitations that such a book imposes. My heartfelt thanks go to our many unsung police officers—like everyday hero Sergeant Bruce A. Prothero of the Baltimore County Police Department in Maryland.

A father of five, Sergeant Prothero supplemented his income as a policeman by working part-time in a jewelry store as a plainclothes detective. His wife, Ann, was supportive but worried about the risks he faced on both his jobs. When four gunmen walked into the jewelry store, which was full of customers and employees, Prothero complied with their demands and watched as the thieves scooped up handfuls of watches and rings. After they left the store, Prothero followed the armed robbers to the parking lot in hopes of getting a license plate number and a description of their vehicle, just as he had done the last time the store was robbed. This time, Prothero was gunned down and left to die in the parking lot. He was pronounced dead on arrival at the hospital. He was only thirty-five years old. His death left a huge void not only in his immediate family but also in his police family and the community at large. He will never be forgotten. His is one of many stories of men and women in law enforcement whose lives were filled with love and a sense of purpose.

In *Police Heroes,* you will be privileged to meet a small handful of police heroes who took their oath seriously and, when confronted with life-threatening circumstances, acted courageously. These are often men and women who have been honored by their departments for their valor. You'll meet two officers serving a search warrant who wound up rescuing a methamphetamine maker from a fire he himself set to destroy evidence of his drug-making activities. You'll read about a patrol officer who, after discovering a house fire early one morning, rescued its inhabitants before the fire department could arrive. Imagine the courage required by one state trooper who single-handedly brought five armed robbers to justice in Alaska's wilderness. One stalwart officer shielded a homeless man with his body from an angry armed mob as his partner helped fend off the attackers. You'll read about some of the bravest officers from California, a state that has lost some thirteen hundred officers, more than any other state. As you read these stories, please keep in mind the hundreds of stories just as dramatic, just as heroic, that play out in cities across our nation each and every day.

On behalf of those of us who do not work in law enforcement, I want to say thank you to each of you for making America a safer place to live, raise our families, and enjoy the liberties our forefathers envisioned for us.

POLICE

HEROES

OFFICER JOHN GRUBENSKY

Oakland (California) Police Department

"Guardian Angel"

"He was my best friend, and he was my partner," said Officer Bariwynn "Barry" Howard. Officer John Grubensky and Officer Howard worked in District 3 in the city of Oakland, California, and as a team they were tight. Looking back, what happened to Officer Grubensky might have been predicted because, as his partner Howard put it, "John had a habit of overworking his guardian angel."

John Grubensky and Barry Howard worked the third watch, covering the evening hours, patrolling the 23rd Avenue corridor of Oakland. They were busy every night. "You've got to understand," Howard said, "that we were in a high narcotics area, and the drug sales would be made right in front of our police car." Officer Grubensky had a knack for making drug arrests. He was aggressive, but not in the tough cop way one might imagine. "To him it was more like a game, more like fishing than police work," said Howard. "We would detain a suspect, knowing their dope wasn't actually on them, and Grubensky would try to figure out where they had it hidden. He'd keep working, and working, and then he'd find it while the dealer was watching. It was like fishing to him, and he was real good at it."

As officers working their beat, Grubensky and Howard knew these dealers well because they'd arrested a lot of them. Officer Howard explained, "Sometimes I had to help him, sometimes he'd help me, but I'm talking about pushing his real guardian angel, because he had no officer safety sense. He really pushed the limits. I think he believed he'd survive whatever hit him."

Howard said that Grubensky developed this sense of confidence relative to his safety with these criminals because he always treated them with respect. He was honest and direct in his reports—even the drug dealers knew he was a fair guy. They treated him with respect too, even though he and Howard were arresting dealers nearly every night they worked. Since he had good relations with the dealers in his district, Grubensky told his partner that if he ever got into a fight, he honestly felt the dealers would come to his aid. Howard said, "I mean it was easy making a felony arrest, because the dealers were all over the place. But imagine, a dealer helping an officer in a fight? I always thought John was crazy for thinking this, but he did. That was him pushing that guardian angel again."

In one instance, Officer Grubensky was pursuing a vehicle when the car abruptly stopped in front of a house and the four armed suspects bailed out of the car and ran inside. Knowing they were armed, and that he was alone, as backup units were still en route, Grubensky still ran up to the house to try to capture the gunmen. The suspects escaped out the back of the house, and fortunately, Grubensky wasn't hurt, but he clearly exposed himself to potential gunfire. For Howard, this was Grubensky pushing that guardian angel too far. "I told him," Howard said, " 'You're going too far! Those guys are going to shoot you.' Well, John didn't hear me, or he didn't believe me, because he never slowed down. He was always pushing things to their limits."

Some described John Grubensky as a perfectionist. He was a hardworking officer. He could be critical in some ways, but he was also very generous to his friends. Howard said, "We got off work late every night and went to breakfast. We talked about everything, and I mean everything—he was my best buddy. We socialized with our families and we were very close. We bonded because we shared the same values. I never worried about his professional ethics. I'd trust John with my life, and I trusted him with my family. I miss him very much. Very much."

Grubensky wasn't with Howard when he died during the terrible fire that started in North Oakland Hills. Grubensky was working overtime on a day when he normally would have been off and at home. Had they been together, maybe John could have survived, or at least maybe Barry could have kept him away from the street that exploded into flames. But truth is, had they been together that day, they would probably both have perished. As partners, they most certainly would have died together, because no one could have survived. The fire was simply too swift, too destructive.

On the morning of the fire, Grubensky noticed the smoke coming from the hills above downtown Oakland. The weather was warm and there were unusually high winds. When the fire took off around 10:30 A.M., it didn't take long for the flames to race through the area. This wasn't the first time a fire had gutted this section of the East Bay. Nor was it the second. Sadly, it was the third time, but it was as though no one had learned the lessons of their own local history.

Oakland, California, sits across the bay from San Francisco. The city grew from a small population in the 1860s to about thirty-four thousand by 1886. A developer had an idea to grow eucalyptus trees to be used for railroad ties and furniture. That was a bust, because eucalyptus wood is too hard and warps too easily to be used for either purpose. But the trees grew fast on the hillsides, eventually starting to choke out the native oaks. Development continued at a fever pitch, and by the turn of the century, beautiful Queen Anne–style cottages covered the hills.

By 1920, the Oakland hillsides were fully developed. There had been a building boom in the East Bay Area because of people relocating out of San Francisco after the Great Earthquake of 1906. On September 17, 1923, a fire broke out in midmorning. Wildcat Canyon was ablaze, and people all over could smell the smoke coming from the burning eucalyptus groves. By one-thirty in the afternoon, the fire was burning in a line about sixteen hundred feet wide, spreading across Berkeley and moving toward Oakland. The narrow roads were clogged with people running from the flames. Panic was everywhere. Although the damage was great, it's a miracle the losses weren't worse.

In all, 584 homes and buildings burned to the ground. Four thousand people were left homeless. The fire burned everything right up to the edge of the University of California at Berkeley. Nothing like this had ever hit the East Bay Area. The fire was simply enormous, and the people were unprepared to fight something so fierce.

Within a few years after the fire, the eucalyptus seedlings had again spread out along the hills. To try to prevent a future fire, builders constructed larger boulevards that could act as firebreaks while designing the hillside neighborhoods to be less dense than before. They replaced the wooden sidewalks, which had brought the fires right into the neighborhoods, with concrete ones. They buried the telephone cables to keep communications open since the phone lines had burned down the last time. But they still missed the mark. They initiated legislation to outlaw wooden shingle roofs and mandate fire-resistant tiles, but it was rescinded before it took effect. Worst of all, the eucalyptus trees with their tall, canopy-style growth were springing up everywhere on the hillsides. They again would be the agents of destruction in the next fire some forty-seven years later.

Between 1923 and 1969, dramatic changes hit the Bay Area. The roads, bridges, and transportation systems, such as the Bay Area Rapid Transit (BART) light-rail system, allowed San Francisco workers to live out in the East Bay. The population of Oakland skyrocketed to nearly half a million people.

In 1970 an arsonist started a fire that was to destroy thirty-seven homes. The hillsides had become covered with old growth trees, and the canyons were dense with brush. The fire burned a large area around the hills before it was stopped, but the necessary changes still weren't made to help prevent future hillside fires. In fact, things got worse. People who moved into the area started planting more trees, adding to the fire hazard. Some natural firebreaks were heavily planted—residents evidently liked the countryside look of the overgrown canyons. The eucalyptus groves spread their seeds everywhere the wind carried them, and residents added Monterey pines to the hillsides' mix of fuel. On Sunday, October 20, 1991, the scene was set for the third and largest fire to hit Oakland.

The fire actually started the day before, on Saturday, when a brushfire hit a canyon and burned about three acres. Oakland City firefighters attacked the flames with picks, axes, shovels, and high-powered hoses that drenched the area. The firefighters thought the fire had been extinguished, but the burning embers in the leaves and dead brush smoldered deep within the canyon. Because the undergrowth was so dense, no one saw that the fire was still lurking, burning slowly through the night. By morning, the warning signs first appeared as dark smoke.

At about ten-thirty on that Sunday morning, Officer Grubensky along with every other officer in Oakland was alerted that a fire had been spotted in the North Hills area near Caldecott Tunnel. Emergency service personnel raced to the scene as firefighters hit the same areas they had hit the day before.

But on that day, conditions were different, and the fire would soon get out of control. The "Diablo winds" that raced through the canyons fanned the flames. Then there was the dense brush. Firefighters couldn't get through some of the areas that were tinder-dry: the flames moved through the grass as if it had been sprinkled with gasoline. The area simply exploded when the fire ran up the trunks of a grove of eucalyptus trees, igniting their leaves. The canopy at the top of the trees allowed the fire to leapfrog from one grove to the next, then from one house to the next. The conflagration was in full force; the flames suddenly controlled the city and its people.

Fire ran up the canyons, while millions of burning embers rained down everywhere. Within one hour of the fire being reported, 790 homes were fully engulfed or completely destroyed. Many of the homes that burned in that first hour were in the exact location of ones destroyed back in 1970. They had been rebuilt, but the owners had again designed and planted their landscape to give it a "natural" appearance with heavily wooded areas and thick underbrush. To maintain the bucolic feel of the area, the roads had never been widened. The lack of fire-resistant materials in the structures, the awnings, the decks, the wooden siding—all contributed to the blaze's fury.

As the fire continued to spread into the neighborhoods, the temperatures reached an astounding 2,000 degrees. At that heat, everything burns. Even the concrete melted away and burned. As the officers drove up Alvarado Road, they could see where the destruction had occurred. Once they actually hit the fire scene, it was clear what was lost; one could see where the million-dollar homes and the forested areas had once stood so stately above the hills. But they had become nothing but fuel for the hungry fire that was consuming more as each hour passed.

Nothing slowed the angry flames. The pine and eucalyptus groves were exploding like bombs above the firefighters. As one tree ignited, another would detonate right behind. Soon the air superheated, and flashovers consumed entire blocks of homes all at once. It was hell on the hillsides of Oakland.

As the disaster grew beyond the city's resources, police and firefighting agencies from around the Bay Area began responding. Firefighters would identify the most likely path of the moving blaze and request that whole neighborhoods be evacuated. The Oakland Police Department took the lead in the evacuation detail.

At about 11:15 A.M., police officers were clearing residents from the Charing Cross and Tunnel Road neighborhoods. Officer Grubensky was on the front lines, choking in smoke, as he helped clear out the panicked residents. Some people were screaming without making sense, others were quietly scrambling to load their vehicles with pictures, artwork, personal records, and whatever memories they could salvage. But no time remained. It wasn't smoke they were running from: they felt the heat in the air as the eucalyptus trees began exploding nearby. Homes down the street erupted into flames. They weren't just evacuating; these people knew they were leaving their homes forever.

The parade of sport utility vehicles, trucks, cars, and motorcycles followed the narrow roads down the hill. Many people abandoned their cars and started to run down the sidewalks. As neighborhoods were engulfed in flames, streets were blocked and alternate routes were jammed up with cars. Some irrational drivers honked their horns as though the road might miraculously open for them. Tempers flared, judgment failed, and order dissolved into chaos. But the police and firefighters persevered, remaining focused. Standing shoulder to shoulder, they were going to save lives. The city would survive.

Many people followed Officer Grubensky out of the fire's path as he bravely led them to safety down the hill. He encouraged them as he directed them around the stranded vehicles and finally to support personnel in a safe zone. Again and again he returned, for he was on a mission. As he drove back up into the hills to continue his rescue effort, he was pushing his guardian angel too far.

Everywhere one looked, cars and burning debris were scattered about from the traffic jams that never cleared. Tires had burned, and huge bright silver piles of aluminum were all that remained of custom wheels and engine blocks. Car frames were planted in melted asphalt. Water lines and hoses, which were connected to hydrants, began to burst. Water, colored black with ash and carrying burned debris, rolled uselessly down the hill. When the electrical system caught fire and burned, the water pumps stopped filling the reservoir. The water system was drained, and everything went dry by 5 P.M. And this fire was to burn for two more days.

As he made his way back up Charing Cross Road, Officer Grubensky found five people who had been driving down the hill around disabled cars and debris but had gotten lost on the side streets. When they saw Officer Grubensky, they knew he would lead them to safety. Slowly they followed him down the narrow street through the thick smoke.

Then, on the hill above him, a garage that had been fully engulfed burned to the point where its support frame failed. When the structure suddenly collapsed, a car that was inside plummeted down the hill. The car became a flaming missile that plowed through the guardrail and careened across the roadway where it stopped in the center of the street, blocking the roadway and preventing any more traffic from coming down Charing Cross Road. Grubensky's escape route was closed.

Undaunted, he ordered the people from their cars and instructed them to follow him down the hill. With the brush on both sides of the hill burning, they proceeded down the middle of the street. The heat was intense, the air temperature had risen to the point where it began to burn their lungs, and the carbon monoxide in the thick smoke began to take its toll. Officer Joseph Kroushour heard Officer Grubensky's call on his radio as John yelled into his microphone, "You've got to get me out of here!"

But it was too late. That would be Grubensky's last call.

As the treetops rained fire from above, Grubensky and his five followers lay down on the pavement trying to find cooler air, but there was no escape. They covered up, trying to limit their exposure, but when the flashover hit, it consumed everything in its path. Even the concrete melted around them. Officer Grubensky and the five people he was trying to rescue were all burned. Their remains were found in the center of the street where they sought refuge. Grubensky's body was found on top of a woman he was trying to insulate from the heat. But there was no way they could have survived the 2,000-degree temperatures.

Barry Howard, now a veteran with seventeen years on the job, talked about his memories of John Grubensky and what a loss his passing was to so many people, especially to his wife and family. Howard said, "You know, I'm black and John was white, and we came from different backgrounds. We talked about race relations and the importance of taking care of people and doing the right thing. He was truly the professional peace officer."

Officer Howard gave a eulogy at Officer Grubensky's funeral. He reflected on the special things that Grubensky brought to the Oakland Police Department. He remembered their days as partners, the great times they had, and how he missed him. "We were young and dumb. We'd come in to work on our days off to check our beats and develop intelligence on the dealers. John would watch the dealers, and without making an arrest, he'd watch deals go down so he could figure out where the dope was being stored. Then we got the sergeant to allow us to take out a detective car so we could make an arrest next time. We got lucky and found a guy who was selling a bunch of stolen guns." And this was on their day off.

Howard knew that his words couldn't bring solace to the family who had lost so much. He choked up a little while talking to me, remembering the time that has passed, and lamented the loss of his partner. He said he would have liked it better if he could have let John's wife, Linda, know how much John cared for her. He said, "He was my best friend, and we talked about everything, including things about our families. And to this day, I don't think he told his wife how much he loved her. How much she satisfied him as a man and how good she was for him. I'll tell you, she was great to him, and he loved her with all his heart, physically and emotionally, he was in love with her. I'd really like it if Linda knew she was everything to him." John was also survived by three children who were very young at the time of his death: John Robert (then seven), Jaime (then six), and Joshua (then four).

No one would question Officer John Grubensky's bravery, integrity, or fidelity as a peace officer. He was credited with personally saving more than 150 lives in the North Oakland Hills fire. He will forever live in the memories of the families he so valiantly protected as well as with the members of the Oakland Police Department whom he made so very proud.

Thirty-two-year-old Officer John Grubensky had been a policeman for a relatively short time when he fell in the line of duty. But in that time, he made a difference for himself, his family, his partner, and his department. He was asked to give a lot on that terrible day in October, but he gave even more. On that day, he gave it all.

2

OFFICER PAUL RAGONESE

New York City (New York) Police Department

"Born to Be a Cop"

Paul Ragonese was born to be a cop. Even as a youngster growing up in an Italian neighborhood called Dyker Heights in Brooklyn, he knew he wanted to serve the public in a caring, understanding way. But as a child, the man who would become the most highly decorated police officer in the history of New York City wanted to be a priest. It wasn't until he was a student at St. John's University that he discovered he wanted to be a police officer. The idea struck him after he watched the movie *The Detective,* starring Frank Sinatra in the title role. Ragonese admired the courage of Sinatra's character who, despite the urgings of his police bosses, revealed that he had helped convict an innocent man who had been executed. The movie showed him that police officers have wonderful opportunities to help people daily.

Ragonese dropped out of college to become a police trainee in May 1970. He was assigned to a communications section where he became a 9-1-1 operator, an area some trainees called "a preview of hell." When he saved the life of a person threatening suicide, he knew he'd made the right decision about his career.

After five months of intense training at the academy, he became an officer in October 1971. Assigned to the 23rd Precinct, twenty-one-year-old Ragonese worked the streets of Harlem in uniform, chasing petty criminals for thefts, muggings, and vandalism while learning the ropes in the department.

The second life he saved was that of a rookie officer who'd been stabbed seven times by an emotionally disturbed parent at a school. The medical staff at the hospital credited Ragonese's emergency first aid with keeping the officer alive until an ambulance arrived. The deputy chief wrote a letter commending Ragonese for his quick thinking, and Mayor Abe Beame sent a congratulatory letter, but as Ragonese stated in his book, *The Soul of a Cop,* "What thrilled me most was that I had saved another life." There would be many such thrilling moments in his distinguished career with the New York City Police Department.

As a result of his actions, Ragonese was invited to join the elite Anti-crime Unit (ACU) in January 1974. Dressed in civilian clothes, ACU personnel blended into the neighborhoods as they patrolled the streets in taxis and other unmarked vehicles. The unit was highly effective, averaging some forty arrests every month. Ragonese reported that 85 percent of the arrests were on observed crimes, the majority of which were robberies.

Ragonese nearly lost his life one night in August 1979. The dispatcher had put out a general alarm regarding a stolen 1979 white Jeep Wagoneer. Ragonese and his partner spotted a white Jeep Wagoneer, its headlights and flashers on, parked next to a phone booth. A young man was on the pay phone. The men drove slowly past the car and verified that its license plate number matched that of the stolen vehicle. After circling around the block, the officers parked a block behind the stolen Jeep to keep it under surveillance. Even though they were in plain clothes in a station wagon, Ragonese noticed that the man in the phone booth was staring directly at them. After a few minutes, the man walked toward the Jeep, hopped in, and waved his arm in the air. A woman and another man ran out of a nearby park and jumped into the stolen car. As the three drove away, Ragonese called for backup as his partner pursued the stolen Jeep.

When the officers blocked the car from entering FDR Drive, Ragonese jumped out of the car with his weapon aimed at the driver, identified himself, and ordered the man to freeze. Instead of complying, the Jeep's driver put the car into reverse, weaving between cars and pedestrians as he sped backward. Several drivers drove up onto the sidewalk as they attempted to get out of the Jeep's way. Ragonese chased the Jeep on foot for two blocks until he came face-to-face with the vehicle when it could no longer move backward.

The driver then shifted gears into forward and drove straight toward him. Ragonese could see the driver's face as he was hit. The fog light on the driver's side slammed into his testicles, jamming them into his stomach, and he was thrown onto the hood, virtually impaled by the light. Instinctively he grabbed the wiper arm with his left hand, then slid his left leg behind the front bumper guard to steady himself. The driver repeatedly attempted to crush his legs and throw him from the vehicle by crashing into the officers' station wagon.

Ragonese's .38 police-issued revolver was in his right hand. As the young driver attempted a fourth time to crush him, Ragonese raised the weapon, placed the muzzle against the windshield, and squeezed off one round. The bullet penetrated the windshield, striking the young man in his chest. The Jeep jerked to a stop, throwing Ragonese onto the street. The driver's door was flung open and the driver fell out, his shoulder resting next to Ragonese's shoulder. As the young man lay bleeding to death on the street, Ragonese passed out from the excruciating pain in his groin.

Jose Ibenez, the young driver, was eighteen at the time of his death. He had been arrested twenty-two times in the prior two years for stealing cars.

The doctors were amazed that Ragonese survived his injuries and the massive hemorrhaging that resulted. He spent four weeks in the hospital and a month at home recuperating. Once back at work, he stayed at a desk job for nine months before he was able to get back to the ACU.

The police department and a grand jury determined that the shooting was justified. Even though Ragonese knew he had been forced to shoot the young man, he wrote in *The Soul of a Cop*, "You never think you might actually kill someone. Until you wake up one day and say, 'Geez, I killed a guy.' And after all those years of parochial school, the guilty feelings follow. . . . I knew I never wanted to kill a man again. I also knew that if an individual put someone's life in jeopardy and I could save it by shooting that individual—I would do it in the space of a heartbeat. *Like that.* The guilt I'd suffer if I allowed an innocent person to die because I couldn't shoot a killer . . . well that would be far worse."

Like most police officers, Ragonese's service to his community wasn't restricted to his on-duty shifts. One evening after a nice dinner out, Paul was driving his family home when he passed a senior citizens' apartment building that was engulfed in flames, and he stopped to give aid. As he walked into the lobby, the building's boiler exploded, making it impossible to see through the black smoke, but he crawled up the stairs, where he heard crying noises. He found five elderly women on the stairs too scared to move. He led them down the stairs and outside to safety.

Then he returned to the building, again crawling upstairs through thick smoke to a third-floor apartment. Hearing the smoke alarm inside, he broke down the door to find a sixty-nine-year-old woman on the floor. Her seventy-nine-year-old husband was unconscious in the bedroom. Ragonese dragged both of them out into the hallway just as a fireball blasted up the staircase, fully engulfing the stairway and destroying any hope of using it as an escape route. Dragging both individuals as he crawled beneath the ever-increasing smoke, Ragonese finally reached a window at the end of the hallway. It wouldn't open, so he began pounding on the window with his right hand until he finally broke the glass. But he saw no firemen in the courtyard below, and at first no one answered his shouts for help. Then, thankfully, two firemen on a ladder appeared at the window. For his selfless actions, Ragonese received the NYPD Medal of Valor as well as the New York *Daily News* Hero of the Month Award for saving the lives of seven people.

Ragonese became a certified member of NYPD's Emergency Service Unit (ESU) in early 1982, then became a certified emergency medical technician (EMT) a year later. The squad, whose primary mission is to help people, routinely responds to calls such as suicide threats by distraught people threatening to jump from high-rise window ledges or from any one of New York's bridges. While a member of the ESU, Ragonese was selected along with fourteen other ESU members to be trained with fifteen FBI agents for a top-secret antiterrorist team in 1984.

Though the ESU dealt with an endless variety of life-or-death emergencies, all of Paul's training and experience would be tested when he was called to a construction site on a Thursday in May 1985, a day he'd never forget. His bravery and steadfastness of purpose would define his response. This would become one of his most acclaimed acts of heroism.

A thirty-five-ton crane situated next to the excavated foundation of a new building in midtown Manhattan had suddenly overturned, leaving the crane dangling downward into the huge hole. Though the cab itself had flipped upside down, the crane's operator had jumped to safety just as the crane started to topple over. But the moans heard by those surrounding the disabled crane signaled the unthinkable: a woman was pinned below.

No one could get to the woman from above or below. When Ragonese arrived on the scene, he crawled onto a four-by-eight section of plywood over the huge pit to the crane's front end. If the crane moved, it would mean instant death for both the accident victim and Ragonese. He slipped into a space just two feet by two feet so that he could be close to her. After removing the debris from her body, he could see that her lower legs were pinned beneath the crane. He requested equipment to free the woman and described the situation on his police radio, then turned to her to introduce himself.

The woman told Paul her name was Brigitte Gerney. She was the single mother of two children ages fourteen and eleven; the children's father was dead. She made Ragonese promise to tell her kids that their mommy loved them and that their dad and she would always be there for them in spirit.

Paramedic Terry Smith asked Ragonese to help him get an IV line of dextrose into Gerney, which Ragonese inserted into one of her veins. Then he reassured her that he wouldn't leave her until she was freed. Though she told him she knew she was going to die and encouraged him to leave her and save himself, Ragonese wouldn't budge.

"Cops have to be a calming influence when other people are coming apart," he writes in *The Soul of a Cop*.

At Gerney's request, Ragonese summoned a priest to give her Holy Communion, but the priest was unable to get down to the pair, so he put the Eucharist in a container and lowered it down. Gerney wanted to say the Act of Contrition while they waited, so Ragonese did his best to remember the words and she repeated them after him. Then he silently prayed for a miracle.

Rescue workers lowered down a surgeon in a harness so that she could assess Gerney's physical condition. Whispering to Ragonese that she thought Gerney's legs would probably have to be amputated, the surgeon told him that he'd have to perform the amputation, which he agreed to do. But when the doctor further evaluated Gerney's injuries, she decided that amputation was out of the question.

Ragonese had been at Gerney's side for almost three hours now. Several cranes had arrived to attempt to secure the fallen machine, and Ragonese's boss ordered him to leave what soon would become an even more perilous position. But he refused to leave Gerney, forcing his partner to tie a safety line around Ragonese's chest and pull him up to safety. He had been crouched in one position for so long that he could no longer feel his legs. With the circulation cut off for several hours, his legs wouldn't support his body's weight and went into spasms.

His legs still convulsing, he was lifted into an ambulance and driven to an emergency room, but all he could think about was Brigitte Gerney. When he awoke from his injection-induced sleep a couple of hours later, he learned that she was still trapped, so he had a police car drive him back to the construction site. Before he could reach her, however, the crane had been moved several inches, allowing the trapped woman to be rescued.

Despite being pinned beneath the crane for over five hours, Gerney's prognosis was good: her legs would be saved, and with physical therapy she'd probably walk again. Ragonese told me that one of the first people to visit her in the hospital was her good friend Jackie Kennedy Onassis.

The following Monday, Ragonese would go to the bomb squad as a detective, receiving a rare field promotion for all the exceptional work he'd done.

By the fall of 1986, an antiabortion fanatic suspected of involvement in as many as fifty clinic bombings around the country had set off bombs in several New York City clinics. The bomber always notified the bomb squad with information about the bomb in time for the squad to react and defuse the dynamite. On December 14, 1986, the bomber called. He stated that the bomb squad had ten minutes to disarm a bomb made of fifteen sticks of dynamite placed at a Planned Parenthood office on Second Avenue. Just as the members of the squad felt their adrenaline pump and sweat began to appear, the phone rang again. It was the bomber. He wanted to mention that he'd handcuffed a real estate agent to a pipe in the building.

When Ragonese's squad arrived at the Planned Parenthood office, they found the building already ablaze. Had the bomb already blown? The overhead sprinklers were showering water throughout. The squad split into teams: one to put out the fire, one to search for the real estate agent, one to search for the bomb. As fire and smoke consumed the room, they located a standard time bomb sitting in six inches of water. The bomber had timed the impending second blast to occur while the bomb squad tried to disarm it.

Ragonese had to place his face in the water to see that he was dealing with fifteen sticks of dynamite, a clock, and a battery. Only ninety seconds remained before it would detonate. Still searching frantically for the bomb's blasting cap with only nineteen seconds left on the clock, he finally located the cap and threw it to his partner, Glenn Welch, cutting the bomb's wires with only a few seconds showing on the clock. After searching the device for a booby trap and opening up each stick of dynamite, the men could breathe easily again. This was the largest bomb to date in the history of New York City.

Whether you call it kismet, divine intervention, or a bizarre twist of fate, it turns out that the real estate agent was a magician who had freed himself by picking the lock on his handcuffs. He had walked out into the street before the bomb squad even arrived on the scene.

The Bureau of Alcohol, Tobacco and Firearms (ATF) found a fingerprint belonging to Dennis Malvasi at the Planned Parenthood office. Malvasi surrendered to John Cardinal O'Connor and revealed where he kept his explosives. Malvasi later pleaded guilty to placing a bomb that malfunctioned, receiving a three-year prison term instead of the maximum sentence of twenty-five years to life.

The heroic acts of Paul Ragonese during his extraordinary seventeen-year career as a police officer could completely fill this book. Paul was the first police officer to be featured on the TV show *Top Cops*, and at the time of his retirement he was the most decorated police officer in New York City history. Among his many awards and citations, he received five Medals of Valor with six Honorable Mentions, twenty-three Exceptional Merit Awards, twenty-five Commendations, eighteen Meritorious Duty Awards, and twelve Excellent Police Duty Awards. In 1986 Governor Mario Cuomo presented the New York State Cop of the Year Award to Paul. He also received the New York State Medal of Honor and the New York State Medal of Valor.

In addition to Ragonese's countless heroic acts throughout his distinguished career, his arrest record rivals that of Popeye Doyle, the New York detective made famous in *The French Connection*. Doyle had the distinction of having made more arrests than any other police officer in New York history during his career with the NYPD.

"I never thought of myself as a hero. Firemen and policemen get paid to do what they do. But frankly, I'd have done it for nothing," Ragonese told me.

In 1987 Paul Ragonese retired from the NYPD because of work-related injuries. Although retirement has allowed him to enjoy more time with his wife of thirty years and their two grown daughters, it hasn't slowed him down. In addition to writing *The Soul of a Cop* with coauthor Berry Stainback, Paul has hosted his own television and radio shows. In between his many speaking engagements, he consults with small police departments.

On occasion he'll offer expert insight into police matters for local and national television programs.

Knowing that she had a proud family tradition of heroism and dedication to live up to, Ragonese's daughter Dawn started her career with the NYPD in August 1998. "My daughter was enjoying a three-day holiday visiting her mother and me when the attack on the World Trade Center happened. My wife called me to say that our daughter was going to help out at the World Trade Center. When my wife unsuccessfully tried to talk her out of it, she called me, hoping I could convince our daughter to stay home. When my daughter got on the phone, she said, 'Dad, those are my brothers out there in those buildings. I have to help them.' I understood exactly how she felt, and I just told her to be careful."

For weeks following the September 11 attacks, Ragonese helped police officers and other volunteers sift through the horrific debris from the World Trade Center. "It was one of the hardest things I've ever done," he said.

"I think what happened in New York on September eleventh brought home to Americans what being a police officer is all about. What happened at the World Trade Center shows what the police do every day— they risk their lives."

3

MASTER TROOPERS ALEXANDER PETIGNA AND HOWARD DICKINSON

Kansas Highway Patrol

"On Thin Ice"

Trooper Alexander Petigna

Trooper Howard Dickinson

Douglas Allen had a heart murmur that was getting progressively worse. One of his heart valves was leaking and he needed open heart surgery. At his midmorning doctor's appointment on December 12, 2000, he discussed the upcoming surgical procedure and hospitalization with his surgeon. The whole business was scary to Allen, but he'd arranged to meet a friend for lunch to take his mind off the heart problem for a little while anyway. Allen left the doctor's office around noon. As he turned onto Interstate 635 at Kansas Highway 5, he noticed how dangerous the driving conditions had become since he'd left his house earlier in the day. The old snow had been pushed onto the shoulders, leaving the roads icy and treacherous to negotiate. And it had started snowing again.

Allen had no way of knowing that his life would hang in the balance that afternoon—not because of his heart murmur but because of a slippery road.

"It was a nasty morning," according to Trooper Alex Petigna. The Kansas City Department of Transportation had sprayed salt on the highways, but road conditions were still dangerous. At approximately 1:15 P.M. Trooper Petigna and Trooper Howard Dickinson were dispatched to investigate a series of traffic accidents on a stretch of I-635 near the Missouri River just half a mile from the Missouri state line. Petigna arrived first to find three vehicles—a Jeep, a Saab, and a pickup truck—in the left median ditch. He radioed Dickinson that he was at the scene and asked him to set out flares to slow down oncoming traffic around the sharp curve. He advised Dickinson that the bridge over K-5 (Kansas Highway 5) was dangerously slippery.

Alexander Petigna had decided to become a police officer at age twenty while studying air conditioning and refrigeration in college. In fact, his dad had to purchase his weapon for use at the police academy since he wasn't yet twenty-one. Married with two children today, he knows that his wife, Noelle, worries about him on the highways but that she appreciates his commitment to his fellow troopers and how much he loves his job. Howard Dickinson, a former track star at the University of Kansas, lives less than a mile from Alex. He too is married with two children, both daughters, and both in college.

As Dickinson traveled to the accident scene, he could tell by his braking that the bridge was very icy in spots. As he approached the area, he couldn't tell exactly how far around the curve Petigna and the three vehicles were, so he drove past to determine where best to place the flares. He saw that Petigna was in his vehicle, having already begun an accident report on the white Jeep Cherokee that was in front of his police car. Dickinson radioed back to Petigna that he would drop the flares.

Dickinson then took six to eight flares from his trunk and placed them in his front seat, did a U-turn, and drove back to the other side of the bridge where he began laying them down. After he crossed the K-5 bridge, he pulled up on the embankment behind Petigna's patrol car, which was sitting six to eight feet left of the roadway on the embankment. Trooper Dickinson stopped behind and to the left of Petigna's car. Both patrol cars had all their emergency equipment activated at the time.

Douglas Allen's Saab was the second car in the ditch. He walked over to Trooper Petigna's car, but Petigna told him to return to his car until the arriving trooper could take his accident report. Petigna then advised Dickinson that he'd told the Saab's driver to return to his car and wait until Dickinson finished setting out the flares.

Trooper Dickinson got out of his vehicle and walked back along the shoulder some thirty or forty yards. He stopped just short of the guardrail to set additional flares. As he prepared the flares, he noticed that most of the vehicles were taking the curve and crossing the bridge at the normal speed limit of sixty-five miles per hour, which was way too fast given the hazardous conditions. That was the speed of a light brown Lincoln Continental he saw coming over the bridge in the left lane. Midway across the bridge, the driver hit her brakes and the Lincoln's rear end started fishtailing, swerving back and forth until the car began sliding down the road straddling the right and left lanes. Watching the car heading directly toward him, Dickinson backed up and moved to take cover behind a bridge pillar. The Lincoln momentarily straightened out as it glided by Trooper Dickinson; then it shot straight across the left lane toward the parked patrol cars and Trooper Petigna.

Dickinson saw Allen bending over beside Petigna's patrol car, facing the driver's side window. Trying to warn the men, "I yelled as loudly as I could, but no one heard a word," Dickinson reported. The Lincoln first struck the left rear end of Dickinson's vehicle, pushing it to the right and into the back of Petigna's car, then continued its skid down the entire left side of Dickinson's vehicle.

"A blur of a car went by me," Petigna recalled.

Dickinson looked on in horror as the Lincoln barreled into Douglas Allen. "He pinwheeled into the air fifteen to twenty feet high" before landing head first on the edge of the roadway in front of Petigna's patrol car, Dickinson reported. "I thought I was going to throw up when I saw the man spinning in the air," he told me. "But in my job, inaction is not acceptable." Trooper Petigna remembered, "He came down face first onto the asphalt. My first thought was that he must be dead." The impact was so forceful that Allen's left sneaker remained on the ground next to Petigna's car.

The Lincoln then struck the Jeep broadside, spinning it around clockwise into the left lane of northbound I-635, before careening into the ditch.

Dickinson saw Petigna bound out of his car to assist Allen. Petigna looked in Dickinson's direction but couldn't see him for all the out-of-control vehicles that were piling up.

"No matter what, I couldn't leave the man in the highway," Petigna told me. He grabbed Allen's belt with one hand and one of his arms with the other hand in an attempt to move him, but he couldn't get a good footing on the slippery road. To make matters more difficult, Allen was a big man, perhaps 220 pounds and at least six feet tall. But the trooper pulled with all his strength, finally moving Allen to the edge of the road. Still, neither of them was completely out of harm's way.

Trooper Dickinson advised dispatch that the accident scene was reaching a critical level and asked that the roadway be shut down immediately. At the end of Dickinson's call, Petigna got on his radio and advised dispatch that he believed there had been a fatal accident and that the troopers' two cars were involved.

Other vehicles, including a large semitrailer truck, were sliding by in quick succession. After what seemed like an eternity to him, Dickinson saw a break in the traffic and raced for Petigna's patrol car. The driver of the Jeep met Dickinson as he approached the patrol car and advised him that a man was hit and in bad shape. Dickinson advised the driver of the Jeep to hide behind the bridge pillar, but if he wanted to wait in his car for help, he should run directly behind the trooper.

Finally the two troopers found one another. Petigna informed Dickinson that he was shaken up but all right, although he thought Allen might not make it, since he wasn't showing much of a pulse or solid breathing. Then suddenly, the man who'd cartwheeled through the air surprised both troopers by coughing, uttering a profanity, and opening his eyes.

Amazed that Allen was still alive, the troopers realized that cars were sliding all around them and that the three of them were in a very precarious situation. They grabbed the injured man by his arms and belt and began pulling him up the embankment. Neither officer could get a good footing, however, and Allen was a dead weight, unable to assist in any way.

The troopers had progressed only a few feet when they noticed a gray Pontiac sliding across the road toward the three of them. The troopers pushed Allen out of immediate danger, but the car was approaching them so quickly that they did not have time to reach the same spot themselves— it would mean crossing directly in front of the vehicle. They did the only thing they could do: they tried to run up the frozen embankment. As they clawed into the ice, trying to gain traction but seeming to take three steps forward only to slide two steps back, their efforts paid off. Instead of hitting them, the Pontiac struck the right rear of Dickinson's patrol car, spun around, then struck the right front of his vehicle. The force of the collision knocked Dickinson's car into Petigna's car yet again. When the driver of the Pontiac stepped out of his car, he stood in the road until the troopers yelled at him to get off the highway.

Though the troopers had saved Allen from the sliding Pontiac, he was still not safe where he lay, so they slid down the embankment and began pulling him up toward the top. He surprised them by asking, "Can you untangle my legs?" They were thrilled that he was still alive and able to speak.

Petigna and Dickinson had moved the semiconscious man eight to ten feet up the embankment when yet another car—a purple Ford Crown Victoria—slid off the road and headed for them. Thinking quickly, Dickinson shoved Allen's head into the snow as the trunk of the Ford slid directly over Allen's upper torso. Petigna watched as the car came just a few feet from Dickinson's legs.

Dickinson knew he was in imminent danger. "Maybe she'll get a leg, but I am going to live," he thought. He broke off all his fingernails as he and Petigna scrambled on their hands and knees up the icy embankment, but the Crown Victoria climbed the hill right behind them. Dickinson continued, "The higher we went, the higher the Crown Vic followed. We kept climbing, and somehow the Crown Vic just missed us, but only by what seemed like inches." Both men were afraid that at any moment they would become the fatalities of this incredible—and growing—pileup.

The purple car finally struck an outcropping of trees and came to rest on top of a rock wall. It took the troopers a few moments to realize that they were both still in one piece. Trooper Petigna went up the hill to check on the driver of the Crown Victoria while Trooper Dickinson went back to Allen.

Dickinson got a blanket out of Petigna's car and covered Allen with the blanket and his parka. He then knelt beside the seriously injured man, speaking to him as he checked his vital signs. Allen's condition was much better than Dickinson had imagined it would be after such a traumatic event. By this time, Troopers Ken Woods and Mitch Mellick had shut down the road just south of the bridge. Finally, cars stopped sliding toward the three men.

Petigna checked out the conditions of the other drivers while Dickinson waited for the ambulance with Allen. Fire and rescue personnel appeared on the scene with several lifesaving teams. The two troopers embraced one another as the ambulance with Allen inside sped off. Physically and emotionally spent, they gratefully turned over the accident scene, involving some eleven vehicles, to their fellow police officers.

Dickinson summed up the scene by saying, "Nothing in my seventeen years of police experience affected me like this one. Everything was out of control." Since his mom had just passed away, he told me, "Later, it bothered me that I didn't have my mother to talk about this accident with."

"We both felt damn lucky," Petigna conceded. He still wears the Saint Michael's medallion he wore on the day of the incident. Saint Michael is the patron saint of police.

"The first call the next day was an accident near where the incident happened. I've gotta tell you that I hated responding to the call!" confided Dickinson. The day also brought more snow and ice. The supervisor that day was a tough and seasoned trooper, an ex-Marine Corps sergeant. After the prior day's incident on the interstate, he expected that several officers would be tempted to stay home.

"How many called in sick?" he bluntly queried dispatch as he pulled out of the trooper station.

"None" was the response.

"You mean to tell me everyone reported in?" he asked.

"Yes. Everyone," the dispatcher said.

"Well, they must be dumber than I thought," the supervisor retorted.

Troopers Petigna, Dickinson, and the other members of the Kansas Highway Patrol are there for each other. They are a team, a brotherhood.

Miraculously, Douglas Allen survived, though he came close to dying in the hospital. His left eye socket was shattered so badly that some of the bone had to be replaced. He suffered from brain swelling and massive internal bleeding. His pelvis was broken in two places and his left ankle splintered into small pieces. He spent the following two months in the hospital, then was admitted to a rehabilitation facility. Four months later he could walk without the use of a walker or cane. At this writing he was still undergoing physical therapy but had stopped using a cane.

Allen spoke to me about what he experienced on the road that day. "I was just trying to ask Trooper Petigna how much longer it would take because I didn't want to be late for my luncheon. I didn't even see the Lincoln coming." The next thing he remembers is coming in and out of consciousness.

"I was surrounded by white. I started walking to find a way out of it. A white light appeared before me, but I wasn't afraid. It was a warm, friendly white light. I could hear two voices talking behind me. One of the voices said, 'This guy is done for,' but I kept saying to myself, 'I'm not dead! Get me the hell outta here!' "

When I asked Allen if the accident had changed his life, he replied, "Yes, in two ways. First, I drive a lot more carefully, and second, if I am ever in an accident again, I intend to stay in my car."

He continued, "Those two officers risked their lives to save mine. I think very highly of them both. I'm just extremely grateful."

On the day of the incident, Trooper Petigna was a thirteen-year veteran officer who knew the radio codes forward and backward. But he disclosed to me that after seeing Mr. Allen hit, he yelled into his radio, "code 1030," which means improper radio traffic, a code typically used when two officers are discussing issues that aren't work-related; he meant to say, "code 1033," which means emergency assistance is required. Sometimes we civilians forget that police officers are people too. They can get just as emotional and excited about emergencies and events that are out of control as civilians do. But good training and past experience kicks in, their sense of duty takes over, and they are capable of unforgettable heroic deeds. These courageous acts frequently go unnoticed, and if asked, the officers involved usually will say that they were just doing their jobs.

Alexander Petigna's and Howard Dickinson's hearts and their respect for human life directed their heroic actions that day, which were publicly recognized. Both troopers were awarded the Kansas Association of Chiefs of Police Silver Award for saving a life and a Silver Award from the Metropolitan Chiefs and Sheriffs Association and KMBC-TV. They received the American Legion Outstanding Law Enforcement Officers Award for 2000.

4

TROOPER BARRY CROY

Alaska State Troopers

"No Hope for Backup"

According to Alaska State Trooper Barry Croy, his wife didn't worry much about him when he was on duty. "She worried more for the people who resisted arrest. 'My husband's a pretty tough guy,' she'd say." Not many people who know Barry Croy would disagree with that statement. Then again, an Alaska State Trooper *has* to be tough.

One-fifth the size of the continental United States, Alaska consists of over 586,400 square miles of harsh mountains, huge glaciers, tundra, forests, over three thousand rivers, over three million lakes, and a coastline of 6,640 miles. The rugged nature of the state that makes it so extraordinarily beautiful also creates significant challenges for law enforcement. State troopers routinely deal with such extreme weather conditions as blizzards, avalanches, winds in excess of a hundred miles per hour, subzero temperatures, hundreds of inches of snow each year, and heavy rains.

The Alaska Territorial Police, established in the early fifties as a response to the need for greater law enforcement in the territory, became a division of the Department of Public Safety, Alaska's primary law enforcement agency for federal, state, and local laws, in 1959. When Alaska became a state that same year, the name was changed to the Alaska State Police, only to be changed again to the Alaska State Troopers in 1967.

The Alaska State Troopers have 240 commissioned troopers and 190 civilian personnel. The troopers' major components are five detachments (in Ketchikan, Palmer, Anchorage, Fairbanks, and Soldotna) and a criminal investigation bureau. Serving in remote areas, Alaska's State Troopers must be among the best-trained police officers in the United States. They routinely face difficulties that other law enforcement officers seldom if ever come up against and bring criminals to justice no matter where they might hide. The Alaska State Troopers are highly respected by Alaska's residents.

When many of us think of a wilderness trip gone bad, the 1972 movie *Deliverance* immediately comes to mind. Based on the novel by James Dickey, the story is about four Atlanta businessmen—played by Burt Reynolds, Jon Voight, Ned Beatty, and Ronny Cox—who take a weekend canoe trip. The trip starts out just as they'd imagined, and they enjoy the serenity of traveling down a scenic river in the woods. But soon their outdoor adventure turns into a nightmare. Two menacing locals stalk the men as they move downstream, raping one of them and killing another. A film with many memorable images, *Deliverance* was great fiction, but the terror endured by the sportsmen was palpable.

Ten men on vacation in the wilderness of Alaska experienced their own terror in early September 1998. The outdoor enthusiasts were camping, hunting, and fishing on the Kobuk River, an uninhabited wilderness area about four hundred miles northwest of Fairbanks, when they were robbed at gunpoint and threatened with death if they did not comply with the demands of five armed Native Alaskans.

The five gunmen—Danny R. Custer, twenty-nine; Larry Custer, Jr., twenty-two; Henry Douglas, thirty-nine; Allen A. Tickett, thirty-six; and Tony R. Tickett, eighteen—were from the small Alaskan town of Shungnak, about fifteen miles west of Kobuk. Their modus operandi was to float downriver until they saw some outdoorsmen who were camping or fishing along the river. Once they'd paddled their skiff to shore, one of the five would quietly check out the men by making small talk about the river and weather. While the sportsmen were distracted, the other four, armed with rifles, would sneak up on them and rob them at gunpoint.

Many of the victims thought these thugs would kill them. They were told to comply with the demands or they would be shot, their bodies left in the woods where no one would find them. It appeared that these five men could do whatever they wanted to do and no one could stop them. According to the information officer of the Alaska Department of Public Safety, during the trial the prosecutor stated that the five armed robbers had thought it was funny that the victims' families might even hire them to look for the missing sportsmen.

The gunmen found three separate groups of vacationers to terrorize. Only one of the vacationers was from Alaska; the rest were from across the lower Forty-Eight. One of the victims managed to radio an outfitter, who in turn contacted the National Park Service, and on September 7, 1998, at 8:00 A.M., a ranger from the National Park Service phoned Alaska State Trooper Barry Croy. In 1997 Croy had been assigned to the small town of Galena, Alaska. With a population of less than a thousand people, Galena lies in the wilderness less than a thousand miles as the crow flies from Juneau, the capital of Alaska. Travel to and from the town is mainly by plane and boat.

Trooper Croy was one of only two officers responsible for keeping the peace in an area of thirty-two thousand square miles. He surprised me by saying that when he couldn't travel to remote villages north of Fairbanks to pick up a suspect, he'd call to ask the person to fly to Fairbanks and turn himself in. Croy told me the suspect usually agreed! "They knew that if they didn't comply, I'd come up and bring them in. When the accused arrived at the jail, he'd tell the jailer that Trooper Barry Croy told him to check in for lockup until a judge could hear the case." No matter how serious the crime, the suspect would be reimbursed for travel expenses, Croy added.

On that September morning, Trooper Croy, armed with his M-1 rifle, six clips of eight rounds each, his standard-issue 10-mm handgun, and armor-piercing bullets, took off alone with a pilot in a small rented Cessna. Ironically, the pilot had flown some of the vacationing victims to the Kobuk River a few days earlier. Flying two hours to Bettles, Alaska, they picked up an unarmed federal park ranger. From there the men flew in a piloted de Havilland Beaver plane on floats another two hours to the site where the incident had taken place.

The victims told Croy that the suspects had escaped in a riverboat. Croy told me that the victims were scared to death. They'd taken what was to be the trip of a lifetime for many of them, only to find themselves at the business ends of rifles, being robbed virtually in the middle of nowhere. Each man would certainly return to his home with more than big fish stories to tell.

The trooper began his search for the gunmen by plane and spotted the eighteen-foot boat in which they'd escaped broken down in the middle of the Kobuk River. He asked the pilot to land near the shore but close to the inoperable boat. By the time the pilot landed, the five armed suspects had managed to paddle their boat to shore, pulling alongside one of the remote observation stations established by the U.S. Navy. Thirty to forty Native Alaskans were standing nearby talking, and the fugitives mingled with the group.

Croy told the pilot and the park ranger to remain with the plane, then walked over to an elderly woman. "Who are the five men who just arrived in that boat?" he asked. The woman pointed to a man in a black cap. Croy approached the man, placed him under arrest, cuffed him, and had him lie down on the ground.

When Croy asked the woman who else had arrived in the boat, she pointed to a man in a multicolored hat. Again the trooper walked up to his suspect and placed him under arrest. With two prisoners cuffed on the ground, Croy placed a third suspect wearing a red cap on the ground. The elderly woman assured Croy that these were the only men who'd come from the riverboat.

Croy returned to the boat, where he discovered a fourth suspect who appeared to be asleep. Curled up on the center seat, his hands were tucked inside his jacket pockets, his eyes shut. Croy wondered: Was the man hiding a gun inside his pocket? Would he turn and shoot?

The trooper came up on him quickly, placing his 10-mm Smith & Wesson between the man's closed eyes as he said, "Slowly remove your hands from your pockets and stand up." When the suspect complied, Croy handcuffed him and had him lie in the bottom of the boat.

With only one suspect remaining, Croy carefully turned 360 degrees to try to discern a likely hiding place. When he asked the man he'd just arrested where the fifth suspect was, the man said nothing but conspicuously stared at a tarp in the front of the boat. Croy noticed some slight movement under the tarp, so he drew his gun and ordered the suspect to come out. Nothing happened.

Croy shouted, "Come out of there now!" Again nothing happened, so he climbed over the man lying prone on the deck and flung back the tarp. Henry Douglas lunged toward Trooper Croy with his fists clenched.

As the two men fought, they kept stepping on the prisoner lying handcuffed under their feet, inadvertently kicking him a couple of times. Desperately trying to eject his opponent from the boat, Douglas hit and pushed Croy, but nothing worked. Instead, Douglas lost his footing and fell into the cold water. Before the current took him downstream, Croy scooped him from the river and handcuffed him. In addition to locating a number of stolen items in the boat, the trooper retrieved six weapons from the gunmen.

Croy marched his five prisoners back to the plane, where they were placed on the floor where equipment is normally stored. Shortly after takeoff, as Douglas became increasingly angry about being captured, he expressed his displeasure by kicking the side of the plane and cursing loudly. The pilot, alarmed by the ruckus, informed Croy that the prisoner's actions could have dangerous repercussions.

Once again Croy pulled out his 10-mm weapon, this time holding it to the forehead of his distraught passenger. Croy didn't mince words. "If you keep it up, I will shoot you. You are not going to cause this plane to crash." Understanding his predicament, Douglas acquiesced.

The flight would not be without additional danger. As Croy looked out the right passenger window, he noticed oil spewing out of the engine. Then the engine stopped completely. Fortunately for all seven passengers aboard, Alaskan pilots are among the best in the world. Oftentimes they repair their own engines, and they're accustomed to flying in extreme weather conditions. This pilot had plenty of experience; in fact, he'd once landed a plane with both engines out. He gave Trooper Croy a thumbs-up signal, indicating that he shouldn't worry, and took the plane in safely using the air currents.

First stop: a camp where all three groups of the victimized sportsmen had congregated. One can just imagine the victims' shock when Croy asked them to come over to the plane to identify their attackers. Handcuffed and sitting on the floor of the plane, the fivesome were no longer so fierce. After the victims made positive identifications, Trooper Croy and his charges flew the two-hour trip to Bettles to drop off the ranger. Fire trucks and an ambulance were standing by as the disabled plane flew in. Following a safe landing, Trooper Croy removed his prisoners from the plane, then handcuffed the five suspects to a railing in front of a country store to await a replacement plane. The charter service sent a twin-engine Navajo to take Croy and his prisoners on the two-hundred-mile journey to Fairbanks.

Around 11:30 P.M.—a little more than fifteen hours after Croy first received the report—he booked the five suspects into the Fairbanks State Jail. They were held on ten counts each of armed robbery and assault in the third degree. All five pleaded guilty to armed robbery and assault with a deadly weapon. Four of the suspects received three-year sentences, while Henry Douglas received a seven-year term in state prison.

What was the motive of the five men? One of the suspects said that the white hunters were on what they considered their land, so they decided to "mess with them," according to a local newspaper report.

Bold and determined, Alaska State Trooper Barry Croy made a daring capture of five dangerous gunmen. His actions epitomize the undaunted, unflinching nature necessary to survive in the Alaskan wilderness.

The National Association of Police Organizations, in selecting Trooper Croy as one of its 1999 TOP COPS, stated: "Such bravery is all in a day's work for Trooper Barry Croy. He rushed to the rescue of the crime victims in an area so remote that there could be no hope for backup." Croy also received a Meritorious Service award.

After twenty years as a trooper, fifty-two-year-old Barry Croy retired on January 31, 2001. As one would imagine, he remains active during his retirement. He tries to play hockey at least once a week, but when I last spoke with him, he was staying off the ice while a broken knuckle—a hockey injury—healed. He and Dora, his wife of thirty-two years and a nurse, have two sons: Barry, Jr., a child psychologist, and David Scott, who works for one of the major airlines.

The Alaska State Troopers surely must miss Barry Croy.

5

OFFICER DENNIS DEVITTE

Las Vegas (Nevada) Metropolitan Police Department

"Facing Down the Gunman"

It would take less than twenty seconds to change forever the lives of the customers at Mr. D's Sports Bar in Las Vegas in the first hours of December 5, 1999. They were lucky that a Las Vegas Metro police officer would put his life on the line for them. And the heroic officer would be lucky if he survived the deadly barroom shoot-out.

Mr. D's was a popular bar frequented by local police officers. In fact, the band playing into the early morning hours that day was Pigs in a Blanket, three of whose members were off-duty police officers. Unlike most professions, the term *off-duty police officer* is an oxymoron because a police officer is never *really* off duty.

Officer Dennis Devitte, forty-one, was a twenty-year veteran of the police force who had come to Mr. D's to be with friends and enjoy the band. He had been there just a short while when he noticed some commotion at the far end of the bar around 1:20 A.M. Someone had tried to jump over the bar. Unfortunately, this wasn't someone who simply had gotten rowdy after too much to drink.

Three armed robbers, their faces covered with T-shirts and bandannas and their weapons drawn, had charged through the back door of the bar. Witnesses heard someone say something like, "This is a robbery." One of the gunmen tried to vault over the bar, hoping to empty the cash register in all likelihood, when several patrons grabbed him and held him down. Then one of the armed robbers shot a patron who was in a wheelchair, hitting him in the shoulder. The third gunman fired shots into the air, then fired into the group of customers holding down the man who'd tried to leap over the bar.

Officer Devitte didn't know it at the time, but of the seven off-duty police officers in Mr. D's, he was the only one that was armed. He had a small .25-caliber off-duty gun that he routinely carried, although he knew the gun isn't very accurate unless it's used at close range. But Officer Devitte and his weapon were the only things that stood between the three gunmen and a bar full of an estimated seventy patrons. He would risk his life to protect those people from the three armed men.

The gunman who shot the man in the wheelchair opened fire on the crowd with a .40-caliber semiautomatic weapon. He would later be identified as Emilio Rodriguez.

In civilian clothes, Officer Devitte identified himself by saying, "Police officer," as he pulled his weapon and walked toward Rodriguez. By doing so, he was redirecting the gunfire to himself. Rodriguez turned and began shooting at the approaching officer, who knew he'd have to close in on his target before he could return the fire. Despite being hit repeatedly, Devitte managed to hold his fire until he was about eighteen inches from Rodriguez. Then he shot Rodriguez eight times before Rodriguez brought him down with a blast to his knee. Mortally wounded, Rodriguez stumbled out the front door, where he collapsed and died without saying a word.

The two men had fired at each other until their guns were out of ammunition. Devitte had fired nine rounds; the ninth bullet was found lodged in the stock of Rodriguez's gun. Ten of the twenty-three shell casings retrieved from the scene belonged to Rodriguez.

The entire incident lasted less than twenty seconds.

Devitte had been hit seven times by Rodriguez's bullets and once by a shot from another gunman. Two shots had gone into his buttocks, two into his thighs, one to his groin, one to his right hand, one hit his torso, and one blew out his right knee. He seemed to be bleeding everywhere.

Officer Mike Richards, a band member and good friend of Devitte's, ran over to the wounded officer. When he saw him bleeding profusely, Richards called for towels and then stuck fingers into two of Devitte's wounds to try to stop the bleeding. Though one of Rodriguez's bullets had ripped into Devitte's right hand, when Richards tried to take the gun out of that hand, Devitte wouldn't let go of it.

"No, there are still two more bad guys," Devitte protested.

Devitte said to tell his wife that he loved her. Then he said, "I did the best I could. I hope I didn't hit anybody else."

To this day, Richards still can't believe the extent of Devitte's heroism. "He was just unbelievable the way he faced down the gunman." Richards had been involved in a shooting before, but this was so much worse.

In addition to the eight rounds shot into Officer Devitte, six other customers had been hit. Mike Richards's neighbor, who'd come to hear him play, was shot twice—once in the neck and once in the shoulder. All of those shot would survive. None of the other customers who were hit were police officers.

Devitte needed six pints of blood, and his knee had to be reconstructed with bone from a cadaver. He'd be in the hospital for a week and endure numerous surgeries. But it's true that you can't keep a good man down. He was back on the job in six months.

One question would arise: Had Devitte been drinking at the bar before the shoot-out? An officer carrying a weapon while intoxicated is subject to disciplinary action. But although Devitte had consumed a few drinks in the course of the evening, he wasn't intoxicated. When he was tested shortly after the shoot-out, his blood alcohol level was .07 percent; the legal definition of intoxication in Nevada is .10 percent.

A seven-member jury at a coroner's inquest cleared Officer Devitte of any wrongdoing on January 20, 2000. The bar's surveillance cameras had videotaped six different angles of the attempted robbery and subsequent shoot-out. Devitte testified that he felt he had no other option but to pull his weapon on Rodriguez, who Devitte stated "was just running through the bar shooting." He didn't think there was any way to disarm him. It took less than twenty minutes for the jury to find him justified in shooting Emilio Rodriguez.

Just who were the three men who'd attempted to rob Mr. D's?

Emilio Rodriguez was a nineteen-year-old registered felon who had a conviction for possessing a stolen car and arrests for several burglaries. He had dropped out of the twelfth grade just before graduation. Kevin

Collins, a cousin of Rodriguez, testified that he and Rodriguez had smoked PCP in the afternoon before the robbery; a toxicology test performed on Rodriguez confirmed the presence of PCP. Collins also testified that Rodriguez had taken Collins's .40-caliber Glock handgun from his car.

Manuel Tarango, Jr., eighteen at the time of the shooting, is alleged to have been the second gunman. On March 16, 2000, second-degree murder charges were brought against Tarango in the death of Emilio Rodriguez. Rodriguez had actually been shot by Officer Devitte; however, defendants have been charged and convicted of murder in cases where someone died during the commission of a crime, even though they may not have been actively involved in the death itself.

Believed to have fled to Mexico following the attempted robbery, Tarango was a close friend of Rodriguez and was identified by a witness who said he was standing outside Mr. D's before the shoot-out. Police say that Tarango was a gang member known as "Demon" on the streets. Search warrants were obtained, and investigators discovered that DNA evidence taken from Tarango's parents matched evidence found at the scene.

The district attorney also charged Tarango with burglary, attempted robbery, conspiracy to commit robbery, three counts of battery for wounding three people, and the attempted murder of Officer Devitte (one of his bullets wounded the officer). The indictment alleged that all the crimes were committed with the use of a deadly weapon.

As of this writing, neither Tarango nor the third gunman—who hadn't been identified—have been arrested.

The Las Vegas City Council presented Devitte with the Medal of Honor. His department gave him its highest award, the Medal of Valor, and a Purple Heart, which were accompanied by a statement that beautifully summed up Devitte's spirit of valor:

> Officer Devitte's extraordinary act of heroism, which extended far above and beyond the normal call of duty, was performed at great risk to his own safety and was directly responsible for the saving of human life. His actions reflect the highest ideals and standards of the Las Vegas Metropolitan Police Department; therefore, he will be presented the Purple Heart and Medal of Valor Awards.

For his unselfish, courageous actions, Officer Devitte received the National Association of Police Organizations' award for the top officer in the country, the TOP TOP COP Award, known as the Citizen's Choice Award. The recipient is selected by over one hundred thousand police officers from across the United States. They honored Devitte for "his quick thinking and raw courage," which saved the lives of so many people.

As he went up to receive the award, Devitte asked Mike Richards to join him onstage. Full of emotion, Devitte told the audience, "He's the man who saved my life when I lay bleeding to death on the barroom floor. To me, this is the Top Cop."

Officer Richards told me that the attempted robbery and subsequent shoot-out changed his life. "I have a whole new outlook about robberies. I think I'm a better officer because of it. I certainly have a lot more empathy now for the victims."

Clark County Sheriff Jerry Keller couldn't have been prouder of Officer Devitte. "When the three thugs attempted to rob the nightclub, Officer Devitte didn't find cover or shoot from a safe place," he said. "He pulled his weapon and faced down the gunman head on."

The sheriff told me that when he visited him in the hospital right after the shooting, Devitte said, "I'm sorry, Boss, I did my best." Keller couldn't believe it. "Can you imagine? I felt so proud of Dennis at that moment in time. He is one great cop."

The International Association of Chiefs of Police and *PARADE Magazine,* which honor the bravery and dedication of the country's police officers, also named Devitte the 2000 Police Officer of the Year.

To save the lives of other people who were clearly in danger, Officer Dennis Devitte put his own life in jeopardy. Those he protected will never forget his fearless actions.

Devitte has had several operations on his body, hand, and knee to readjust the bones and remove fragments. He said he's facing another surgery on his hand, but hopefully the work on his knee is done. "It's still very painful, but what are you gonna do?" Despite numerous personal tragedies that have befallen many of his close relatives, Devitte remarked, "We're a real good family. I don't know why these things happen to us."

His dad is a double-amputee from World War II who was featured in HBO's *Band of Brothers.* Dennis Devitte learned a lesson of survival and perseverance from his father: "What are you gonna do. You just go on. I learned that from my dad. You just gotta go on."

On regular street patrol now, Devitte drives a black-and-white. "I still go back to work every day. I'm a street cop. That's what I like to do."

"I am the luckiest man in the world," Sheriff Keller told me when I interviewed him. "I have over four thousand of the most dedicated, hard-working people in the world working for me. My police officers are every-day heroes. It's their natural instinct."

Apparently Dennis Devitte would agree. What was his reaction to all the fuss about his courageous actions? "It's hard to believe it became such a big deal. It was sorta shocking that I was named TOP TOP COP of the Year. Guys do that every day, and you never hear it on the news."

6

DEPUTY SHERIFF
RICHARD CARMONA, M.D.

Pima County (Arizona) Sheriff's Department

"To Protect and Preserve Life"

You can probably count on one hand the number of police officers in the United States who are also medical doctors. When the same person who is honored as his county's Physician of the Year is also honored as a TOP COP in America, the nation's SWAT Officer of the Year, and the only recipient of the two highest Valor Awards in his department's history, you can be sure the person is Deputy Richard Carmona, M.D.

Not too bad for a former gang member and high school dropout.

One of four children, Richard Carmona was born in Harlem to alcoholic parents. His mother never received much support from his absentee dad, so she sometimes had to turn the kids over to relatives when the burden of raising them became too great.

"To survive," Carmona told me, he joined a local gang known as the Social Lords, more for protection than anything else. He hung out at the corner candy store with his friends, but unlike many of the other kids, he didn't steal or drink alcohol, much less do any drugs. He credits his mother with doing a good job of instilling in him a sense of right and wrong.

He had attended Dewitt Clinton High School for Boys in the Bronx enough days to complete the ninth grade before counselors finally gave up and showed him the door for the third and last time.

Major Saul Hasson, a Green Beret who'd grown up in the neighborhood, visited the candy store every day during a leave. Hasson told Richard that without a high school diploma or GED equivalency certificate he would never go anywhere or do anything. Impressed by the bearing of the major, seventeen-year-old Richard and his friends enlisted in the Army. Within two years Richard Carmona, Green Beret, was in Vietnam, where he became a medic and weapons specialist on a twelve-man "A" team. He was soon treating gunshot wounds and amputating limbs. Carmona himself was wounded twice in Vietnam.

After a three-year hitch, he decided to return to the United States and complete his education. His Army superiors urged him to go to college when he was discharged, and he credits them with teaching him how to succeed in life. After he received his GED, he enrolled at the City College of New York, which had an open enrollment program for Vietnam veterans. During this time, he married Diana Sanchez, a woman he'd met when they were fourteen. She would help him get through college and medical school. He lovingly calls her "a gift" and "the best thing that ever happened to me."

Richard and Diana moved to the Los Angeles, California, area where he attended California State University at Long Beach. He completed his medical degree, residency, and fellowship at the University of California in San Francisco. He graduated in 1979 as class valedictorian.

Fast-forward to 1992. Living in Tucson, Arizona, Carmona has become the chief of trauma services at Tucson Medical Center and a surgeon and assistant professor of surgery at the University of Arizona, and he commutes to the Uniformed Services University of Health Sciences in Bethesda, Maryland, where he's a consultant and faculty member. He's a member of the Pima County Sheriff's Department search and rescue team and a commissioned peace officer as well. As a SWAT team leader, he has helped redesign the structure of the unit to include a doctor as a fully certified tactical member.

On March 6, 1992, a Medivac helicopter with a pilot and two nurses on board was headed toward Mount Graham Community Hospital to pick up a patient suffering from chest pains. The pilot had checked the weather conditions before taking off, but as he reached the mountains, the weather changed for the worse. The helicopter crashed around 7:30 P.M., killing the pilot, Dale Matthews, thirty-two, and flight nurse Susan Newton, twenty-six. The only survivor was thirty-four-year-old paramedic Glenn Velardi. He woke up trapped against the helicopter ceiling, soaked in fuel; he had fractures in his back and left ankle and wounds on his head.

The crash site was about a hundred miles northeast of Tucson and virtually inaccessible. Initial rescue attempts by a Customs Service helicopter and a Department of Public Safety Ranger helicopter were unsuccessful because they couldn't land on the steep terrain. Fourteen hours after the crash occurred, a four-man rescue team from the Pima County Sheriff's Department search and rescue team arrived in a helicopter.

After surveying the terrain, the team decided to execute a "long-line lift-out." Deputies Tom Price and Richard Carmona rappelled down into the crash site on a sixty-foot line tied to their helicopter. Arriving at the site first, Price stabilized Velardi, then examined Matthews and Newton for any signs of life. Then, with the helicopter hovering overhead, Carmona tied a special harness connected to a lifeline to both the wounded paramedic and himself. When Carmona signaled, the helicopter rose a mile and a half above the ground, taking its harnessed passengers with it. As Carmona held his wounded passenger, the helicopter pilot leveled off and slowly traveled about one mile to a clearing where the helicopter lowered the two men to the ground.

This is one of the most dangerous methods of rescue. The harness can break, the safety line can get caught in a tree, the victim can go into shock, a hard landing can cause further trauma, and there is always the chance that the precious human cargo dangling one hundred feet below a huge moving object can hit something during transport. Bad weather and high winds can only add to the inherent danger. It takes real teamwork to pull off a successful lift-out, requiring a rescue team member who remains in the helicopter to "spot" for the rescue and coordinate the efforts along with a highly skilled pilot.

For his role in the rescue, Deputy Richard Carmona was touted as a hero in the local press and honored by his department with a Medal of Valor. The rescue helped earn him the title of national SWAT Officer of the Year in 1993.

Deputy Carmona was not on a rescue mission or SWAT assignment when his courage and strength were once again challenged. He was on his way to a University of Arizona football game in his unmarked police car in bumper-to-bumper traffic when he came across an accident, so he stopped to provide medical assistance. He radioed for backup and to expedite any medical assistance required. Though he'd taught a course on unexpected high-risk encounters at the national SWAT school, he never imagined that his police training would be called into service at the scene of a fender-bender that day.

At about 5:45 P.M. Jean Pierre Lafitte, twenty-seven, had been driving his pickup truck near one of the busiest intersections in Tucson when he rear-ended a woman driving a Dodge Intrepid. As she got out of her car and approached the truck to get Lafitte's driver's license and vehicle information, he grabbed his gun and threatened her with it. He proceeded to bang her head on the side of his pickup and tried to pull her into his truck, according to witnesses.

When Deputy Carmona pulled up next to the truck, the woman managed to get away. Bystanders began yelling to Carmona to run and hide because the man in the truck had a gun, so Carmona returned to his car and picked up his Duty Colt .45.

"I'm on sensory overload at that point," Carmona told me. In civilian clothes, he pulled out his badge and showed it to Lafitte, who was about sixty feet away. "People are hiding behind me, yelling and screaming. I yelled for the man to come out, that I'm a police officer."

But Lafitte wasn't complying. His door opened, then closed, opened again, then slammed shut again. Then he got out of his truck with his back to Carmona.

"Let me see your hands," Carmona yelled to the suspect.

When Lafitte turned around, he had a semiautomatic pistol with its muzzle pointed toward the ground. Carmona repeatedly told Lafitte to put his weapon on the ground.

"The suspect started to crouch, and initially appeared to comply," Carmona recalled. "Just as I said, 'Step back from the gun,' he picks up the weapon and shoots out the windshield of my car." Another shot grazed Carmona's head.

"Survival is the strongest instinct," Carmona said as he reflected on the incident.

Afraid he might hit bystanders during a shoot-out, Carmona weighed that possibility against the risk that Lafitte might kill those around him. Then he returned Lafitte's shots in a running gun battle, firing seven rounds, three of which struck Lafitte, who went down. He'd been hit in the right leg, left arm, and abdomen. Carmona approached the man to attend to his wounds, but the shot to Lafitte's abdomen had traveled to his heart. He was pronounced dead at University Medical Center at 7:39 P.M. Carmona was devastated by the shooting death.

Jean Lafitte's grandfather, Carl Lafitte, found his fifty-three-year-old son, Carl Marion Lafitte, dead in his bed in his Tucson Mountains mobile home that same day. He had been stabbed multiple times. A bloody knife and 9-mm shell were found nearby.

Court records show that in 1998 Jean Lafitte had been diagnosed with severe anxiety, suicidal tendencies, depression, and paranoid schizophrenia. Symptoms of paranoid schizophrenia include anger, violence, and delusional thoughts. His father tried to make sure he took his medicine as prescribed three times a day.

Jean's sad history is replete with disturbing episodes that chronicled his violent nature. From a broken home, he was cited for shoplifting when he was only nine. At the age of ten he was placed in a shelter after he'd beaten his mother twice with a pair of nunchacku sticks (a martial arts weapon), which his father had made. Three years later when he was arrested for assaulting his father with the same weapon, police found a knife in his sock. Just a month later, his girlfriend's mother reported that he'd held a revolver to his girlfriend's head. His father committed him to a hospital for treatment that same year. He was released less than a month later, his mental health records sealed.

Five years later, he choked his girlfriend in court as she testified against him regarding an assault. Though he received a five-year sentence for the courtroom attack, he was released three years later on community supervision. In 1998 he was indicted on two counts of aggravated assault when he allegedly stabbed a man at a party.

Carl Lafitte had admitted his son to Kino Community Hospital the week they would both die. Faith Valenzuela, Jean's mother, stated that less than two days later, the young man was discharged. Three days later, Lafitte apparently murdered his father and then attempted to kill Deputy Carmona. According to a former girlfriend of Jean's, his father was trying to get Jean committed the day they both died.

Several years before, Jan Bernardini had been appointed to represent Lafitte when he was being held at Kino Community Hospital. In a letter to the *Arizona Daily Star* published on September 21, 1999, she stated that

Jean was a very disturbed, violent young man in desperate need of psychi-atric treatment. She wrote that he had told her he had showered in the dark so he couldn't see the blood pour out of the showerhead.

Lafitte had been ordered by the court to receive mental health care. Bernardini wrote that this generally "means the patient receives a cursory review of his mental health and legal history by an overworked case man-ager, a bag of meds, and an order to check in with his mental health provider from time to time." In her letter she lamented that there was no long-term treatment facility in Arizona for people like Jean Pierre Lafitte, who are mainstreamed back into society: "Although I am not a mental health professional, I had no doubt that Jean would kill someone, some-day, soon. I am saddened that it was his father, who seemed to be his only real advocate and friend. What we need to ask ourselves is not whether Dr. Carmona was justified in killing Jean, but how many other 'Jean Lafittes' are out there, without adequate treatment."

Deputy Carmona was cleared of any wrongdoing in the shooting death on September 22, 1999, and complimented for his actions by the county attorney. It's an odd coincidence that Dr. Carmona had run Kino Com-munity Hospital—where Lafitte had been hospitalized and from which he had been released just three days before their shoot-out—for two years as head of the county health-care system. He doesn't believe there's any-thing wrong with the hospital but that lack of an adequate health-care pol-icy and necessary resources were to blame.

The National Association of Police Organizations honored Deputy Carmona with one of its ten TOP COPS Awards in 2000 for his courage under fire. Today he is a professor at the University of Arizona in addition to his ongoing involvement with law enforcement.

"I'm bound to preserve and save life. I protect and preserve life in a dif-ferent way as a policeman."

Something tells me we haven't seen the last of this incredible individ-ual. In March 2002, President George W. Bush nominated Dr. Richard Carmona as the next Surgeon General of the United States.

7

DETECTIVE DAVID FOSTER

Newark (New Jersey) Police Department

"Human Shield"

"Thinking that you're going is a nerve-shattering experience. Your life goes right before your eyes. I still check behind shower curtains even at home," admitted David Foster. In November 1998 the forty-four-year-old detective, an eighteen-year veteran of the Newark (New Jersey) Police Department, was working in the Domestic Violence and Sexual Crimes Unit.

"The first time I met Malikah Jamison was at a hospital in Montclair, New Jersey. The Bloomfield Police Department contacted our unit with a report that a rape victim had been taken to the hospital. I drove over and took a crime report. Malikah agreed to an examination and rape kit to test for semen samples."

But a stranger didn't rape Malikah—she knew her attacker very well. "Malikah stated that her ex-boyfriend raped her at knifepoint early in the day and she wanted to file a complaint," Foster recounted to me.

The next day Malikah, twenty-two, and her father were at the station from 9 A.M. until 4 P.M. going over the events that led up to the alleged rape and kidnapping. The pair told Detective Foster that Adrian Howell, Malikah's ex-boyfriend and the father of her child, had been harassing her since she broke up with him, despite a restraining order. Malikah's rejection apparently had been an emotionally devastating hit to Howell, a twenty-seven-year-old substitute teacher who Foster recalled had a police record for selling marijuana. Withdrawn and despondent over the breakup, he had written a two-part letter describing how he was going to murder Malikah, according to Foster.

Malikah told Detective Foster that while she was getting ready for work on November 23, Adrian broke into her apartment by picking the lock on her front door, then, holding a knife in his hand, told her that he would kill her if she didn't have sex with him. Knowing Howell as well as she did, Malikah knew that the threat was real. Howell kept the knife at her throat during most of the two-hour sexual assault. He then abducted his former girlfriend, taking her to his apartment. Not willing to go inside, a scream-ing Malikah managed to fight off her kidnapper and run into the street where a passerby with a cell phone called 9-1-1. Police responded quickly and took the shaken and bruised woman to the hospital. Rather than return to her apartment, Malikah decided to spend the night at her father's home.

Detective Foster typed up warrants for the arrest of Adrian Howell. The next day a local judge would be asked to sign them, and Adrian would be arrested at his home, or at school if necessary. Malikah asked Detective Foster if he would accompany her to her apartment. She wanted to pick up some clothing and personal items and retrieve a photo of her attacker for identification purposes. Foster agreed.

It would be a life-altering decision and a defining moment in David Foster's life.

When Malikah didn't see Howell's vehicle in front of the building, Foster admitted, "I thought about sending the young lady into the apart-ment alone, but decided I should go in with her." As they approached the front door of the apartment, Foster noticed the tampering around the lock but couldn't tell if the marks were evidence of the earlier break-in or were new. "I thought that Adrian Howell may have, in fact, returned to retrieve incriminating evidence or maybe hurt Malikah. But when she wasn't home, he left." As it turned out, such a scenario was just wishful thinking.

When Malikah opened the door, she thought she heard a noise inside. Foster moved in front of her and instructed her to stay behind him, so she hung back as he stepped alone into the dark apartment. He sensed something was wrong. "I could feel my heart beating," he told me.

Curtains covered the openings to each bedroom. Despite the sunny day outside, the 25-watt low-density lightbulb left the three-foot-wide hallway so dark that Foster had to squint to see. He raised his radio to call for backup as he slowly walked down the narrow hall toward the bedrooms.

The eerie quiet was abruptly erased when Adrian Howell burst through a curtain.

Howell took two steps and, without speaking a word, aimed his .22-caliber gun at Foster and started shooting. Howell's first round hammered into Foster's shoulder. As Foster turned to find cover, Howell pointed his gun directly at the detective's head. Foster felt a bullet zip through his hair. His police radio was still in his left hand near his face, which would be a life-saving placement; the next bullet headed for Foster's head from less than two feet away but hit the radio instead, lodging in the battery. As Howell again pulled the trigger, Foster backed up and hunched over in an effort to dodge the next round, which entered his upper back. As he pitched toward the floor, he fired one shot from his .38-caliber service revolver into the attacker's left elbow and a second shot to his chest.

Howell crumpled. As Foster fell to his left knee he remembers hearing Malikah, apparently in a state of shock, running down the hallway screaming, "Someone just shot my boyfriend." Her screams for help compelled a resident to call 9-1-1.

"Officer down! Officer down!" Detective Foster radioed for help. Then he turned to Adrian Howell. "I tried to help him," Foster said. But Howell's chest wound was fatal.

A police unit soon arrived. In the confusion following the assault, Foster believed that Howell had fired as many as ten rounds instead of four. As the detective assessed his physical condition, he became concerned about his wounds; he knew that a .22-caliber gun shot at close range can be extraordinarily dangerous since the bullets can ricochet inside the body. Foster related to me that even a shot to a nonkill body zone could bounce off a bone and end up in the heart or brain, whereas a shot from close range from a larger caliber weapon such as a .38 usually penetrates whatever it encounters and exits cleanly.

"The anticipation of death is probably worse than death itself," Foster believes, and he wanted to breathe fresh air one more time. "I didn't want to die in the dark apartment," he told me. "I told an officer, 'Let me get outside.' " As the paramedics transported Detective Foster to the hospital, Officer Al-Terique Whitley, who'd been in the neighborhood on patrol, was pulling up. A police officer for two years, Whitley is David Foster's son. He didn't know until he arrived at the scene that his father was the officer who'd been shot.

Fortunately for David Foster, none of the .22-caliber rounds had ricocheted, but he suffered through several surgeries and a rehabilitation ordeal that lasted a year. "I've still got two bullets in my body. There was too much damage to the muscle and bone to take them out. My movement is still limited, and I feel pain when it's cold." Still, Foster feels blessed. "I'm a living witness of what God can do. He may not be here when you want him, but he's right on time."

Foster had pulled his gun in previous law enforcement skirmishes, but he had never killed anyone before. "I was nervous and scared," he confided. Unfortunately, his department did not offer counseling for post-traumatic stress disorder at the time. Many officers feared asking their supervisors for counseling because such a request might result in being relegated to what Foster calls "the rubber gun squad"—police jargon for a desk job. To some police officers who enjoy outside police work, a desk job is a fate worse than death.

Foster knows that he had no choice but to shoot Adrian Howell; if he had not returned Howell's fire, he surely would have been killed. Still, he shares the anguish of Howell's family. Howell's mother would later admit that her son had been acting strangely, according to Foster, but "I can't help but think about the guy's family. They won't see him again," he said.

What if Foster *hadn't* accompanied Malikah Jamison home that afternoon or had decided to stay outside when she went in? He is positive that she wouldn't be alive today. And that would have been a lot harder to live with than the pain he still suffers from that November afternoon.

In 1999 the International Association of Chiefs of Police and *PARADE Magazine* honored Detective David Foster as Police Officer of the Year. That same year he won the Newark Police Department's highest award, the purple and gold Medal of Valor, and the New Jersey Medal of Valor. The mayor of Newark presented David with a Purple Heart Award and officially proclaimed November 6 David Foster Day. For his courageous actions Foster also received an award from philanthropist and businessman Russ Berrie, who annually recognizes New Jersey citizens who make a difference in the lives of others.

Foster never regained full use of his left arm, which still has only limited range of motion. After eighteen years of exemplary service, he turned in his shield and weapon and retired with a two-thirds pension on September 1, 1999. He's now director of transportation at an adult medical day-care center and is waiting to get his private investigator's license.

"The end of my career came as unexpectedly as it started. I applied to join the Newark Police Department along with dozens of others. The others appeared more qualified to me. They were a tough-looking group of applicants. I went through the motions of taking the physical and mental aptitude tests but never in a million years thought they would call me. They did call, and I worked hard to become a good police officer," the retired detective affirmed.

"Being a police officer was a dream come true. I miss it. I was a good investigator, and I really enjoyed helping people and solving crimes." And the citizens of Newark miss Detective David Foster, a truly great American hero.

8

OFFICERS GLEN McGARY AND JAMES SWEATT

Portland (Maine) Police Department

"Saved Twice"

Officer Glen McGary

Officer James Sweatt

It didn't take much to persuade Kevin Caufield to leave the area in front of Paul & Val's Firehouse Tavern in Portland, Maine. The passive Caufield gave Officers James Sweatt and Glen McGary no reason to think that he was a violent man.

James Sweatt, thirty-one, a veteran police officer on September 17, 1999, and his wife, Lisa, also an experienced police officer, were dedicated to doing a good job. The two met at work and dated despite the usual warnings about the disasters that can result from dating a coworker. After a short courtship, they tied the knot. In truth, James was actually a bit envious that Lisa, at five feet two inches and 105 pounds, routinely collared bad guys, always seeming to be in the right place at the right time. An avid horseback rider, she's a mounted police officer in the summer months.

On the day they met Kevin Caufield, Sweatt's partner, Glen McGary, twenty-four, was a rookie with only a year on the job, and Glen's wife, Elsa, was eight months pregnant. Elsa and Lisa were both from Vermont, while Glen and James were both from Maine. The couples even shared the same anniversary date, although they married in different churches.

Partners for eleven months, Sweatt and McGary were part of a five-man community policing unit. Sweatt was also a SWAT team member, while McGary had worked as a deputy for the county and had extensive training as an emergency medical technician (EMT) and mountain climber.

On the morning of September 17, 1999, Lisa was in the barn brushing down her police horse as she talked with her female police partner. Lisa was going out of state with some friends on an antique-buying trip that day. Before leaving for work, James came down to the barn in his uniform to say good-bye to Lisa and tell her to drive safely. James and Lisa never showed affection for one another around other police officers while on duty because they thought it was inappropriate. But "When I simply said, 'Good-bye. Have a nice trip,' Lisa's partner asked me if I was going to kiss Lisa good-bye. I laughed and kissed her, even though we don't usually do that around other officers. Lisa's last words to me were, 'Be safe, and I'll see you in a few days.' "

Lisa had taken several of these trips with her girlfriends in the past, and James never bothered to ask her where she would be staying or how to reach her if he needed to. It never dawned on either of them a life-threatening emergency would make her race home that very night.

Sweatt and McGary started their shift at 1 P.M. that Friday. Their first call was a domestic disturbance. They helped fellow officers chase and arrest a suspect whom they drove to the Cumberland County Jail.

The second call would change both their lives forever.

Around 6:45 P.M., the manager at Paul & Val's Firehouse Tavern reported that a man was creating a loud disturbance in front of the bar. McGary radioed back that they would respond since they were only two or three blocks away. Outside the bar they found a forty-five-year-old man, somewhat well attired in an oxford shirt and blue jacket, on a bicycle. He'd been bothering people in the bar, but he was on a public sidewalk and not really bothering anybody when they arrived. Still, he'd been acting strangely, according to the tavern owner. All the officers could do was urge the man to move on.

The bicyclist's ID indicated that his name was Kevin Caufield and he lived in Portland. He was very cordial to the two officers and gave them no trouble. He pedaled away on his bike.

Minutes later the officers heard another radio call concerning the same tavern. This time Officer Bob Pelletier responded to the call and wrote up a field call report about the incident. The bar manager said Caufield had threatened to blow up the bar or set it on fire because the cops had been called out earlier. Officer Pelletier radioed Officers McGary and Sweatt, who were already on their way to Caufield's home, to arrest him if they located him.

Caufield was living with his sister and his mother, who was suffering from respiratory disease and constantly required help breathing from an oxygen unit. As the officers approached the home around 7:00 P.M., they could see Mrs. Caufield inside, and she told them to come in. She said that Kevin had gone to the pharmacy for her. Kevin's sister told the officers that he might be in his room in the basement, so with the mother's permission, Sweatt cautiously proceeded downstairs.

Caufield wasn't there. Though it seemed strange that he slept in the basement on a cot, Sweatt saw nothing suspicious. There was a workbench in one corner, a dresser in another corner, and a trunk. Later, investigators would find many disturbing and damning items in the basement, but now they only wanted to find Kevin Caufield.

If Caufield were arrested, he'd probably have to spend a night in jail and would be released on his own recognizance in the morning. If charged with a crime, it most likely would be a misdemeanor. The officers told Mrs. Caufield to call them when Kevin came home and they would make the arrest with a minimum of fanfare and trouble.

The officers left the house and were back in their cruiser when they noticed Caufield riding toward his house on his bicycle, holding a bag in his left hand. McGary got out of the car and began pursuing Caufield on foot, telling him to stop and put down the bag. Instead of stopping, Caufield turned his bike into his driveway and headed for a detached garage behind his house.

Sweatt radioed that a pursuit was in progress and asked if there were any other units that could lend a hand. Then he tried to cut off Caufield with his car, but Caufield had gotten inside the open garage and closed the door behind him.

When McGary pulled up the garage door, Caufield swung at him with the bag he was carrying (which, it was later learned, contained a six-pack of beer). McGary instinctively jumped back, and Caufield again shut the garage door, this time locking it. At this point Sweatt joined McGary, only to find themselves standing outside in the rain, staring at Caufield through the glass panes in the garage door.

Even though the door had four panes across the top, it was difficult to see inside the darkened garage. The officers yelled to Caufield to come out, but he only glared back at them. Sweatt then removed his baton to break out a pane of glass. When he smashed through the glass, Caufield stuck his arm through the broken pane in an attempt to punch the officers. Sweatt sprayed pepper spray at Caufield, who then darted to the rear of the garage and out of sight.

The officers ran around to a second garage door, but it wouldn't open fully because it was blocked by the stored materials inside. It took the combined weight of both officers to push it open far enough for Sweatt to press through the narrow space created. Once inside the murky garage, Sweatt—pepper spray at the ready—followed Caufield up a set of stairs. Caufield started throwing anything he could find at Sweatt, who covered his head and face as he crept up the stairs.

Meanwhile, McGary was struggling to push through the same blocked door, which had required the coordinated efforts of two officers to open just moments earlier. Unknown to him at the time, however, his radio fell off as he squeezed through the makeshift opening.

By now Sweatt had reached the top of the stairs where he once again sprayed pepper spray at Caufield. But Caufield spun around with an eight-inch knife in his hand, slashing the officer's neck and face and stabbing him in the chest. Sweatt yelled for his partner to help him.

"Shoot him," Sweatt yelled. "He's stabbing me."

McGary yelled back that he couldn't get a clear shot—he was afraid he would hit his partner instead of Caufield. Again McGary heard his partner yell for him to shoot Caufield, but all McGary could see were two silhouettes, arms flailing in all directions. Then one of the bodies fell backward down the steps, and McGary clearly saw one of the silhouettes raise his arm high in the air, knife in hand.

"There was a very small light shining through the window. I could see Caufield's mustache," he recalled as we spoke.

McGary finally had a clear shot, and using the night sight on his gun, he fired four rounds. Then "Everything went quiet," he said. "It was eerie . . . it was so silent."

Caufield fell forward down the stairs on top of the fallen officer. Pulling Caufield off his partner, McGary checked the man for a pulse and quickly determined that he was dead. His partner was alive—but barely.

Sweatt could not move. With each heartbeat, he felt a warm, wet sensation as his blood pulsed from his body. Blood was everywhere. He instinctively knew that he was in serious trouble and would die if he didn't get immediate help.

"I jammed my hand into Jimmy's neck and pressed with my fingers on two spots," McGary remembers. Thanks to his EMT training, he was able to grab the bleeding jugular vein in his partner's wound and apply pressure to minimize the blood loss.

With his other hand, McGary reached for his radio to call for help, but it wasn't there. He tried Officer Sweatt's unit, but it had been broken during the scuffle and subsequent fall. All he knew was that he couldn't leave his partner alone to bleed to death.

Suddenly Officer Jeff Viola, responding to Sweatt's previous call about a chase in progress, yelled out, "Glen! Jimmy! Where are you guys?"

Several officers rallied around the wounded officer to carry him from the gloomy garage. Sweatt still remembers the chaos as his fellow officers carried him quickly through the debris and clutter, all the while shouting at him to stay alive. He managed to unfasten his gun belt, which fell to the ground, reducing their load by some ten pounds. The emergency medical unit soon arrived to take Sweatt to the emergency room.

Sweatt told me that he felt relief because he recognized the paramedics and knew they were among the best. All the way to the hospital, he kept repeating that he had ordered Glen to shoot, that Glen had done the right thing. In case he died, he thought he'd better make sure the world understood that the shooting was justified. On what he thought was his deathbed, all he could think about was protecting his partner.

Covered in Sweatt's blood from head to toe, McGary returned to the station. He knew that Lisa was out of town and wanted to make sure that she was paged about her husband's condition. Then he cleaned up, changed his clothes, and called his wife.

"Elsa, I'm still at work. I'm okay, but I'll be late."

"Is there something wrong?"

"I can't talk about it right now."

Then he hung up and arranged for two friends who were both police officers to go to his house and tell Elsa what had happened while he drove back to the hospital to be with his partner. Elsa and Lisa would join James and Glen at the hospital.

Sweatt had a 180-degree cut through the jugular vein in his neck and a 95-degree cut through another major vessel. A vertebra was broken in his neck, and he was paralyzed on his right side. Luckily, the metal plate in his bullet-proof vest had protected him from Caufield's stab to his chest. The doctors worked for six hours repairing the damage. When I spoke to Sweatt, he told me that as a result of "Caufield's psychotic rage," as he put it, the doctors had to put sixty staples around his head and over a hundred stitches in his neck.

McGary really saved Sweatt's life twice that night. Not only did he stop Sweatt's attacker but he also stopped Sweatt from bleeding to death. The doctors agreed that Sweatt would never have survived if McGary had not controlled the bleeding at the scene.

Though Caufield had a history of run-ins with the Portland Police Department dating from 1984 when he led police on a high-speed chase, his most serious offense prior to the deadly September 1999 incident was a physical assault on a man in order to steal his bike. Most of his encounters with the police had been for fighting and disorderly conduct.

Caufield's family said he was schizophrenic, McGary told me. Though he had medication to treat the symptoms, he didn't take it when he was drinking—and he was a binge drinker.

When investigators searched Caufield's home after the shooting, they found no guns, but they found a loaded crossbow under the covers on his bed, pipe bomb materials, and books about how to kill people. One of the books explained the best techniques to use when killing someone with a knife from behind, similar to the way Caufield had cut Officer Sweatt. They also discovered a personal note believed to have been written by Caufield. Excerpts from the note read: "Columbine will look like a picnic. Sawed-off shotgun should be easy enough to sneak in. Hostages will be fun to torture and maim. This is my destiny." Another notation stated that the right ammunition in a sawed-off shotgun could "wipe out 10 to 15 immediately."

We'll never know what Kevin Caufield intended to do. Following his investigation, Brian MacMaster, chief investigator for the attorney general's office, concluded that McGary's decision to use deadly force on Caufield was reasonable under the circumstances.

True to what being a real partner is all about, each officer kept worrying about the other during that violent evening. Even as he was being carried out of the garage, James Sweatt wanted to make it crystal clear to anyone who would listen that Glen McGary had fired on his orders. McGary, however, was only concerned that his partner survive his attacker's wounds. "He's my partner and my best friend," McGary told me on the phone.

While McGary will tell you that Sweatt is the only hero who emerged during the incident, Sweatt says McGary is an authentic hero. McGary responds, "I feel uncomfortable being called a hero. For me it was just a day at work. It's part of the job."

According to Chief Michael Chitwood, they are both heroes. In fact, it was the chief who submitted their names for inclusion in this book. As a result of the violent encounter, Chief Chitwood requires all officers to wear their bulletproof vests while on duty. He's also made EMT training available to any officer who wants it.

For his bravery and quick thinking, Glen McGary received a Valor Commendation from the city of Portland and was presented with an award for heroism from the South Portland chapter of the Military Order of the Purple Heart, a veterans organization, which also gave a Citation and Meritorious Service Award to James Sweatt. The officers received a TOP COPS Honorable Mention, awards from the chief of police, and a letter of commendation from the state legislature.

Even though he would be declared disabled with his spinal cord injury Sweatt regained movement in his arms and legs. He would return to work a year and a half later and insist on returning to patrol duty. He's been promoted to sergeant in the Portland Police Department.

"It's what I love and what I do best," Sweatt said. But he suffered from what he believes was post-traumatic stress disorder, and confesses now that the events of that September night in 1999 have made him worry more than he used to about the inherent risks of his job. Both Sweatt and McGary attended a program in Minnesota for officers involved in critical incidents, which they found valuable.

When James Sweatt thinks about how Caufield almost took his life, he worries about Lisa more than he did before the incident. He now knows all too well how quickly things can go wrong on the streets, even when pursuing a courteous, well-dressed, apparently friendly person.

"Any thoughts of retiring?" I asked Sweatt.

"Not really. Both Lisa and I love what we do," he replied. "I'm just grateful I have a second chance to do what I love."

9

CHIEF ROBERT J. MORTELL

Paxton (Massachusetts) Police Department

"Officer Presence"

"I got three guys running across the road right now!" Chief Robert J. Mortell yelled into his police radio. He had spotted three men running from a neighborhood that had just been burglarized. He knew these were the right guys. Known to his friends as "Bobby," the chief of the Paxton Police Department had responded to a mutual aid call for a burglary in progress put out by the Holden Police Department, a neighboring jurisdiction. Also a K-9 handler, Chief Mortell's bloodhound Ginger was a new partner who was just completing state certification.

Detective Al Bourget, an officer with the Holden police, was the man who called Mortell into service. "I asked him to respond and told him, 'Bring your new mutt,' referring to Ginger." Al and Bobby were long-time professional friends; they worked next door to one another between the two small jurisdictions.

It was February 1, 1994, a Tuesday, and, as they say in New England, it was "wicked cold." Three known felons were burglarizing a home in

Holden when a witness who saw them kicking in the door to a house alerted the police to the crime. As Detective Bourget recounted, "We had been experiencing a rash of burglaries in our area for some time, and we formed sort of a loose task force to deal with it." The various agencies around the Holden and Paxton communities all participated. When a burglary call hit one agency, the neighboring jurisdictions all swarmed in to set up a dragnet.

"It worked," recalled Bourget, referring to the success of the task force. "We'd caught other burglars in the act. In fact, Bobby Mortell loved catching B&E [breaking and entering] guys, and he was good at it. Bobby was good for the town and good for the cops. He really was a good guy, and everyone loved him. I loved working with the guy. And he really was very good at police work and at handling crime scenes."

Chief Mortell had developed quite a reputation for apprehending burglars, according to former Paxton police chief Robert P. Sheehan. "Bobby hated housebreakers. He had this thing about them. He'd chase them to his last breath." In one storied arrest, Mortell went into the woods, chasing two suspects on foot for three miles. An avid distance runner, Mortell and his young tracking K-9, Ginger, simply stayed with the suspects until they fell, totally exhausted. Mortell then held one man down while holding the other at gunpoint. Mortell didn't know the man he was atop was holding a gun hidden underneath his body. It was later discovered when the backup officers came to transport the suspects to jail.

As another example of Mortell's skill at finding burglars, Bourget told the story of being all the way over in Worcester when he heard Mortell on the radio calling for assistance on a burglary in progress. Evidently, Mortell had discovered signs of forced entry, but it wasn't clear if the crime was recent or not. As he approached the house, two gangsters who were capering inside watched as he walked up to the door. One of them later told police that he had Mortell in his gun sight but he didn't shoot at that point because he heard the approaching sirens, and there were lots of them. He just wanted to get away.

The suspects ran out the back, only to be confronted by the chief. He told them to lie prone on the ground while he maintained his safety by keeping back, not getting in too close. He held them at gunpoint, called in on the radio for help, and never took his eyes or his attention off them. At the time, Mortell didn't know the suspects were armed; they'd hidden their guns under them as they lay down on the ground. They planned to ambush the chief if they could get the drop on him.

But he wasn't giving them that opportunity. He showed the suspects that he was in command and control, maintaining that cool, composed demeanor that policemen like to call "officer presence."

Bourget and his partner heard the call and knew Bobby would need their assistance, so they rolled all the way back to Paxton. Meanwhile the two suspects, prone on the ground, were sizing up the situation with the chief, wondering if they could take him. They tried to draw Bobby toward them, but he wasn't buying. He stood his ground, keeping his pistol trained on them. The suspects were taken into custody without incident and sent to prison.

"That was a year ago," Bourget said, "and then this thing on Kendall Road happened; it was awful."

The metropolitan and suburban areas surrounding Worcester, Massachusetts, are a mix of urban neighborhoods and upper-scale communities. In this part of the country, the sprawling neighborhoods have ranch-style homes that are built on large lots. Some of the towns are less affluent, but others are clearly upper-middle-class enclaves. Most have quiet downtowns, and often they leave an outsider with a small town feel reminiscent of a fabled little village near Raleigh, North Carolina, where crime is someone else's problem. But that image would be false. They have real crimes in these communities, just like everywhere else in America. They need professional peace officers like those joined together in the self-proclaimed "loose task force" around Holden and Paxton, Massachusetts. And they need real heroes like Chief Mortell to patrol their streets and protect their neighborhoods.

On this fateful day in February at about ten forty-five in the morning, Detective Bourget heard the call of the burglaries that had just occurred. A radio car officer arrived on the scene and described the violence of the break-ins. The homes had the outside doors kicked in, and the interiors were totally trashed. The suspects had trampled through the homes, ransacking nearly every drawer and every closet. They vandalized with every step and destroyed things they didn't take. Bourget realized the suspects were on Kendall Road, which was a dead end. He knew there was a real chance of catching these guys, but only if the officers moved quickly and set up a good perimeter. So he called for help from his neighboring city's police force, and Bobby Mortell rolled into the town of Holden to help his brother officers. It was to be his last call as a policeman.

The suspects in these Kendall Road burglaries were all known felons who had been terrorizing the central Massachusetts communities just outside of Worcester. The ringleader was Michael D. Souza from Seymour Street in Worcester. Souza had been in and out of court and jail for almost all his adult life. Now at the ripe old age of twenty-five he was a hardened career criminal, totally amoral, totally asocial, and a total predator. He was a thief for the most part—he'd done time for other residential burglaries—but he also had a history of illegally using firearms. As his crimes graduated to robbery, he practiced what he would do if he surprised a homeowner or met up with a responding police officer. He'd planned and prepared for how he would take a life. As it turned out, he was training himself for the day he would kill a policeman. The other two suspects, Kenneth N. Padgett and Jamie Richards, both twenty-three, were also from Worcester, and they too were well known to the local police.

Souza, Padgett, and Richards were somewhat organized in their criminal endeavors, and they'd planned this caper for the Monday following Super Bowl Sunday. But all three of them partied over the weekend, getting high on cocaine and drinking all day Sunday, so on Monday their hangovers forced them to stay home. They'd wait until Tuesday.

On Tuesday Souza drove them over to the town of Holden where they ended up on Kendall Road. On the prowl, they were determining which homes to hit, looking for easy marks in the well-to-do neighborhood. Kendall Road is about a mile long and dead-ends near a reservoir. It runs parallel to Route 31, which is the major thoroughfare that connects the town of Paxton to Holden. Some say the Kendall Road residents added to the police's problems by not locking up their homes due to a false perception that they were immune from crime, that crime happened in other communities, not theirs. Naive residents commented that they didn't need to lock their doors or windows. The neighborhood might as well have put out the welcome mat to criminals.

Near the end of the street and adjacent to the neighborhood is the Kendall Reservoir, which supplies drinking water to the area. Souza drove the three men down to the end of the cul-de-sac near the reservoir, where they started their crime spree. They were pretty clumsy with their entries. Souza simply kicked open the doors, which caused wood and glass to shatter into the homes. It also left telltale forensic evidence pressed microscopically into the suspect's clothes, trace evidence that ultimately could be used as evidence to place Souza at the scene of the crime.

Glass shards, wood fibers, oil stains, and paint fragments could be the fingerprint-quality evidence used to convict all these men. Better than eye-witness testimony, which is always disputed, or stolen property found in the suspect's possession, which is generally explained away as circumstantial and not connected to a crime, the forensic connection to a suspect and the original crime scene is usually the evidence that convicts. If Souza were to be found with microscopic glass shards, wood fibers, and paint chips in his clothing that all matched the damaged items at the victims' homes, how else could he plausibly explain their presence? Most seasoned detectives will tell you that when you're talking crime scenes, forensics isn't just important to consider, forensics is everything.

Once inside, the men were interested in money and easily fenced items like televisions, stereos, VCRs, and jewelry, which could support their lifestyle of drug use and partying. They were on Kendall Road long enough to ransack three homes before a neighbor saw them. The police rolled into action when a witness called to report that a break-in had occurred at 93 Kendall Road. Just as responding officers were pulling up to investigate, another call came in to dispatch that a carjacking had just occurred on a service road near Pine Hill Reservoir.

The suspects, fleeing the area, had evidently lost control of their stolen van when they hit some black ice near Pine Hill Dam. Careening out of control, they sideswiped a Worcester city water department truck that was parked near the roadway. The suspects then abandoned their getaway vehicle and ran over to the workers who were near their truck. At gunpoint, Souza and the others demanded the truck's keys from the city crew.

Initially the crew didn't respond, and the foreman didn't want to submit. In either disbelief or defiance, the foreman started to walk away. Souza responded by firing a shot and said, "Give me the fucking keys or I'll blow your head off!" The foreman realized Souza would kill him if he didn't cooperate and gave up his keys to the truck. He told his crew to run off into the woods, where they waited until the police arrived.

The suspects sped off in the water department truck, and in their haste, they lost control of that vehicle too, running it into a ditch. With the truck mired in the snow and mud, they were forced to abandon their second stolen vehicle. Fleeing on foot, they ran about a mile across a frozen portion of Kendall Reservoir, heading toward Route 31.

When Detective Bourget called Chief Mortell into service for this particular call, there was nothing routine about it, even though working together was very much routine for the two men. In small town America, local officers work with neighboring city police, county sheriffs, or state troopers the same way major city officers work with their beat partners. Most people in America don't realize that the majority of police agencies nationwide have less than fifteen officers. Police departments with two or three officers have to use outside mutual aid assistance on virtually every emergency they handle. Searching for criminals that were this violent, this predatory, required scores of police officers to provide the necessary tactical advantage.

The situation was well above the staffing capabilities of most police departments in the country and clearly beyond any of the departments in the immediate Worcester area. The Holden Police Department did the only thing they could do in this case: they put out the call for mutual aid.

When he got to the area where the suspects were last seen, Detective Bourget started to track them through the snow. The snow wasn't particularly heavy in some spots, so the footprints weren't always plainly visible. Bourget recalled, "I'm chasing after these guys, and I realize I might lose them." He was hoping Chief Mortell would get there soon with his dog, Ginger, and they could take over the tracking. Besides, Al knew how good Bobby was at chasing housebreakers and how he hated them. That would give the officers the edge they'd need to capture these dangerous men.

When Chief Mortell responded to the call for assistance, he was updated on the subsequent carjacking, the robbery, and the shots fired. He knew the level of violence doesn't get much worse. He had his K-9 partner with him as he rolled to the area. Paxton is southwest of Holden, and Mortell had to take Route 31 to get to the scene where the suspects were last seen. As he was driving into Holden, he heard Holden police officers broadcast that they had the suspects running into the woods. At this point Souza and his gang had made their way across the frozen reservoir and were running up the embankment to the highway just as Chief Mortell was approaching. The suspects didn't slow for traffic as they ran across the road and into the woods on the other side.

"I got three guys running across the road right now!" the chief yelled into the radio. Then he left his police cruiser and his dog behind and pursued the men on foot, broadcasting that he was chasing the suspects through the woods. Ginger wasn't a patrol dog, she was a tracker, but she was upset at being left behind in the police car. After bonding with Bobby Mortell, she wanted to be at her partner's side. They'd always been together before, and she could probably sense the danger. When the chief didn't take her, she wailed and yelped while she sat alone in the cruiser.

As Mortell ran up the embankment into the woods, the three suspects split apart. Padgett and Richards ran off to the chief's right, but being the good runner that he was, he stayed with them, catching up to them as he got to the top of the hill. The chief soon had the tactical advantage over the suspects. As he positioned himself for the capture, he repeatedly yelled out, "Freeze! Police!" Padgett and Richards helped draw Mortell's attention away from Souza, and for that, they would be just as responsible for what was about to happen.

Souza moved in the opposite direction from his crime partners so that he could work his way behind the pursuing officer. He was searching for the high ground one needs to be effective as a sniper. He used his crime partners to draw the chief into a position of false security and clear vulnerability.

When Mortell yelled out, "Freeze! Police!" for the third time, Padgett and Richards stopped to surrender. With the momentary cooperation of the two suspects, Mortell became distracted. In the excitement of overtaking the suspects, he lost track of Michael Souza.

Like the predator he was, Souza, lying down on the ground in a sniper's attitude, had set the trap for the pursuing officer. Souza opened fire, shooting twelve rounds at Chief Mortell, hitting him twice in the left side of his chest. The rounds tore into Mortell's heart and ripped into his aorta, causing massive bleeding. Gravely wounded, Mortell didn't retreat from the fight but turned and opened fire on Souza, getting off six shots and causing Souza to retreat back down the hill. Mortell took a few steps after him, but he had lost too much blood. As he slipped into unconsciousness, the chief went down.

Momentarily, it was strangely silent. Only Ginger could still be heard crying from Mortell's car.

Within a few minutes, Paxton Police Sergeant Michael Ahearn called on the radio to report that Chief Mortell had been shot. Princeton Police Chief Charles Schmohl and West Boylston Police Detective Francis Glynn tried to comfort Chief Mortell. Several officers worked together to pick him up and carry him down to the roadway. An emergency medical crew feverishly worked on Mortell as they transported him, but he was bleeding internally, and nothing more could be done. Chief Bobby Mortell was transported to the University of Massachusetts Hospital, where he died in the emergency room.

By now, twenty police departments had sent over 150 officers to the scene where a perimeter was set to capture the suspects. The forest had been buttoned up; there was no segment of the woods or roadway that didn't have officers within eyesight of one another in what was the largest dragnet in Holden or Paxton history. State police helicopters with heat-seeking cameras were brought in to assist in the search.

"We'll freeze them out," one officer remarked to his partner as they stood at their post and waited. The officers tapped their feet and moved about in the wicked cold trying to keep their blood circulating, but they were taking pleasure in the cold at that point, knowing that the suspects were freezing too. As the afternoon passed, it felt like twenty below.

As officers combed the area, Souza made his way over to Lindgren Lumber, an old sawmill on Reservoir Street. He was walking down a road near the woods when Paxton Police Sergeant Donald Ball and Massachusetts Trooper James Jaworek saw him. The officers had the advantage as they closed in on the suspect from behind. With their guns drawn, they ordered Souza to stop. But Souza, ever defiant, refused to stop or turn to acknowledge the officers' commands. Again and again, Sergeant Ball ordered Souza to stop, but the man continued to walk away. Finally, the officers engaged him in hand-to-hand combat, subduing and disarming him without seriously injuring him. Without firing a shot, the officers were able to take away Souza's 9-mm pistol, the weapon he used to kill Chief Mortell. The officers retained their dignity by handling the suspect with appropriate professional demeanor, never letting their emotions over the death of Chief Mortell override their good judgment. Within hours, the other two suspects were also captured without incident.

All three went to trial and were convicted for their roles in the murder of Chief Mortell. Souza was sentenced to life without the possibility of parole. His coconspirators each received fifteen years to life with the possibility of parole.

An officer had fallen in the line of duty. But Chief Mortell is not just a hero for the way he died. He is a hero for the way he lived his life. Ironically, as Detective Bourget was responding to the scene that February day, he passed Mortell's wife. He had known Pamela Mortell for a number of years, and he also knew the Mortell's three children. The high school sweethearts had a very good marriage. When Al Bourget passed Pam on the road, he couldn't know what was ahead, but he knew that Pam was always supportive of Bobby's career as a policeman and that she was very proud he had been made chief. Bourget told me, "Bobby was always on duty. He slept with one ear to the scanner, and if one of his guys was on a car stop, and it didn't sound right to Bobby, he'd throw on his gear and ride over to back up the cop. He was that kind of guy." Always there for her husband, Pam loved him for being that kind of guy. He was a wonderful husband, father, and son.

Chief Bobby Mortell worked every day to protect and serve the city of Paxton. A very professional peace officer, he was highly experienced and well educated. He earned a B.A. degree from Anna Maria College and was pursuing his M.A. degree when he was murdered. In his routine duties he was committed to providing quality service to the people of Paxton. He was courteous and friendly, and those who knew him loved and respected him.

Bobby Mortell was not the only hero in what happened that day. To start, every officer who had a hand in the manhunt for the criminals could be considered a hero. The officers who stood the post for the perimeter on that brutally cold day in February should be on the list of heroes also. The officers who tracked down the burglars and captured the gunman are on the list too. And the men who carried Chief Mortell down from the hill will take the memories of that day with them to their graves. Detective Al Bourget is a hero not only for the good job he did that day but also for the excellent follow-up work he did to help put the killers in prison. They are all top drawer in anyone's book.

Others are uncelebrated heroes. On that day, Holden Police Officer Richard Westerback, a twenty-five-year veteran of the force who responded to the original burglary scene, is a reluctant hero. He was very upset he wasn't participating in the manhunt, angrily saying, "I should have been out on the perimeter. I should have been there for Bobby." Anyone can understand how Officer Westerback felt, but he was needed to control the original crime scene. He had to protect the very evidence that could convict the suspects of the first-degree murder of a police officer. And as it turned out, some young crime scene investigators had started to muck up the evidence before Officer Westerback refocused their procedures. His role was no less important than Sergeant Ball's and Trooper Jaworek's when they captured Souza. Though Ball and Jaworek took Souza into custody, without Westerback's crime scene work it might have been difficult to convict the man and put him in prison for the rest of his life.

The loss of Chief Bobby Mortell is too well known to members of his family, who are heroes for carrying on his name and his traditions of service to the community. An officer's family is always forced to pay a premium for our police service. In so doing, they ultimately pay the premium for our freedom and for our way of life. An officer's family may resent the failure of society to fully understand or appreciate the devastation that hits a household when a police officer falls in the line of duty. No words can explain the pain that results—the missing touch of a loved one, the loss of an approving smile, the absence of a father or mother no longer there to watch the children grow. Mortell was murdered while trying to protect someone he'd never met; in this case, it was some homeowners over on Kendall Road. How will they remember him ten years from now?

The Paxton Police Station is named after Robert J. Mortell. The Massachusetts Police Association awarded Chief Mortell the Medal of Honor, while the New England Association of Chiefs of Police awarded him a Posthumous Commendation. Visitors to the Paxton Town Center can view a granite and brass plaque that memorializes the ultimate sacrifice Mortell made for his fellow citizens. Quinsigamond Community College has an annual charity golf tournament for a college scholarship program known as the Mortell. Some of the funds support the creation of the school's Public Safety Memorial Garden, which is being developed to honor students who pursue public safety careers and die in the line of duty. At Anna Maria College, the Institute for Public Safety is now called The Mortell Institute for Public Safety. And remember Route 31, the main thoroughfare connecting Holden to Paxton? It's now called the Chief Robert Mortell Memorial Highway.

There was a final loss for the Paxton police family. Immediately after Bobby Mortell's death, Ginger, his K-9 partner, stayed a week at the home of another officer before being taken back to Pam and Bobby's house. But after living another week without Bobby, she passed away in her sleep. Detective Bourget described Ginger as being lost without Bobby's companionship.

Bobby's widow, Pam, agreed. "She died from a broken heart."

10

DEPUTY TERRY LAWSON

San Diego County (California) Sheriff's Department

"In Harm's Way"

In harm's way—three simple words that aptly describe the dangers faced and the sense of purpose for a peace officer, that define the commitment, drive, and determination required to serve as a peace officer, that explain the values shared by peace officers. Bravery comes in many forms for the peace officer. The police do for society what individual citizens could never do on their own. Each day, as officers step into their radio cars, walk the corridors of their jails, or pick up case files, they place themselves in harm's way.

The expression itself dates back to the year 1661 and is attributed to Thomas Fuller, a British scholar, preacher, and prolific author of the seventeenth century. Fuller used it to describe avoiding danger—by staying *out of* harm's way. The first recorded use of this expression in America, however, occurred in a naval context, in a letter from Captain John Paul Jones to French leader Le Ray de Chaumont. John Paul Jones set the American standard when he wrote on November 16, 1778, "I wish to have no Connection with any Ship that does not Sail fast for I intend to go in harm's way."

Throughout America's history, police officers have gone in harm's way to serve and protect our country. And the dangers abound. The threat for police officers is the unknown—what they don't expect and can't predict. The police respond to radio calls or make traffic stops, they break up family fights or street brawls, and they don't know friend from foe. That unknown element is the real danger because officers can't approach a person assuming they are going to be killed. That would be too aggressive, too oppressive, in a free society. It would be viewed as unprofessional by American standards.

To stay safe, officers must approach suspects not as though they are going to be killed by them but instead as though they *could* be killed by them. This subtle difference will keep officers on their toes, and ultimately that might keep them alive. The old slang term *flatfoot* described the neighborhood foot-beat officer, but it could also describe an officer caught off guard, as in "He was flatfooted." A police officer caught flatfooted could end up dead. Yet police departments throughout the country made very few changes in their procedures for decades.

Then along came the Newhall tragedy on April 6, 1970, the darkest day in the history of the California Highway Patrol (CHP). Situated just north of the San Fernando Valley in Los Angeles, California, the area is now better known for the Six Flags Magic Mountain amusement park in nearby Valencia. But that's not what Newhall means to the police. To the police, Newhall is the place in America where tactical training for the patrol officer began. It's the place where four highway patrolmen were gunned down during a high-risk felony car stop. The Newhall tragedy is well known to almost every peace officer in America.

In the early morning on April 6, 1970, CHP Officers Walter C. Frago, Roger D. Gore, James E. Pence, Jr., and George M. Alleyn were all killed in Newhall. Officers Frago and Gore were working the morning watch, or graveyard shift, out of the Newhall CHP station. The main highway that they patrol is Interstate 5 (I-5), known in Southern California as the Golden State Freeway. The officers responded to a report of a suspect brandishing a weapon from a vehicle. Bobby Davis, the driver of the suspect vehicle, and Jack Twinning, the passenger, were both ex-convicts with extensive criminal histories. Davis, driving recklessly, cut off another car on the I-5 freeway. Jack Twinning waved his gun at the driver of the car that had been cut off. As soon as Twinning brandished his weapon, the other driver pulled off the freeway, went to a pay phone in a gas station, and called the CHP. The dispatchers immediately broadcast "Attention all units: a 417 [man with a gun] just occurred." Area road patrols swarmed in and began to search for the two gunmen.

Officers Frago and Gore spotted the car, called for assistance, and initiated a car stop before their backup arrived. When the suspects pulled over in a parking lot, the driver was told to get out and place his hands on the hood of the car. Gore approached the driver as Frago moved to the passenger side of the car. But the passenger door unexpectedly swung open, and a man came out shooting. Frago fell with two shots in his chest; he was dead when he hit the ground. When Gore realized what had happened to his partner, he turned to open fire. But the driver, Davis, was able to draw his weapon and shoot Gore twice at close range. Both officers, who were just twenty-three years old, were dead at the scene.

CHP officers James E. Pence, Jr., and George M. Alleyn, both twenty-four years old, were partners that night on the graveyard shift. They heard the call for assistance and where the stop was going down, so they raced to the scene. They pulled into the parking lot in a minute or two. They saw the CHP black-and-white sitting there with its old-style round amber flashing light pulsing through the rear window. It must have been a little blinding because they saw nothing else. The officers weren't there, and no suspects were to be seen. Pence and Alleyn didn't know their brother officers had already been murdered. In a flash the two suspects opened fire as they came out from behind the radio car. Pence put out an "officer needs help" call on his radio, alerting everyone to respond, then took cover behind his car door. Alleyn grabbed a shotgun before crouching behind their own black-and-white. The officers and suspects exchanged several shots in a running gun battle. Even though the officers hit one of them, the suspects gained the high ground and were able to shoot both officers, who died at the scene.

After driving a short distance, the suspects dumped their car and split up. Officers set up a dragnet, combing the area for hours. Suspect Twinning broke into a house and held a man hostage while officers surrounded the property. As the officers teargassed the house, Twinning killed himself using the shotgun he had stolen from the police car. Davis was later captured and convicted on four counts of murder. He was sentenced to die in the gas chamber, but the U.S. Supreme Court's decision to overturn the death penalty as "cruel and unusual punishment" in 1972 spared his life. Davis was resentenced in 1973. He's currently serving a life sentence in Pelican Bay State Prison, which houses the state's most dangerous criminals, in the northwest corner of California.

Each of the four CHP officers had been on the job for less than two years. They were rookies, really. In the pants pocket of one of the dead officers, detectives found six expended cartridge casings. It seems he had a habit of dumping his empty casings into his hand and putting them into his pants pocket as he reloaded, a habit that had begun when he qualified on the firing range. The practice served dual purposes: it kept the casings off the range master's grass, which was planted in between the shooting lanes, and it meant the rookie didn't have to bend over to retrieve them. But this practice also added precious seconds to his reloading time, which ultimately contributed to his death. It was while he was reloading his weapon that one of the suspects came up from behind and shot him.

The events at Newhall changed the profession forever. The four young rookies gave their lives, but their loss was not in vain. To some, the critical review after the shooting was just a way to fix the blame for the top brass, but to others, it was a chance to analyze procedures and design new weapons systems to enhance an officer's tactical advantage. It was also an opportunity to set new mandates for police academy training. Most important, it changed the mind-set of a tradition-bound profession that had been too slow to learn. The emotion-charged investigation and after-action report led to revamped training programs for officers throughout the United States. These four CHP officers ultimately sacrificed their lives for every recruit who came after them, as each was told about every movement and every mistake that was made at Newhall.

San Diego County Deputy Sheriff Terry Lawson can be grateful for the lessons of Newhall because those lessons ultimately saved his life some thirty years later. Lawson is a tall, handsome guy who has been a deputy sheriff for San Diego County for over twenty years. He is good-natured, somewhat on the quiet side but with an active sense of humor. He looks for the good in a situation, and he's generally known for keeping cool under pressure. He's also well liked by his peers. Like most deputies, Terry wanted to work patrol, staying clear of the jail assignments in the custody division. After he successfully interviewed for a coveted traffic assignment, he was transferred to the Encinitas Sheriff's Station in North San Diego County. Things had gone pretty well for him in his career.

During the late afternoon hours on June 1, 1999, Deputy Terry Lawson was working his traffic car on routine patrol out of the Encinitas station in the city of Solana Beach. At approximately 5:35 that afternoon, Albert

Alofa Suna, aka Felix Suna, entered the Wells Fargo Bank in the city of Solana Beach. Suna was a long-time criminal who was suspected in ten bank robberies throughout San Diego County. Also a known criminal, Christopher Snow, his accomplice and driver, was out on parole for armed robbery. The two had planned on doing a bank job in Solana Beach and then making their way home to Oceanside, just a short drive north on the freeway.

The incident occurred in an upper-class area of San Diego County known as Rancho Santa Fe, which consists primarily of estate properties and ranch-style neighborhoods. It's populated by wealthy, retired business professionals and the occasional Hollywood celebrity. The beautiful homes back up to rolling greenbelts that are connected to quiet country roads, which provide a rural feel to the community. As it does with most local towns in North County, the San Diego Sheriff's Department contracts for local law enforcement services.

As Suna entered the bank, he threatened tellers with a chrome handgun. Six feet tall and 255 pounds, Suna was an imposing man whose aggressive behavior struck fear in the hearts of the people in the bank. They had the impression he would shoot them as soon as look at them, and evidently they were right. Suna hit the two teller stations that were open. Christine Marks was a teller who was robbed. She was fairly composed when she described Suna: "He was Samoan. He was wearing a blue bandanna across his face, and he had a silver handgun." Suna fled the bank with just twelve hundred dollars in a white Ford Thunderbird driven by Snow.

Sheriff's dispatch first broadcast that they had received a silent robbery alarm but quickly upgraded the incident to a "robbery just occurred" at the Wells Fargo Bank. As the suspect ran outside, a witness on the street thought it suspicious that a man was running from a bank. An exploding dye pack is timed to explode a few minutes after it's pulled from a teller's drawer. When the man saw the dye pack explode, he knew a robbery had just occurred. The witness put in a call on his cell phone to the sheriff's dispatch center. He provided a vehicle description and the license plate of the car as he watched the two suspects speed away.

Because patrol deputies were already tied up on other calls, the dispatchers were trying to locate a unit to respond to the bank. When Deputy Lawson realized he was only two blocks away, he immediately drove to the scene. As he pulled up to the bank, the dispatchers began broadcasting a description of the suspect and his possible vehicle, as related by the witness on the cell phone. The same witness flagged down Deputy Lawson personally to describe the man he'd seen. He also pointed out the suspects' direction of travel. Lawson remembered, "I had heard information in roll call about these guys. I knew they were good for nine or ten bank jobs in North County . . . now we had a chance to get them. I mean we were right on top of this." Lawson told the witness to stand by for responding officers, then gave chase after the gunmen. Still alone, Lawson didn't realize yet how far away his backup units were at this point.

Deputy Lawson drove up Santa Helena Drive but was unable to locate the suspects on the main drag, so he started checking side streets. He then heard dispatch advise that the suspects' vehicle was registered to an Oceanside address. Lawson concluded, "I knew they would have to make their way back north to get home, and they were trying to do it on the back roads to avoid the Interstate 5 freeway." Heading north from Solana Beach, Oceanside is the last major city in San Diego County where it sits next to Camp Pendleton, western home to the United States Marine Corps.

Lawson stated, "I tried to follow what roads the suspects would take to get out of Rancho Santa Fe, and that's when I pulled onto San Marino." As he got to the intersection at San Marino and Highland, right in front of him he saw the suspects' T-Bird. Lawson confirmed the license plate and broadcast on the radio, "I've got a white T-Bird, California plate; 3, Tom, Charles, Lincoln, 5-3-9." The adrenaline coursed through his veins when he knew he'd located the suspects.

The deputy made a U-turn to follow the gunmen as they drove through the upscale community of Rancho Santa Fe. Calling for assistance, he was advised by San Diego dispatch: "The nearest patrol unit is several miles away, with an extended ETA [estimated time of arrival]." To add to Lawson's problem, his backup units were trying to make their way through evening rush hour traffic, which was awful. They might as well have been two hundred miles away.

Deputy Lawson was alone, and he knew it. He could have given himself some distance, could have avoided pushing the encounter, but that would have given the suspects too much of an opportunity to escape. He was aware that they could easily flee toward a neighboring residential area or make their way to the nearby country club. He wanted to prevent that, so he stayed close. But he didn't want to get close enough to provoke an incident either, so he contemplated his difficult situation with its limited options. He knew the lessons from Newhall, so he stayed on his toes. He continued to follow and continued to update his location while waiting for assistance that was still too far away. As the suspects drove through Rancho Santa Fe, Lawson realized he was pulling away from his backup. Time was working for the suspects.

In Newhall, the suspects had picked their location for the stop. Just like any predator, they were laying the trap for their prey, and the four CHP officers fell victim. Deputy Lawson didn't want the gunmen to be able to pick the location for the stop or to have any opportunity to plan. He felt they were gaining an advantage, so he decided to pull the T-Bird over in a safe spot and simply wait for his backup. By initiating a car stop, Lawson thought, "I'd pull them over, but not approach. They'd expect me to come up on them, but I was going to keep my distance. All I'd need was a few moments and my backup would get there. I just needed to keep these guys off guard."

It was risky, but what in police work isn't risky? Wasn't it safer than allowing the situation to escalate into a vehicle pursuit? Wasn't it better for Lawson to pick his spot as soon as he could rather than let the gunmen make the choice? Lawson weighed his choices, then made his decision. When he activated his emergency lights, the suspects' vehicle abruptly pulled over. But things didn't go as Lawson planned. Christopher Snow, the getaway driver, immediately jumped out of his car, then abruptly moved back toward the patrol car. The suspect yelled out, "He made me do it!" and then asked the deputy not to shoot him. Out of his car with his gun drawn, Lawson confronted Snow and ordered him to lie prone on the street. Snow immediately went down on the pavement as he repeatedly yelled that Suna made him do the robbery.

With Snow obviously complying, Lawson decided to hold his position. Then he gave an order for Suna to get out of the car. But Suna wasn't going to surrender—he slid across the front seat, got behind the wheel, and sped off down the road. At this point, many things could have occurred. Deputy Lawson could have finished his involvement by taking Snow into custody, although he wasn't sure of Snow's role primarily because Snow did not fit the description of the robbery suspect and had immediately complied when the deputy stopped the car. But Lawson did get a look at the other suspect, who fit the description. For peace officers, decisions that are made in milliseconds can have results that last a lifetime. This was one of those decisions.

Lawson took control of Snow but left him at the scene, ordering him to stand by for his backup. Lawson's commanding presence must have been impressive because that's precisely what Christopher Snow did: he remained to be taken into custody by a backup unit. Then Lawson, still alone, turned on his lights and siren and went in pursuit of Albert Suna, who was now well out of sight.

Suna had driven off at high speed. A light rain had fallen that afternoon, and as he drove down Puerta Del Sol, he failed to adjust for the wet roadway. Traveling too fast for those conditions, he failed to negotiate the turn at Las Palomas Drive and skidded off the road, hitting a tree head-on. Momentarily stunned, Suna remained in the driver's seat.

Deputy Lawson wasn't far behind, but he was taking the wet road conditions into account. As he approached the intersection he stopped. He could see that the suspect's vehicle had plowed through a split rail fence and hit a tree. He could also see the suspect still in the car, but he didn't know if Suna was seriously injured or playing possum. Lawson got out of his patrol car and stood by his door; he was approximately fifty feet away from Suna's car. He gave a command for Suna to get out of the car and show his hands. He shouted the command several times but to no avail.

Suddenly Suna got out of the car and began to move around to the front and side of it. Lawson continued his commands as he sized up the situation. He realized Suna had the Morgan Run Golf Course—filled with golfers and their carts—directly behind him.

Bob Armstrong, living in Orange County just north of San Diego, was golfing with his friends that day when the incident unfolded. He said, "I know this word is overused, but it was surreal. We heard screeching tires and a siren following behind from a distance. I looked up and saw a white T-Bird that was flying, and I knew it was going too fast for the turn. We didn't know what was going on." Though Armstrong found himself in the front row of an impending shoot-out, he still didn't sense the personal danger.

Deputy Lawson was assessing the chances that Suna was going to run, and if he did, what Lawson himself would do. Lawson reported, "I didn't know who else might be in the car; I didn't really know what Suna was going to do. Was he going to give up? Was he thinking about it? Or was it that he was getting ready to kill me?"

Suna didn't run. Instead he moved back toward Deputy Lawson, who could see his shirt and shorts and nothing in his hands. Lawson held his ground as he held his fire. Suna still failed to obey any commands, though—it was clear he was factoring in all the information he could before he attacked.

The situation had become a standoff.

Lawson could tell he was in grave danger; he could feel it as he watched the encounter unfold in slow motion. He remarked, "I couldn't get him to surrender. He just kept pacing back and forth. He was the hunter waiting out his prey. He was laying the bait, waiting for me to bite, waiting for me to make the first move." Lawson decided to keep his distance, thus keeping the tactical advantage of higher ground. The lesson from Newhall was a critical choice for the deputy.

In real police work, rarely does an officer find himself alone in a protracted standoff. Most officers work with partners or in teams. They try to stay close by, to join together in policing. If they're working a single-man unit, or an "L" (for lone or loner) car, they call for backup before moving. They get their resources together, line up reserves, and formulate a plan before they engage—that's what was learned from the Newhall tragedy. Lawson was going to do just that . . . that is, Lawson *would have* done that if he'd had the time.

Suna went back to his car and reached inside. He pulled out something covered by a towel or cloth of some sort. He hesitated, then stepped to the front of his car as he made plans for his final moves. While Lawson continued shouting commands for surrender, Suna pulled away the cloth and opened fire with a Tech 9 automatic assault weapon.

Armstrong was still standing nearby on the golf course. He said, "I couldn't believe it. I had been watching him and thought he was going to surrender, and then this happened. He pulled out a rag or some shirt or something. It was maroon or red, and it looked like cloth. That deputy was yelling at the man to get down on the ground, but he kept moving. And that's when the towel came off and I could see he had a gun."

Suna fired continuously for several seconds, peppering the deputy's patrol car with bullets. Deputy Lawson wasn't hit, but Suna fired a second volley of more than twenty shots at him. Lawson was able to return fire, causing Suna to retreat to his car. Meanwhile, the golfers on the nearby course were huddling behind trees, trying to avoid being shot.

Witnesses described the gun battle that followed. After the initial firefight where several dozen shots were exchanged, the gunfire slowed into sporadic shots. Then fierce bursts of fire were repeated. Suna kept up his attack, but Lawson never withdrew. Armstrong described the deputy's actions as heroic: "The officer never retreated; instead he kept up his fire and pinned the suspect down. I've never seen anything like it. It's like I'm still there, hiding behind a tree and watching the bravery of this man. The

officer kept his position and kept shooting back at the suspect. It was surreal. That's what it was, surreal."

Using twenty-round magazines, Suna had reloaded twice. He shot up
the front end of the deputy's car, which caused the radiator to erupt. With
steam blowing out directly in front of him, Lawson was momentarily
blinded. Suna took advantage of the steam by starting to reposition to the
west away from his car. As he moved he opened fire, again trying to kill
Lawson, but the rounds tore into the car's windshield and body, missing
their intended target.

Rarely in police work does a shoot-out last this long. In most police
shootings, the officers don't have time to think about what is happening
to them; they only have time to react. Most incidents are over in milliseconds, not seconds; they certainly don't last for minutes. Deputy Lawson
was able to call for help twice. In one plaintive call for assistance, he
yelled, "I need all kinds of help! All kinds of shots fired!" He had gone
through two magazines and was down to his last one. His plea sounded
mournful over the air, but the dispatchers could do nothing more. They
knew one of their own was out there on the firing line and help still
hadn't arrived.

But the dispatchers also felt that Lawson's voice held purpose, determination, and courage. The deputy sheriff was a brave man. He wasn't
going to retreat—he was going to attack and survive. Like so many others,
he had learned from those brave officers at Newhall, and he was ready to
apply what he had been trained to do.

Lawson moved quickly away from the venting steam of his patrol car to
regain his view. He also regained his bearing: he decided he was no longer
just going to react to this assailant; instead, he began making a plan to
resolve the threat. Lawson said, "I watched the suspect firing again and
again and he continued shooting while he ran. Suna moved away from
cover, and I carefully took aim and opened fire." He went on, "It was just
like in training at the academy. It was as though my range instructor was
talking to me, 'Focus on your gun sights! Acquire your target, get your
sight picture, take aim, and then fire.' And all of a sudden I kind of
calmed down."

Lawson was ready as he calculated his attack: trigger control, slow
breathing, take aim, fire. With one round, Suna was knocked to the
ground, but he scrambled to a small rise in the earth. Suna kept popping
up and shooting repeatedly, and unfortunately, Lawson couldn't get
clear aim.

Then a remarkable thing happened. Lawson remembered an unusual demonstration of "skip shooting" from his academy days. "I remembered that recruits were shown how a ricocheted bullet's trajectory followed a flat line parallel to the ground." Lawson knew the tactic was intended to quell a deadly riot by disabling the attackers' legs without killing them. But he was thinking about how it might help him now. "I couldn't seem to get a good enough aim at the suspect; I was shooting around him. I was too far away, and I kept missing him. That's when I remembered skip shooting. I figured I might be able to at least hit somewhere in front of him. Maybe I could walk a bullet right in front and take him out."

Lawson took careful aim and waited for Suna to look up. As the suspect moved, Lawson was waiting for the all-important sight picture. Again and again the gunman popped up from the ground and opened fire. Lawson remained ever so still and focused his gun sights toward the last spot where he'd seen the shooter. Even under fire, Lawson remained calm until he was ready to take his shot. The next time the suspect fired, Lawson laid a single round directly in front of the earthen barricade. The skip-shot round followed a flat line, just inches off the ground, traveling over 102 feet before hitting Suna directly in the head. Suna died instantly. The firefight was over.

Many civilian witnesses on the scene that day observed this fierce firefight. Some described the paralyzing fear they felt, saying there was nowhere to escape without running through a killing field. But they were all taken with the courage displayed by Deputy Lawson as they watched him square off, one-on-one, in a running gunfight with Albert Suna. Undaunted, Lawson was determined to improvise, adapt, and overcome any adversity. He revealed not just his will to survive but his will to succeed.

As a peace officer, Deputy Terry Lawson clearly holds the values of devotion to duty, selfless service, honor, and personal courage. His heroic actions while facing sustained hostile gunfire were clearly above and beyond the call of duty. He received the San Diego Sheriff's Department Medal of Valor and was named 2001 Officer of the Year by the California Robbery Investigators Association.

In harm's way—three simple words of deep resolve that so aptly describe the sense of purpose, the shared values, and the commitment required to serve as a peace officer. And in this case, Deputy Terry Lawson sailed fast and sailed well as he went in harm's way.

11

SERGEANTS DANIELL GRISWOLD AND MARK FEDDERSEN AND PATROL SPECIALIST GARY LOCK

Tacoma (Washington) Police Department

"Kidnapped"

Sergeant Daniell Griswold　　Sergeant Mark Feddersen　　Patrol Specialist Gary Lock

"Mom, if you don't come down here, she'll wanna kill somebody, ya hear. You better come down here. She wants your kids, but if you don't hurry up and get you to come down here, or she'll even kill me if you don't hurry up and get you to come down here. You wanna kill me?"

An emotionally distraught Sheryl Ann Custor left this chillingly incoherent message for her mother, Viola Custor, at 6:20 P.M. on Sunday, February 14, 1999. Sheryl, twenty-nine years old and mentally disabled, had been kidnapped by Tina Lee Weaver, twenty-four, the foster child of a family friend. Weaver was holding Sheryl at gunpoint; her goal: to kill Sheryl's mother when she came to pick up Sheryl.

Sergeant Daniell Griswold responded to a report that there was a female with a gun threatening to kill someone at the King Oscar Motel. She'd had many dangerous encounters with criminals in which she had to fight for her life, but this one would be especially memorable. Her training and experience as a hostage negotiator with the SWAT team would be invaluable. At the motel she joined Sergeant Mark Feddersen, who'd already arrived at the scene. The two knocked at the door of room number 31 and identified themselves as police officers, but there was no response. After knocking again and repeatedly announcing their presence, Griswold heard a female voice inside.

When Patrol Specialist Gary Lock arrived, he saw Griswold and Feddersen at the door, talking to the woman inside. Lock would act as the cover officer for Griswold and Feddersen as they negotiated with the armed kidnapper. Several officers from the Tacoma Police Department and the Pierce County Sheriff's Office had also responded to the dispatch. These officers would provide backup to the first officers on the scene.

The sergeants stood directly in front of the motel room door, aware that the subject inside was armed. Sergeant Griswold advised the woman to open the door so that they could make sure everyone in the room was okay. She attempted to negotiate with Weaver for several minutes, all the while fearing that the victim was in imminent danger. When Griswold heard what could have been either muffled laughing or crying behind the door, the officers decided to enter the room and obtained a passkey from the motel's security guard. But as Sergeant Feddersen attempted to open the door with the key, he found he couldn't get into the room—Weaver was holding on to the dead-bolt knob, relocking it as soon as Feddersen unlocked it and tried to unlock the door's second lock.

When Feddersen finally unlocked both door locks, Griswold tried to push open the motel room door. Twice she was able to push it open a few inches, only to have Weaver push the door shut from the other side. With each push, Griswold could hear Sheryl Custor screaming for help. Officer Lock then kicked open the door, which initially threw Weaver backward. As the door swung open, police could see Weaver, an unkempt brunette dressed in dirty jeans and a sweatshirt with holes, running toward the back of the room where her captive sat duct-taped to a chair.

"It's not every day you see someone strapped to a chair," Feddersen recalled. "You might see it in Hollywood but not in real life. When you do see it, you don't expect to see it again."

Griswold, Feddersen, and Lock chased the kidnapper, hoping to keep her from retrieving one of her weapons and harming Sheryl, who was screaming loudly. A loaded Winchester 12-gauge shotgun sat just inside the door. A large black-handled knife and a small knife were within six feet of the victim.

According to Lock, "Weaver was beelining for a shotgun propped up on the dresser." After the officers subdued and handcuffed her, she fell to her knees yelling and cursing and refusing to walk. Lock said, "I literally picked her up and carried her back to my car," which was about 150 yards away. Because she wouldn't walk, at one point Lock grabbed her by her belt, carrying her "suitcase style" part of the way to the police car.

Officer Lock advised Weaver of her Miranda rights, which she waived. Then he obtained a full confession from her. She admitted that she had duct-taped Sheryl to the chair so that Viola could see she meant business when she came to pick up the girl. Weaver also gave police her consent for them to search her motel room.

Weaver told the officers at the scene that six months earlier she had planned to commit suicide by overdosing on drugs, but first she'd asked Viola to take her four children. This was the woman whom Weaver called "Grandma" and who she claimed was her foster grandmother. But then Weaver's suicide attempt failed, and according to Weaver, she and Viola had been engaged in an ongoing custody battle over her four children ever since. Weaver said that recently Custor had refused to give back the four children because one of the children claimed that Weaver had assaulted them.

Viola Custor revealed to the police that the Thurston County Courts had awarded her custody of Weaver's children on February 12. The same day, Tina Weaver and her foster sister had visited several pawnshops because Weaver wanted to buy a shotgun. She had told her foster sister that she didn't know if she could buy a gun if they ran background checks; she said she had been a patient at Western State Hospital, where she said she was told not to buy a gun, that no one would sell her a gun. According to the foster sister, Tina bought a shotgun and knife that day with no problems. The foster sister stated that Tina threatened to harm her if she told anyone of her plans to hurt Viola.

Police would also find a Kmart receipt dated February 12, 1999, for two rolls of duct tape, one notebook, one pair of scissors, one knife, and one lock box. Weaver rented a motel room at the King Oscar Motel in Tacoma that day.

On February 14 at about 3:00 P.M. Weaver picked up Sheryl Custor and took her back to the motel. Weaver told officers that she called Viola to get her to come to the motel to get Sheryl. Weaver said that once Viola was in the room, she planned to kill both Sheryl and Viola with her shotgun.

Sheryl Custor, who Viola stated had the mental capacity of a third grader, had been taken from her home by a ruse. Weaver had told Sheryl that her mom wanted Weaver to take her to church. Even though Sheryl questioned Weaver about the matter, she eventually agreed to go. But as soon as Sheryl got into Weaver's car, Weaver bound her hands in front of her with tape. Sheryl would later report that Weaver started yelling profanities at her, threatening to blow off her head if she didn't keep her mouth shut. Sheryl shut up.

Weaver drove Sheryl to the King Oscar Motel, where she taped Sheryl's torso, wrists, and legs to a chair. Weaver kept Sheryl quiet by placing duct tape over her mouth. As Weaver became more enraged, she took out her anger on Sheryl by physically assaulting her. Weaver also told Sheryl that the police beat up people, which is one of the reasons Sheryl was screaming when she saw the officers rush into the room. It took quite a while for Sheryl to calm down.

Weaver told police that she had called Viola Custor and also let Sheryl speak with Viola. Sheryl told her mother that Weaver was serious and had a gun. When Weaver called Viola again, the answering machine picked up the call, and Sheryl left her mom the desperate plea for her to come to the motel. Sheryl told police that Weaver kept saying she was going to kill her and that she was going to blow Viola's head off and cut out her heart because Viola had taken her children from her.

Viola Custor called the police after receiving several disturbing phone calls from Weaver telling her that she had Sheryl and a gun and that someone was going to get hurt if Viola didn't come to the motel.

According to Sheryl, a man named Eddie had come to the room shortly after she was taped to the chair. Ed Canady, fifty, was Tina Weaver's mom's former boyfriend. According to Sheryl, who'd never seen Canady before he appeared at the motel room, Weaver gave Canady a bag and told him to leave before she blew off his head too. Sheryl said Canady clearly saw her as she sat bound to the chair. Sheryl also reported that Weaver spoke to Canady on the phone later.

When police asked Weaver where her red Dodge Shadow was, she said that Ed had picked it up at the motel to repair it because it was leaking antifreeze. She said that Ed never came into the motel room, and Ed would deny ever seeing the victim in the room. When he was brought to the scene, however, Sheryl identified him as the man she'd seen. He was arrested for complicity in the kidnapping.

Police would find the following handwritten notes in the motel room. Tina Weaver confirmed that she had written them.

1. call Viola
2. cry—tell her to come down here.
3. when she gets here point the gun at her, tell her to sit down in the chair.
4. tape her to the chair. cut her and ask does that feel good. She hurt me so I'm hurting her.
5. Let her call Hubert and say good-by.
6. Shoot her in the head.

go to Sherrals house. hold gun to her. have her call Viola to come down here. Say a friend gave her a ride. the do above!

Another page begins:

I'm not sure what I'm doing . . .

Then continues:

I'm going to make this very painful for Viola be for I kill her: tape her to a chair, cut her <u>deep!</u> When I feel she felt enough pain I'll shoot her in the face so she can see my face as she dies.

On another page a more sorrowful Tina writes:

I miss my kids so much. why did this have to happen to me. what did I do that was so wrong. I would never hurt my kids like that. Every time I see on tv kids my eyes water. I need my kids. They need me. What am I supos to do, make more kids no way. I want my kids back.

If anyone would feel how I feel they would know why I'm going to kill Viola. I'll go to prison. Oh well maybe some one will kill me.

Weaver also reveals that Viola isn't the only woman she wants to seek revenge against:

I've even thought of buying a ticket to Alaska kill my Mom. She cause me pain too. Fuck that bitch. I need to figure out time. Monday By by Viola.

Two days after the kidnapping, Pierce County Deputy Prosecutor James S. Schacht formally charged Tina Weaver with kidnapping and two counts of attempted murder. Eddie Canady was charged with kidnapping in the first degree. Canady pled guilty to a lesser charge of rendering criminal assistance in the first degree. With no prior criminal history, he served a six-month sentence.

Deputy Prosecutor Schacht reported that in March 1999 Western State Hospital found Tina Weaver competent and described her as having "a borderline personality disorder with antisocial features." She pled guilty to attempted murder in the second degree with firearm enhancement, second-degree assault with firearm enhancement, and second-degree kidnapping. She was sentenced to over twenty-four years in prison.

In a letter to the Tacoma Police Department, Deputy Prosecutor Schacht commended Sergeant Daniell Griswold, Sergeant Mark Feddersen, and Patrol Specialist Gary Lock for putting themselves at great risk and saving the life of kidnap victim Sheryl Custor.

Sergeants Griswold and Feddersen were aware that Tina Weaver was armed as they stood at the door of the motel room and negotiated with the suspect. In doing so, they placed themselves in immediate peril. Griswold, Feddersen, and Lock exposed themselves to even greater peril when they charged into the room and confronted the suspect. Because of their bold acts of heroism, Sheryl Custor's life was spared and Tina Weaver was taken into custody. Miraculously, the incident concluded without loss of life.

The City of Tacoma Police Department awarded Griswold, Feddersen, and Lock Medals of Valor for their courageous actions.

Looking back, Sergeant Griswold told me that she had wanted to be a police officer for as long as she could remember. "Dani," as she likes to be called, joined the Army after graduating from high school and attending college for a short period of time. At the age of nineteen she became a military police officer, serving in that capacity for three years. During her military service career, she worked in Panama and the jungles of Honduras. After receiving an honorable discharge in 1991, she joined the Tacoma City Police Department, starting out as a patrol officer.

In 1994, Sergeant Griswold's father, Dennis, was murdered in cold blood during a holdup at the pub he owned. The harrowing story of the murder of Dennis Griswold was featured on the television shows *Primetime* and *Justice Files.*

Although Henry Marshall Lewis pleaded guilty to the murder, his conviction was overturned as he sat on death row. At this writing, Lewis is scheduled to be retried for the murder and is awaiting trial in jail just two floors above Dani's office. Dennis's wife, Jan Griswold, and his daughter will again be forced to relive the horrible circumstances surrounding his untimely, horrific death.

Following an assignment with the SWAT team, Sergeant Griswold was promoted to sergeant in 1998 and accepted assignments in firearms training and ethics training. Griswold is currently assigned to the Tacoma Police Department's Training Section. She lives with Shirley, a dental hygienist who worries about Dani, especially when she is on patrol duty. The sergeant makes it a point to not discuss her police work at home. Together they are raising two fine teenage sons, Cameron, thirteen, and Christian, sixteen.

Sergeant Griswold told me that she hopes to go back to patrol duty soon. She loves working on the streets. When I asked her what she thought about being included in *Police Heroes*, she said, "I know a hundred police officers more deserving."

Sergeant Mark Feddersen looks philosophically on his work: "I'm not taking credit for what I do because I think God put me in this place for a particular reason a long, long time ago." Feddersen decided he wanted to go into police work at the age of thirteen when an officer spotted a fire in his home, then alerted the six or seven family members there at the time. He said that being a policeman was "all I ever wanted to do. So I tried to educate myself and get as much experience as I possibly could." In high school, Feddersen became a Kitsap County Sheriff's cadet. He joined the U.S. Army Reserve when he was a junior in high school and went to boot camp after graduation. He was with the military police for five years as a reservist while he got his education, earning a B.A. in Criminal Justice. After working at a naval submarine base in Washington, he left as a sergeant in 1991 to join the Tacoma Police Department. He graduated from the police academy first in his class.

Feddersen received another Medal of Valor when he and his partner safely rescued a mother and her two children from a burning house. While driving in Tacoma, the officers had smelled smoke and tracked it to the basement of a home. Mark believes he was meant to find the fire. "God put that fire in my life when I was thirteen so I would be there for someone else when I was thirty." The sergeant has received two Lifesaving Medals as well as a Medal of Merit. In 1995 the Tacoma Police Department named him Officer of the Year. The national Veterans of Foreign Wars presented him with their Officer of the Year award for the state of Washington that same year.

A family man, Mark and his wife have two children with one on the way. "When I leave the house my wife is concerned about me returning or not. We pray together." He went on to say, "The foundation by which I live is that the job is difficult, so you need more than yourself to survive."

Patrol Specialist Gary Lock is now Sergeant Lock, having been promoted since the Tina Weaver incident. Lock joined the police force in December 1988 after getting out of the Navy in May of that year. A neighbor who was a Seattle police officer got him interested in joining the department. Though he was single at the time of the Weaver incident, he's now married to a police dispatcher. He says they don't talk about work at home.

Although Lock received departmental commendations in the mid-1990s for his work in narcotics, winning a Medal of Valor for his role in capturing Tina Weaver took him by surprise. "I was just at the right place at the right time," he says.

Lock's humble attitude, typical of so many everyday heroes, was apparent as he told me, "I never thought I'd get a medal out of this. I certainly wasn't expecting it. It's just day-to-day business."

12

K-9 HEROES

"Guardians of the Night"

Police dogs are valuable members of police departments throughout the United States. These K-9 officers are admired not only for their physical skills but also for their unwavering loyalty and willingness to sacrifice everything for their partners. The bond between a K-9 officer and his or her handler is a unique one. They work and train together as a team, and the dog is usually part of the handler's family. Retired K-9s generally live in the home of the handler.

Training for a K-9 begins around age one, when the dog has matured and learned basic obedience. Only those dogs that have the drive and perseverance to perform certain repetitive tasks are chosen to enter into the twelve- to fourteen-week training course. The success of a handler and his or her dog depends on the strength of the bond between them. It is a proven fact that the most productive teams are those that are together for the life of the dog.

Russ Hess, National Executive Director of the United States Police Canine Association, Inc. (USPCA), a nonprofit organization concerned with establishing minimum standards for police dogs through proper training, spoke to me about the importance of a strong bond. "An officer spends more time with his dog than anyone else, so a strong bond is a critical foundation. The better the bond, the better they'll work together. It's like an ESP that develops. The dog knows what kind of day he's gonna have by observing his handler's behavior when he gets up. It's essential that the bond is developed through training to the greatest degree possible."

According to the USPCA, police dogs that are properly trained and handled are one of the best non-lethal aids for crime prevention and detection. When I asked Hess why dogs were so important to police work, he responded, "Dogs can assist in doing things that an officer can't. Because of their sense of smell and hearing, they make the job safer for officers. A police dog isn't meant to replace an officer but to give him the capability to do a job safer and a lot quicker. A dog can find danger before a cop can."

K-9 officers are trained to search areas for unauthorized individuals, suspects, and lost children as well as to sniff out evidence, narcotics, explosives, and human remains. Hess told me that "a dog is still the most reliable tool we have today in finding narcotics, even with the newest scientific tools." They are taught to apprehend suspects with a minimum amount of force. A well-trained police dog will apprehend a suspect only upon command and in the protection of the dog's handler.

The German shepherd is probably the most popular working police dog, but because K-9 officers do more than just locate and apprehend suspects, many other breeds have also been trained as police dogs. Retrievers and pointers are often used for tracking and detection, while bloodhounds, Dobermans, Rottweilers, border collies, mixed breed dogs, and schnauzers locate narcotics, detect illegal aliens crossing our borders, chase down escaped convicts, save lives in burning buildings, and perform a myriad of other law enforcement duties.

The first documented evidence that dogs were used by law enforcement was in 1899. Since then, the number of K-9 programs in the United States has increased to more than three thousand, according to Rick Boling's article in *Animals* magazine, a publication of the Massachusetts Society for the Prevention of Cruelty to Animals. According to Boling, statistics show that dog handlers and their dogs work more night shifts and are involved in or called out to more violent confrontations than other officers. Today's K-9 and handler are just as important in fighting crime as any other law enforcement partners. Their very lives depend upon one another. It takes great dedication, extensive training, and proper funding to have a successful K-9 division.

K-9 teams responded to assist in the rescue and recovery efforts following the terrorist attacks of September 11, 2001. Police officers and their canine partners volunteered to help search and rescue teams tirelessly climb through the smoldering debris to search for survivors. When the dogs found no survivors, dogs trained to locate human remains were brought in. Dogs working the scene were treated for dehydration, eye irritation, and cuts and scrapes. Breathing in the air at Ground Zero for even a few minutes caused sore throats in humans. Unlike the people working on the WTC scene, the dogs couldn't wear facial masks since it would impair their ability to sniff. It's not known what, if any, long-term effects the dogs will suffer from inhaling so much smoke and dust.

When a K-9 officer dies in the line of duty, he or she is treated with the respect and dignity given to other officers. Police dogs everywhere have had monuments erected in their honor. They are truly "guardians of the night," in the words of an unknown author whose poetic tribute to K-9 officers has been widely circulated.

Stories of K-9 heroism are abundant. Cero, Sevo, and Atlas are just three of these stories.

K-9 CERO
Ashtabula County (Ohio)
Sheriff's Department

Deputy Sheriff William R. Niemi and K-9 Cero

K-9 Cero of the Ashtabula County Sheriff's Department in Jefferson, Ohio, is just one example of a hardworking police dog. Like many K-9s and their handlers, Cero, a husky German shepherd, and Deputy William R. Niemi shared a close bond. According to Deputy Niemi, Cero didn't fit the stereotype of a German shepherd; he was not aggressive unless he was commanded to be so. "He was just like a kid," Niemi confided.

Around 7 A.M. on March 25, 2000, Deputy Niemi and K-9 Cero were the first officers on the scene in response to a call about a shooting on a residential street; the two had just finished a shift and were about to head home. The shooter had killed Walter Olson, who had been out for a routine dawn walk. Though there were lots of people around, Deputy Niemi observed a man in a black raincoat who was later identified as Levi Ridenour. The barrel of a long gun appeared to be sticking out from the bottom of his coat. Other officers from the Ashtabula County Sheriff's Department responded, as did officers from the Jefferson Village Police Department. When the Sheriff's Department sergeant and another deputy arrived, Ridenour stopped walking. Several times the sergeant ordered Ridenour to put down the gun. Instead Ridenour turned around and began shooting. He shot out a patrol car's windshield and rear window; shots also hit other patrol vehicles and nearby houses. Officers ran for cover and returned fire.

After he emptied his gun, Ridenour threw the shotgun down in the street and fled, taking cover behind a tree. Deputy Niemi ordered K-9 Cero to apprehend the suspect. Cero grabbed Ridenour's arm, distracting him from two officers who were out in the open.

Ridenour then pulled out a .22-caliber revolver and shot Cero in the chest. Cero let go of Ridenour, who began firing at officers again. This time, the officers' bullets hit Ridenour, who fell to the ground but continued to fire. Eventually, Ridenour's weapon dropped from his hand. Officers secured him and called for rescue units. Ridenour was pronounced dead on arrival at the hospital.

The department vet was called to the scene but was not able to save Cero. The bullet had lodged in his heart. He was the first law enforcement K-9 to be killed in the line of duty in northeast Ohio. Cero, the first K-9 Niemi had ever worked with, was only two years old when he died. He had been with Niemi for only six months.

On March 31, 2000, hundreds of people in a crowded funeral home and hundreds more standing in the parking lot, on the lawn, and on the sidewalks, paid tribute to K-9 Cero. Mourners from Ohio, Illinois, Kentucky, and West Virginia were present, including over three hundred police officers.

Deputy Joseph Niemi, the brother of Cero's handler, said, "He was as much a police officer as any of us. Cero sensed the danger, and he died saving my brother's life, and for that I thank him. But he also saved other people's lives because we didn't know who else might have died if not for his sacrifice." And there were tears from hardened police officers when he told them that, after Cero was shot, he crawled back to William Niemi's side long enough for Niemi to praise him with one final "Good dog."

Deputy William Niemi, present along with his wife and children, told the mourners, "Cero was a member of my family, and he loved my children and wife, especially my wife. We'll all miss you. Daddy loves you, Cero."

After the ninety-minute service, a second, longer service was held at the Ashtabula County Fairgrounds. The funeral procession passed by the scene of the shooting and by the county courthouse, where flags flew at half-staff. During the second service, a Cleveland police bagpiper played "Amazing Grace," two trumpeters played taps, and there was a twenty-one-gun salute. The seventy dogs that were present went up to the urn one at a time with their handlers to pay their respects to a brave dog named Cero.

"It was a tragic moment," Deputy Niemi said as he remembered the incident. "The event gave me a new perspective on how fragile life is."

He continued, "At the time he died, I was devastated. He was a great dog." But Niemi also remembers the support he received from the public. "It was out of this world. I heard from handlers out of state, even from Italy. I'm totally thankful for the people who responded. It's good to be reminded why I'm out there . . . that you're appreciated."

K-9 SEVO
Topeka (Kansas) Police Department

K-9 Sevo

Shortly after midnight on September 24, 1998, the Topeka (Kansas) Police Department received a call from a woman who said a male acquaintance was kicking the front door of her home on SW Central Park. An officer who arrived at the house called for backup, said the suspect had left the scene, and gave a description of the man. Officer Scott Gilchrist and K-9 Sevo were on their way to back up the first officer when Gilchrist saw a man walking near SW Hampton and Buchanan who fit the description of the suspect. He called in and was told to stop the man.

Sevo and Gilchrist got out of the car. Gilchrist identified himself as a police officer and told the suspect more than once to stop. The suspect, forty-one-year-old Victor Wright, cursed, said he wouldn't stop, turned away from Gilchrist, and reached into the waistband of his pants, pulling out a knife. Gilchrist drew his service weapon and ordered the suspect to drop the knife.

Wright not only continued to disregard Officer Gilchrist's order to drop the knife, but he kept moving toward the officer. Sevo took out after Wright, biting and holding on to his arm. As Sevo persisted, Wright suddenly grabbed him by the neck and began stabbing him in the chest.

Gilchrist shot the suspect twice. Wright shouted, "I'm shot," but kept moving toward the officer, who shot him two more times. Only after he had been stabbed five times did Sevo let go of Wright. When other officers arrived, Wright was sitting with a knife in his hand. The officers discovered that he was wearing a leather belt holding seven other knives with blades four to sixteen inches long, including a meat cleaver and butcher knife. He was taken to St. Francis Hospital and Medical Center for treatment of dog bites and four gunshot wounds to the upper torso.

Though Wright was charged with aggravated assault on a law enforcement officer with a weapon and inflicting harm, disability, or death on a police dog, he was found incompetent to stand trial on December 8, 1998. After making his ruling, Shawnee County District Judge Thomas Conklin placed Wright in Larned State Security Hospital until he was found to be capable of standing trial.

Court records showed that this was not Wright's first run-in with the Topeka police. He was convicted of misdemeanor theft in 1980. Two years later, he resisted arrest after refusing to comply with orders to submit to being frisked for weapons; in the same case, he was charged with misdemeanor obstructing the legal process and two counts of misdemeanor criminal damage to property. The case was delayed because he was placed in Topeka State Hospital when he was unable to help with his own defense. After two and a half months, he pleaded guilty. His stay in the hospital was credited to his thirty days' jail time and he was given six months probation. In 1997 a restraining order was taken out against him for squatting at a house on SE Hudson. An odd twist is that Wright was not the person involved in the call on September 24, 1998; that intruder was never arrested.

Sevo was rushed to Western Hills Veterinary Clinic. Remarkably, his stab wounds healed and he returned to work. But when Gilchrist and Sevo were searching a building, it appeared that Sevo wasn't able to smell. He kept going left when he needed to go right. "He wanted to do it, but he just couldn't," Gilchrist said. He wasn't able to perform test exercises the next day. The vet said that Sevo had swelling in his brain from the blows he'd taken to his head. Sevo had to be put down.

"He was a sweetheart," Gilchrist told me. "It was like losing a family member."

Sevo had been in the department for three years. When his first handler transferred to another unit, he made an easy transition to Officer Gilchrist, according to Corporal Bobby Schwerdt, Sevo's trainer and head of the K-9 teams. "Sevo had a tremendous work drive. Really easygoing. He socialized well with people and was very good with children. You didn't have to worry about him getting confused about being a working dog versus socializing. He was very responsive to verbal commands."

On June 19, 1999, Officer Gilchrist accepted the K-9 Medal of Valor for Sevo and himself from the North American Police Work Dog Association at a training conference in Kansas City, Missouri. Sevo posthumously received a K-9 Medal of Valor from the Topeka Police Department in November 1999.

Gilchrist was activated in the National Guard on October 1, 2001. Currently he's a staff sergeant in the Air Force Security Forces Unit. Gilchrist admits, "I'd love to go back to work with K-9s. I miss working with them. There's no better partner in the world."

K-9 ATLAS
Simi Valley (California) Police Department

Officer William Sterling Johnson and K-9
Atlas

K-9 Atlas responded to almost seven thousand calls, searched 2,227 homes
and cars for drugs, and nabbed 536 suspects during his six years with the
Simi Valley (California) Police Department. A German shepherd reared
and trained in Germany and purchased for ten thousand dollars, Atlas
more than proved his worth.

As a team, he and his handler, Officer William Sterling Johnson (who
became a sergeant in 1999), competed in the World Police and Fire
Games, winning gold medals in both 1989 and 1991 in the police service
dog competition—something no other police dog has done. The competition involved jumping over obstacles such as a six-foot-high chain-link
fence and finding a suspect hidden in one of five boxes. What is also
remarkable is that Atlas earned his second gold medal at the age of nine
and a half, six months after most police dogs retire. Fortunately, Atlas suffered no serious injuries on duty. The longest Atlas was ever off duty for an
injury was four hours after he was hit with a baseball bat.

"He had an unbelievable desire," Johnson said of Atlas. "He was an
amazing dog."

Atlas set the tone for Ventura County. His success prompted the county
to add more dogs, going from seven to twenty-five K-9s. Atlas was what
Johnson called "dual purpose"—trained in narcotics and patrol. In addition, "He knew when he was working and when he was just a regular dog,"
Johnson said.

In February 1992, Atlas retired from the police department and continued to live with Johnson and his family. But Atlas had a bit of a hard time adjusting to retirement, Johnson reported. When Johnson put his new K-9 partner in his patrol car, Atlas went over the fence and chased the car. He still wanted to work.

Atlas was one of the first police dogs in the country to receive a pension upon retirement. In 1991 the Simi Valley Council adopted a policy allowing retiring K-9s to be bought by their partners for one dollar. The city pays a flat five hundred dollars per year, and the veterinarian contracted for by the police department offers his services to retired K-9s.

Atlas died at the age of fifteen in May 1996. Although Sergeant Johnson is no longer a handler, he has managed K-9 units and teaches all over North America through the K-9 Academy for Law Enforcement. He instructs handlers in K-9 trauma care, narcotics detection, and tactical deployment. He is on the Simi Valley Police Department's SWAT team, serving the team as both paramedic and team leader. Fellow officers selected him 1994 Officer of the Year.

13

OFFICERS HILTON HENRY
AND STEPHEN KEHOE

Los Angeles (California) Police Department

"The Accidental Partners"

Officer Hilton Henry

Officer Stephen Kehoe

Officers Hilton Henry and Stephen Kehoe, two uniformed Los Angeles Police Department (LAPD) officers, exhibited courage and determination as they attempted to rescue a small child held hostage by an armed robber in the famed and fabled land of Hollywood in April 1993. The incident revealed bravery under extraordinary circumstances, exemplifying the police term *will to survive*. But this story is not only about two courageous LAPD officers. While it is about their actions when faced with extreme danger during a running gun battle, it's also about the department that trained them to fight as one. It's a reflection of the nearly ten thousand men and women who serve the citizens of Los Angeles.

"This is the city: Los Angeles, California. I work here. I carry a badge." In those words, TV personality Jack Webb began the television show *Dragnet*, for many years the program that defined the public image of the LAPD. *Dragnet* was followed by his other popular police drama, *Adam-12*. Both series were written with the approval of LA's police chief. To detractors, the shows were departmental propaganda; to the members of the LAPD, the shows represented their dogma. The television images from these programs declared that the officers of the LAPD were the best of the best, the finest peace officers anywhere in the world. But was it reality?

Webb's relationship with the LAPD began in the 1950s with Chief William H. Parker, the man credited with modernizing the city's police force and an individual whose influence is felt to this day. If asked, police officers might privately acknowledge that Webb's programs influenced their interest in a police career. It was clear that Webb was a booster for all law enforcement, but he had a special fondness for the members of the LAPD. Many LAPD officers would publicly thank him for projecting a positive image of the men and women who serve the citizens of Los Angeles. He left a remarkable legacy. Today his memory lives on in a prominent teaching facility that bears his name on the grounds of the police academy.

The LAPD is a world-class law enforcement organization that has weathered many storms. The Watts Riots in 1965 and the LA Riots twenty-seven years later following the acquittal of four LAPD officers accused of beating Rodney King understandably left a bad impression on many. Then a series of scandals hit that culminated in the Rampart corruption investigation. The negative images of these incidents began to take a toll on the dedicated officers who faithfully serve the citizens of that great city. The support that Webb had worked so hard to establish withered under the intense media coverage. Webb wasn't naive about policing; there were certainly problems and peccadilloes during his time, but he never thought the misconduct of a few should define the work of many.

The various chiefs who followed the venerable W. H. Parker searched for ways to maintain the luster of the public image he left behind. With Jack Webb's publicity machine at Parker's disposal, he would be an almost impossible act to follow. Some of his successors were more successful than others. Daryl F. Gates was cut from Parker's cloth, and interestingly enough, for a short time he served as Parker's driver and aide.

Chief Gates was certainly one of the most innovative and insightful leaders in American law enforcement. He was the man who originated the special weapons and tactics team concept, naming it SWAT. The LAPD model helped establish emergency response details in police departments throughout the country. (For more information on SWAT teams, please see the story about Salem, Oregon, Police Officers James Anglemier and Larry Roberts.) Gates commanded the department during the 1984

Olympics, started the original DARE (drug abuse resistance education) program for elementary schools, and restored order after the infamous 1992 LA Riots. Chief Gates personified Webb's LAPD image, and he projected that to the men and women who served with his department. He was with the LAPD for more than forty years, and to his officers, he was simply known as "The Chief."

One of the most prominent aspects of Gates's tenure was the department's focus on training and standardizing field operations. The LAPD's academy was already considered one of the best in the world, and the in-service training program for veteran officers was unsurpassed. The academy created advanced technical firearms training where officers could experience real-time "shoot/don't shoot" video scenarios. Countless presentations reviewed critical incidents for the staff. Roll call discussions that reviewed shooting situations were standard fare. Training staff drilled field officers in tactics so that everyone would respond the same way when trouble erupted. Such training would prove critical to Officers Kehoe and Henry, who found themselves in a life-or-death situation together in 1993.

The LAPD produced high-quality docudrama videos recreating officer-involved shootings that demonstrated the will to survive that is so necessary if an officer is to remain alive after getting shot. Throughout the country there had been incidents where police officers were wounded and died even though their injuries were not viewed as life-threatening—as if the officer had given up because of the trauma of being shot. The LAPD training films depicted incidents where officers who had been wounded refused to give up or give in, and that mind-set led to their survival.

Captain III Richard Wemmer, host of each film, carries the officers through each incident, allows them to air their views or concerns, and reminds the audience of the need to maintain the will to survive. Wemmer, formerly the commanding officer of the LAPD's Training Division and a widely recognized expert in field tactics and officer-involved shootings, has personally examined the circumstances surrounding the murders of more than three hundred California peace officers. His message is crystal clear: if this officer can get shot and survive, so can you; and you must if you are to endure. The lesson is not just to survive, but to prevail. Rich Wemmer ultimately carried this LAPD mantra to peace officers throughout the country: "Never quit, never give up, and never give in. Don't let them leave you in some dark, stinking alley. Keep fighting and maintain your will to survive."

One of the most enduring films the department produced involved the famous Limas-Roberge shooting. Epitomizing the will-to-survive message, the film is presented to almost every basic police academy class for recruits throughout California. In 1968 Officers Roberge and Limas were in a wild ambush shoot-out with members of the violent Black Panthers gang. Both officers were shot and seriously wounded, but they survived. During the gunfight, Roberge fought back again and again, ultimately killing his attackers. Unfortunately, Officer Limas was unable to return to duty. But beyond expectations, Norm Roberge fought to return. A medical pension wasn't for him, surrender was not in his creed. And return he did.

Norm Roberge was ultimately promoted to sergeant. He became an accomplished detective and was transferred into the venerable and storied Robbery-Homicide Division of the LAPD. He completed his full career, earned his service pension, and did something very special on his last day with the department. On February 20, 1993, he patrolled around the city one final time, taking a last look as a police officer at the many neighborhoods he'd spent a lifetime protecting and serving. He'd given most of his life to the city, and on that day in 1968, he nearly gave all of it. As he drove around, he gave thanks to his Creator for giving him the will to survive. When his tour was finished, he pulled his detective unit into Parker Center and ended his duty shift over the radio. With everyone in the department listening, Detective Sergeant Norm Roberge came on the air and simply said, "4K31: For the last time, end of watch." What a way to go.

Norm Roberge's strength of character and his devotion to duty would help save the lives of two of his brother officers. As you'll see, Officers Hilton Henry and Stephen Kehoe are two heroes who truly define what the LAPD is all about—in the glory days of *Dragnet* and *Adam-12* and now. As Jack Webb might have put it, the story you are about to read is true.

It was Friday, April 30, 1993. Officers Stephen D. Kehoe and Hilton C. Henry were both working PM watch (3:30 P.M.–11:30 P.M.) out of the West Traffic Bureau. They knew each other; they both worked out of the old Venice area police station on Culver Boulevard. But even though they worked out of the same station and worked the same watch, they were assigned to different details and had never worked together before. Kehoe was a motor officer, while Henry worked accident investigation. Henry, the younger officer, was looking at the beginning of his career, whereas Kehoe, a seasoned veteran, was serving in the twilight of his. But both officers were LAPD blue to the core.

Hilton Henry had just five years on the job. Single with no children, he had been working as a traffic officer for some time out of the West

Bureau, covering accident calls in several west side LAPD patrol areas, including the Pacific, West LA, Hollywood, and Wilshire stations. Henry enjoyed patrolling the vast area the bureau covered, and he liked working a traffic car. When he left roll call that afternoon, he set up his police car, keyed his radio microphone, and said, "6TL59, PM watch clear." The 6 in his call sign designated the divisional assignment, the T identified his detail as a traffic accident investigator, the L indicated he was a loner unit—meaning he had no partner with him—and 59 was his patrol car number for the shift. With that, he drove north into the Hollywood area to start his day.

Stephen Kehoe was an old salt, a veteran motorcycle officer who got his first police Harley-Davidson back in 1974. As a west side motor officer he had his own unique radio call sign: 7M25. The M identified Kehoe as a lone motorcycle officer. Just like Officer Henry, Kehoe had finished roll call and gone into the field, driving off to the Wilshire area just east of Hollywood where he began to work traffic enforcement.

Kehoe was known to move at his own pace. Not to be hurried, he was confident, thoughtful, and deliberate in his actions. At this point in his career he was also a bit of a sage as he helped train new officers in the bureau. Through accident or misfortune, several times he had "gone down" on his motor (the iron horsemen's lingo for having a wreck). He knew what it was like to be seriously injured on duty. Life was very precious to him, and he always thought about his wife, children, and grandchildren as he prepared himself for duty. Tactically, he would keep himself firmly grounded with his mind clear while planning his response to a critical incident. When he talked about training police officers, Kehoe showed his deep philosophical bent as he said, "When times of crisis arise, the truth and trivia of life are soon separated."

Kehoe explained that he believes there are four things that influence how a police officer handles a critical incident. "Physical preparation, mental preparation, luck, and divine intervention decide how the events will unfold. That means you've only got control over fifty percent of the factors that can impact you in a crisis. So you'd better prepare yourself." A former U.S. Army captain and an active leader in his local church, Kehoe was as prepared as he could be. Though he was confident for all the right reasons, however, a little self-doubt would creep into his thoughts from time to time, which is pretty natural for most people who walk in harm's way. Like most officers, Kehoe wondered to himself how he would respond when it was his time to face true peril. Would he do the right thing at the right time? Would he survive? Would he be able to prevail? Knowing himself, Kehoe suffered not so much from self-doubt as from a state of wonder at the unknown variables in any breaking situation.

As Officer Stephen Kehoe understood so well and Officer Hilton Henry was about to learn, what an officer *doesn't* know is often what kills him. The police train, prepare, and respond to unknown trouble. If Officer Kehoe is right, they can control just 50 percent of the elements that impact the outcome of a critical incident. What prudent businessperson would enter into a proposition with so many variables and such limited opportunities for success? A businessperson doesn't make a profit by relying on luck. But a peace officer is different. Sometimes good preparation allows the officers to prevail; sometimes it's luck; and maybe sometimes it's divine intervention. For police officers, things can go either way, as these two accidental partners would see firsthand.

At approximately 5:50 P.M., a lone gunman entered a restaurant on North Western Avenue in the Hollywood area. The suspect, Victor Lopez, was a twenty-three-year-old from El Salvador who had a prior criminal history. Lopez walked into the Rinconcito Guatemalteco Restaurant at 501 North Western Avenue, sat down, and ate a meal. After finishing, he pulled his gun and ordered five people to the floor. This was a takeover robbery. The customers and staff immediately complied, trembling as they moved under the chairs and tables. Each knew what was happening and prayed that the man didn't start shooting. Lopez cleared out all the cash from the register, then went over to a waitress lying on the floor and took her wedding ring off her finger. The ring was worth more than anything else taken in the robbery, and to the victim it was priceless with a lifetime of memories, but Lopez didn't care. He fled with about six hundred dollars in cash and jewelry and was last seen running down Western Avenue.

As the restaurant was being robbed, Officer Henry had been dispatched to a traffic accident in the Hollywood area. As he responded to the accident call, he drove closer to the path of the robbery suspect.

In the restaurant, the victims frantically dialed 9-1-1 and got LAPD's emergency communications center. Even with some language difficulties it was evident that an armed robbery had just occurred, so the dispatchers began to compile information for a "hot shot" or serious emergency radio call. Meanwhile, Lopez was on his way on foot over to Maplewood Avenue, just south of Western. There he saw Bob Hu getting into his car. Knowing that the police would be coming soon, Lopez needed to get out of there quickly, so he ran to the passenger side of Hu's car and, threatening Hu with a gun, shouted, "Open the door. Now!" Hu thought Lopez was going to kill him, so he jumped out of the driver's seat and ran off down the street, taking his car keys with him. Left with an abandoned vehicle and no keys, Lopez was stymied, so he again took off on foot.

As Lopez moved down Western Avenue, Hu followed from a distance, keeping him in sight. Aware that he was being followed, Lopez turned several times to challenge Hu. Then Hu saw Officer Henry driving nearby and began waving frantically at the officer, whom he approached in search of assistance. Hu was unable to speak very well in English, so his native Korean came out instead. Still, he was able to get out the words, "Man, gun, gun, gun!" As he pointed at Lopez, who was hurriedly walking away, Hu acted out Lopez pointing the gun at him during the robbery attempt. When Officer Henry realized what had happened, he immediately broadcast his activity and requested assistance. Shouting into his microphone he said, "6TL59: 415 [disturbance call] man with a gun. Suspect is a male Hispanic, five feet five, one hundred-fifty pounds, wearing blue sweatpants." The dispatchers had yet to put out the "robbery just occurred" call from the restaurant, so the officer was unaware that Lopez was also wanted for that crime.

Officer Henry maintained surveillance by slowly following the man as he walked down the street. Following officer safety rules, he waited until a backup unit arrived to approach the suspect. Henry explained, "I saw Lopez walking away. I saw he was carrying a bag, and I wanted to keep him in sight, but I also didn't want to provoke him. This situation was unfolding, and it was very dangerous to approach a suspected gunman without assistance."

Officer Henry continued to drive slowly behind Lopez, who had walked off Western onto Elmwood Avenue. As Lopez turned the corner he picked up his pace. The block was filled with apartment buildings enclosed by tall fences. It would have been difficult for Lopez to try to force his way into one of the buildings, so he was left to walk away from the police. Henry noticed that Lopez looked panicked as he furtively glanced over his shoulder at the officer.

Then Officer Henry heard the radio broadcast for the restaurant robbery: "Any Hollywood unit, any Hollywood unit: a 211 takeover at the Rinconcito Guatemalteco Restaurant, 501 North Western Avenue." Henry recalled, "I heard the broadcast, but I really didn't think I had the same suspect. I didn't know there was such a time delay in putting out the call." He pulled closer to the suspect, who was still walking quickly down the sidewalk on Elmwood Avenue.

Henry's plan was to keep Lopez in sight until backup arrived but, unfortunately, Lopez moved first, creating a scenario that became the officer's worst nightmare. Lopez ran into the front yard of an apartment building where children were playing. Fearing the suspect might harm a child or escape into the building, Henry got out of his patrol car and stood near the door. Knowing the suspect was armed, he drew his weapon as he ordered the suspect to drop his bag and raise his hands.

Lopez bolted, ran a few yards, then grabbed twelve-year-old Susana Guerra, held the gun to the girl's head, and threatened to kill her. Using his handheld radio, Officer Henry broadcast, "Officer needs help, man with a gun, hostage situation!"

Henry remembered, "I knew he was going to kill that little girl. Lopez had a wild look in his eyes." Fearing for the girl's life, the officer kept his distance. Little Susana screamed for her mother. The suspect placed a headlock around the child's throat as he continued to hold the gun to her head. Henry calmly told him to drop his weapon and release the little girl, but Lopez responded by telling the officer to drop his gun or he would blow Susana's head off. The standoff continued for several moments with Officer Henry repeating his commands to the suspect.

Henry said, "I couldn't get a shot off at his head. The suspect was hiding behind the girl. I was too afraid I'd hit the little girl."

Lopez aggressively approached the officer at his car while dragging Susana as a human shield. Henry moved to keep the police car between himself and Lopez. Lopez, trying to provoke the officer, forced him to back one full circle around the car. Henry said, "I knew I couldn't shoot under the circumstances, so I did a tactical retreat. I honestly thought I might have to shoot through this girl to stop this man." It was clear the officer didn't want to provoke the gunman for fear he would kill the child. Henry's fears were focused on little Susana, not on protecting himself. "The part that was the most nerve wrenching was the danger facing the girl. She was so scared her eyes were like saucers. I wanted to get my hands on him, but he kept me at bay with Susana."

When Officer Kehoe heard Henry's first call for help, he immediately responded from the Wilshire Division area. He was a few miles away, but he quickly made his way through traffic. He estimated he was two or three minutes out, but when he got onto Elmwood, he saw only the one black-and-white patrol car down the block. To Officer Kehoe this was very odd. "I'd been on the job for twenty years, and I'd been to dozens, maybe hundreds, of help calls, but this was the first time I was first in on the call. I mean, I was the only officer to get there, and now it was me and Henry against this guy with the little girl." Kehoe pulled his motorcycle up onto the sidewalk as he drove toward Henry's position, using the parked cars as cover from the gunman.

With Henry crouched behind the radio car, Officer Kehoe cautiously approached. When he saw that Lopez held the child in a headlock and still had a gun to her head, he moved to a position of advantage behind the rear of Henry's car. Both Kehoe and Henry made a conscious but unspoken decision: this man was not getting away with little Susana Guerra, not on their watch, not while they were both alive.

Lopez heard Officer Henry yell to Kehoe, "He's got a gun!" Lopez yelled back, "If you shoot, I'll kill her!"

Realizing he had no escape, Lopez jumped inside the police car, forcing Susana onto the front seat. Struggling for her life, Susana tried to pull away from the suspect. The terror felt by this child cannot be imagined. Concerned with what was unfolding and fed up with the suspect controlling the situation, "I decided it was our turn to take control," Kehoe told me.

Henry heard the grinding noise of his car's starter and realized that the suspect had attempted to start the engine although it was already running. Fearing the child would be killed by the suspect if he escaped, Henry decided to shoot out the rear tire. Then he warned Officer Kehoe, who was behind the car's trunk. Kehoe initially thought the suspect had shot Susana before realizing it was Officer Henry's shot. When Henry's bullet hit the right rear tire, the suspect immediately opened fire at Officer Kehoe.

Kehoe recounted, "Lopez shot out the rear window of the police car. I looked up and saw two bullet holes close enough to graze my helmet."

Kehoe didn't want the suspect to be able to shoot at both of them at the same time, so he directed Henry to the opposite side of the police car. Kehoe wanted Henry to move to the front of the car, but only from the passenger's side. Kehoe moved to the left of the rear fender so he would come up from behind Lopez, intending to shoot him in the leg. Kehoe said he wanted to keep clear of Susana's position but, as he moved to the left of the driver's door, he realized Lopez had been tracking him in the rearview mirror.

In an instant, Lopez leaned out of the car to shoot at Officer Kehoe. Kehoe told me, "He shot me in the leg. I felt the bullet fly out and hit my holster. First, I felt like getting hit with a hammer. Then I thought about having to wear a body cast with no bodysurfing that summer. Funny how your mind works, you know?"

Kehoe returned fire, shooting twice at Lopez, and then three more times through the window. The gun battle continued as the suspect fired a second time at Kehoe. Able to take aim through the broken window, Officer Henry opened fire at the suspect, emptying the magazine of his Beretta 92F. As chaotic as it was, both officers were careful to avoid the child, who was lying on the floor of the car.

Kehoe wanted to shoot again but realized he needed to reload his revolver. As Officer Kehoe was reloading, the suspect shot him a second time. The officer said, "That second round went straight into my shoulder and it spun me to the left. I initially thought I had only been grazed."

Wounded twice but still reloading, Kehoe turned to face the suspect, who was walking toward him, and found himself looking down the barrel of Lopez's gun. As Lopez prepared to execute Kehoe, they stared at each other. Lopez pulled the trigger, the hammer fell, but the gun didn't fire. Kehoe watched as Lopez again tried to shoot him. A second time the hammer fell, but still the gun failed—evidently it was empty. Kehoe was shouting for Officer Henry to fire, but Henry was also reloading. "I was yelling, 'Take him out! Take him out!' I didn't know Henry's gun was empty," Kehoe recalled.

The officers thought that Lopez was trying to reload his pistol when he ran back toward the police car. Unbeknownst to the officers, Susana Guerra had escaped when the suspect got out of the car to shoot Kehoe.

Lopez began to drive away, but because of the flat tire he was unable to drive very fast. As he passed Officer Henry, Henry opened fire, shooting four more rounds in an attempt to prevent his escape. Then, fearing for the life of the little girl who he still believed was held hostage in the car, Henry ran after the suspect, firing seven more rounds. Henry refused to give up.

As Henry opened fire at the suspect, a couple of things crossed his mind: "I thought, 'Lopez is not taking that little girl, and he's not stealing our police car!' I was starting to get mad, and I reloaded again to go after that guy." As Kehoe watched the suspect drive off, still thinking little Susana was inside the car, he thought about the lessons from Limas and Roberge, and knew he was not done, at least not yet.

With no regard for his own life, wounded in his right leg and left shoulder, Kehoe got on his motorcycle and pursued the suspect. He knew he was bleeding severely, so he used his radio to put out a call for a rescue ambulance for a shot officer . . . only he never said that *he* was the officer who'd been shot.

The two officers, Kehoe on his motorcycle and Henry on foot, followed the suspect, who drove a short distance west on Elmwood to the intersection with St. Andrews, where he collided with another car, then slouched forward in the seat. It turned out that he had been shot at least twice by Henry, but he didn't react to his wounds until the crash. A total of forty-five rounds were exchanged in Kehoe and Henry's gunfight with Lopez.

Only when the two officers approached the car did they realize the girl had already escaped. And only then would Kehoe allow himself to be transported to Cedar Sinai Hospital in West Los Angeles for treatment of his wounds.

Victor Lopez was transported to Hollywood Presbyterian Hospital. En route to the hospital, his heart stopped, but the Los Angeles Fire Department paramedics revived him. Once in the emergency room he suffered cardiac arrest a second time, but the hospital staff was able to revive him. Lopez fully recovered to be tried and convicted for robbery, carjacking, kidnapping, assault with a deadly weapon, and two counts of attempted murder of a police officer. He's now in prison serving two life terms for his violent crime spree.

Officer Kehoe went through surgery and returned to full duty. He later transferred to a detective assignment working accident investigation follow-up. He participated in several training events where he shared his will-to-survive story, helping repay the favor to Limas and Roberge. When Kehoe talks to recruits, he vividly reminds them that they can impact 50 percent of the problem through physical and mental preparation. "I got shot from nine feet with a .38-caliber pistol and it didn't knock me down," says Kehoe. "I tell the officers, if I survived, so can you!"

Kehoe served a full career and retired on a well-earned service pension. As testimony to the man's spiritual beliefs, his church and his family have always been at the forefront of his life. At the time of this writing he was celebrating thirty-five years of marriage to his wife, Candi, and they have four children: Stephen, thirty-three, a motor officer for the LAPD; Ty, thirty-two, a lawyer and accountant; Mark, twenty-nine, a Secret Service agent; and Susan, twenty-five, a former lifeguard for the city of San Clemente. Stephen and Candi have been blessed with eleven grandchildren.

Officer Hilton Henry returned to duty as an accident investigator and was soon promoted to the position of motor officer. He's now a seasoned veteran who trains younger officers, and he loves riding "motors" and working traffic. Single, he lives in a beautiful neighborhood in the hills above the San Fernando Valley. As luck would have it, from time to time he rides with Kehoe's son, Officer Stephen Kehoe II.

Stephen Kehoe and Hilton Henry were never assigned to be partners; they became partners by happenstance. But once thrown together by accident, they moved together as one. They both focused solely on saving Susana Guerra and stopping Victor Lopez. They followed the training lessons instilled by their LAPD mentors, and by all accounts, they did their job and did it well. *PARADE Magazine* gave them both Honorable Mention awards at the International Association of Chiefs of Police Officer of the Year awards in 1994. For their actions above and beyond the call of duty, Officer Stephen Kehoe and Officer Hilton Henry were awarded the agency's highest honor: the Los Angeles Police Department Medal of Valor.

Their brave and heroic actions under fire demonstrated the abilities of Henry and Kehoe to improvise, overcome, and adapt under extraordinary circumstances. Their courage, both physical and moral, was put to an extreme test. Both men showed the leadership skills that allowed them to survive. They made conscious decisions to refuse to give up or give in. They showed the world why they're the best of the best.

14

OFFICER WILLIAM J. HANSON

Tucson (Arizona) Police Department

"Firetrap"

"I came from Chicago and was a firefighter's kid. My dad died as a result of injuries suffered from a fire." Officer William J. Hanson apparently inherited some of his dad's instincts for firefighting, which would prove very fortunate for three individuals on the morning of May 13, 1995.

Around 6:55 A.M. Patrol Officer Hanson noticed a column of smoke coming from a house. The thirty-six-year-old officer pulled up in front of the house, then ran to the front door and banged on it, but he got no answer. Then he ran to the front window and yelled inside that the house was on fire.

"I went to the house and banged on the door. The door and window were all encased in wrought iron. The window covers were all the old style and had no release," Hanson told me.

A neighbor, Steve Price, had heard an explosion and saw the smoke coming from the house. He started banging on the front door in concert with Hanson's efforts to rouse anyone who might be inside.

"What's the matter?" asked a woman who emerged from the front door. "Your house is on fire!" the two men yelled back.

Shelby McConnell started screaming and ran back into her home.

Officer Hanson chased down the hall after McConnell, pulling the woman back to the front of the house and outside. Running back into the house, he thought he heard someone in a bedroom. He checked the door-knob for heat; it was cool to the touch. When he tried to enter the room, however, he discovered that the door was locked.

"I found a locked bedroom door and tried the knob. The knob was turning in my hand as if someone was turning it, so I waited for the door to open, but it didn't. The smoke was heavy, and the back of the house and roof were engulfed. I kicked in the bedroom door and found a seventy-two-year-old woman inside."

Hanson took Nora Lee Gibson outside. She appeared dazed and dis-oriented.

Officer James McShea, forty-one, on patrol at 7:00 A.M., had responded when Hanson advised dispatch that there was a residential fire nearby. "I saw a huge amount of smoke from about two blocks away. There was no fire department there when I arrived."

When McShea pulled up in front of the house, Gibson was sitting by the front door. "Bill was already in the house saving the occupants. Bill had broken down an old woman's door and brought her out," according to McShea.

McShea entered the home with Hanson to search for additional people. But they found no one, so they came outside. Then the officers dis-covered that McConnell's eight-year-old grandson was missing.

Officers Hanson and McShea ran back to the blazing house. McShea told me, "We had to run through the fire in order to find the child. The air was so filled with smoke, there was no visibility. I couldn't see in the closets and rooms, so we checked on our hands and knees, feeling our way." They felt along the tops of the beds, checked under the beds, sifted through clothes on the floor, and felt inside closets. One bathroom was so engulfed in flames and smoke that it couldn't be entered. When the heavy smoke again forced them outside, they had located no one else. McConnell then said that her daughter, Felice Scholes, couldn't be found and might be inside the house too. The two officers again went back into the burning building, searching for the eight-year-old and Felice in the now completely dark living and dining areas. Once again the intense smoke drove them from the house empty-handed. As the men came outside, the Tucson Fire Department arrived to put out the blaze.

"He's been found!" someone yelled. Officer Hanson found Shelby McConnell hugging the little boy in the backyard. The boy had lived with his grandmother since he was a baby. Felice Scholes and her two teenage sons also lived at the house but, as it turned out, Felice had not come home the previous night, and neither of the boys was home at the time of the fire.

Hanson, who had entered the burning house five times to evacuate those inside, suffered from minor smoke inhalation as well as cuts and bruises. McShea sustained minor smoke inhalation, as did Steve Price, the Good Samaritan who'd helped the officers that morning. The fire department administered oxygen to the men at the scene.

None of the occupants was injured by the blaze. Afterward, McShea revealed, "The most frightening fact was that the window and door wrought iron had no inside releases." All the family members in the house would have perished if Hanson had not acted as he did when he did, according to the fire department. When thanked by the fire's victims, Hanson responded with his usual contagious smile, then decided to finish his shift.

The apparent cause of the fire: arson. Clothing and cardboard had been ignited on the back porch. It appeared that someone had been playing with matches in the backyard. Each year an estimated seven hundred people are killed by arson. Arson accounts for 25 percent of all fires in the United States, according to the U.S. Fire Administration, and juveniles account for approximately 55 percent of all arson arrests.

A week after the fire, Shelby McConnell told police that her eight-year-old son finally admitted that he started the fire but said that it was an accident. Most of the items set on fire had belonged to him; they were in a box that was to go to Georgia, where he was being sent to live with his mom and her new husband.

The boy left Tucson the following day with his mother.

Both Officer Hanson and his brother, Steven Hanson, served in the Arizona Air National Guard at the time of the incident. Steven was asked to write a column about his brother's heroic act for *The Copperhead,* the base newsletter. Few siblings have such a golden opportunity to toast—and roast—a younger brother publicly in print. What follows is the article exactly as it appeared. You don't have to read between the lines to understand how much Steven loves and admires his brother.

MY BROTHER, THE HERO
by Steven J. Hanson, Sr., Tsgt. Boom

My Flight Commander, Rick Hinojosa, has been after me to write an article that I promised him awhile back, so here is where I bear my shame. I can't promise anything. Last year sometime my older Brother Bill, also of the 161 ARW Logistics Office, also known as Billy, a.k.a. Francis, call me Psycho Hanson, was working as a sworn Police Officer on the midnight beat in the busy, gang infected town of . . . Tucson? As in any job where there are adrenaline junkies employed, after a certain point their sugar level starts to decrease and the body becomes dysfunctional. Knowing he was coming dangerously close to this level Bill stopped to replenish his hypoglycemic condition (Dunkin' Donuts). After downing his free donut (oops), Bill was drinking his coffee when he heard a call for help from a fellow officer over his radio, something about a fight with a drag queen or something. Not spilling a drop of coffee he vaulted into his new Chevy police cruiser, with its Corvette engine, and at speeds only imaginable to F-16 pilots (and could make a navigator puke) he arrived at the scene, only to be turned away with a wave and a thank you from the lipstick and cheap makeup covered officer. After drinking his sixth cup of coffee for the evening Bill was looking for a lonely stretch of road with a bush; when he looked up and saw a column of smoke in the distance. Bill started heading for the smoke column, hoping to bust somebody for illegal burning, and make a couple of bucks for the City of Tucson. As he turned the corner he saw smoke and flames coming from under the eaves of a home. He immediately transmitted a message asking for the Tucson Fire Department to respond. Since Bill grew up in the household of a Chicago fireman, he remembered the stories he had been told as a child about great fire rescues and let instinct kick in. Working on pure adrenaline now Bill parked his police car, and, after five minutes or so, he parallel parked between two cars so tight that no fire hose could fit between them. He then dismounted, holding his baton (cop term) and, knowing lives may be in danger, sprinted to the rear of his car where he opened the trunk and grabbed some road flares. After making a runway out of road flares long enough that you could land a B-52 without popping the chute, and could be seen by any satellite, Bill then ran toward the home and began tapping with his baton on the front windows. Well, this disturbed the woman inside the house enough to make her go to the front door and ask him what the hell he wanted. Bill then informed her that her house was on fire, to which she screamed, turned and ran back inside. (A lot of people scream when they see Bill.) After skillfully throwing his baton at her ankles and making her trip, Bill dragged her back outside to safety. She then informed Bill that there were other people inside the house. So Bill entered the home again, now with smoke and flames rolling around the ceiling enough to burn your hair off (maybe that's why his hair looks like that). Moving through the house, searching on his hands and knees, Bill found another woman, and while she put up a good fight (she was leaving anyway), Bill carried her and her walker to safety. With news of more children inside Bill once again entered the home, the smoke was down to the floor now and Bill searched valiantly until he had found all persons in the house. When he returned outside, Bill found out that some of the people he had been searching for had already been outside for quite some time. After they got Bill to put his weapon back in his holster, he sat down for some well-needed oxygen. Bill was now on his way to the hospital to be treated for smoke inhalation, and a possible concussion from the woman hitting him with her walker, and might well have gone, if his sergeant hadn't asked him if he wanted overtime.

For his act of bravery Bill was awarded the Tucson Medal of Valor.

The reason I say I have to bear my shame is that I'm the fireman in the family, and it seems that all I do is go on calls to help a senior citizen who has slid off the toilet and gotten wedged between the wall and the commode.

The State of Arizona Division of Military Affairs awarded Technical Sergeant William J. Hanson the Arizona Medal of Valor for his courage on May 13, 1995. The award reads in part, "By his prompt action and humanitarian regard for his fellow man, Sergeant Hanson has reflected credit upon himself, the Air National Guard, and the State of Arizona."

For heroic action above and beyond the call of duty, Hanson received the Tucson Police Department's Medal of Valor, as did Officer McShea, who is now a police lieutenant. Steve Price's heroism in the incident was recognized by the Tucson Fire Department.

Prior to joining the Tucson Police Department, Bill Hanson was with the Mojave County Sheriff's Office for three and a half years, where he was a field training officer and SWAT team leader. Married with five children, Sergeant Hanson is currently a police detective. He's also a member of the honor guard, a detective trainer, an ethics instructor, an instructor at the Basic Academy, and member and assistant squad supervisor for Mobile Field Force One. A first sergeant for security forces in the Arizona Air National Guard, he was activated for Operation Enduring Freedom in September 2001. In January 2002, the Air National Guard selected Hanson First Sergeant of the Year for the state of Arizona. He retired from the service in 2002.

★ 15 ★

SERGEANT RORY TUGGLE AND OFFICER ANDREW RAMOS

Las Vegas (Nevada) Metropolitan Police Department

"Fright Night"

Sergeant Rory Tuggle

Officer Andrew Ramos

On April 29, 1992, a Simi Valley, California, jury that contained no African-Americans acquitted four white Los Angeles police officers of the beating of black motorist Rodney King. On March 3, 1991, King had been beaten and sent to the hospital with numerous broken bones when police stopped him after a fifteen-minute high-speed chase. The eighty-one-second videotape of the beating—with twenty-four officers in attendance—was shown repeatedly on television and brought issues of racism and police brutality in America to the front burner.

Within hours of the acquittal, violence broke out in Los Angeles. But the jury's decision would also have serious repercussions on the streets of the fastest growing city in America, too.

On the day following the acquittal, more than two hundred people protesting the verdict marched a mile and a half north of downtown Las Vegas starting at around 3:00 P.M. What began as a protest against police brutality simmered into civil unrest, then boiled over into a full-blown riot in little over an hour.

According to Sergeant Rory Tuggle, "The core group that started the march grew quickly from five or seven to fifteen or twenty and, within minutes of starting this 'march,' attacked an Equal Opportunity Board bus containing physically and mentally challenged children. They beat and pelted the driver with rocks and bottles, hospitalizing him and terrifying the children. This group moved on, gaining strength in numbers, swelling to over two hundred, all the while victimizing residents they passed and news crews that followed."

One officer described the scene as "hell on the streets." The evening would later be known as "Fright Night."

Among those protesters were hoodlums who wished to take advantage of the mayhem in order to steal and perpetrate other criminal acts. These participants were armed with guns, Molotov cocktails, bats, bottles, and rocks as they stormed toward the downtown area. Innocent motorists were dragged out of their vehicles and savagely beaten. Bystanders were threatened with bricks and bottles; some were robbed. Wholesale looting erupted as the rioters accelerated their vicious attacks, throwing bricks through retail-business storefronts. Buildings were set on fire, and hundreds of rounds of gunfire could be heard. The disorder would last twenty-two hours.

Sergeant Tuggle had been in Defensive Tactics Instructor school earlier in the day with his partner Officer Andrew (Andy) Ramos. Later, they were both testifying before a grand jury on the same case when Tuggle was informed that dispatch was looking for him. Jumping into their personal cars, Tuggle and Ramos drove to work from the courthouse, dressed out, and headed in their patrol car to the intersection of Bonanza and Main, what Tuggle called "the flashpoint" of the riot.

"Hold them at Main Street! Don't let them cross Main Street!" Sergeant Tuggle yelled into his radio as they went. "We've got to form a skirmish line at Main Street." Tuggle knew that allowing the unruly crowd to get into the downtown casinos would be disastrous and would endanger the lives of many additional people. He considered how the casino security guards might react as looters poured into their buildings. They certainly hadn't been trained to deal with rioters. The rioting had to be contained.

It's estimated that rioting happens only once every twenty-five years in the United States. Many police officers can spend an entire career and never get involved in a riot, even in a large metropolitan area. The Las

Vegas Metropolitan Police Department wasn't equipped for what their officers would face in the streets that day.

"We had no shields, no riot batons," Ramos remembers. "SWAT had them, but it took a while to deploy them and get them into place. We just had our helmets and the vests we normally wear, and one day of mobile field force training."

The Metro Police supply sergeant was able to locate a stash of never-used helmets, which were dispensed immediately to officers at the site of the disturbance. There was a line of cops on one side of an underpass and an angry mob on the other side, but no tear gas canisters, bulletproof shields, or rubber bullets were available to the officers.

Just as Sergeant Tuggle and Officer Ramos turned onto Bonanza, a fellow officer warned of the presence of snipers. Most of the shots were aimed at the police and firefighters attempting to restore order and control the fires. At that very moment, the two men found themselves in the snipers' crosshairs.

As shots were fired at them, both officers instinctively ducked down in the car. Tuggle leaned to the right as Ramos leaned to the left. In an occurrence that could be laughable only later upon reflection, "We smashed our helmets together," Tuggle remarks.

Tuggle dropped below the steering wheel, placing his hand on the accelerator to give the car gas while periodically raising his head to see where he was going, then lowering it again for safety. He managed to stop the car behind an abandoned vehicle, where he joined others who were using the buildings and nearby trees for cover.

"We thought the wind was blowing hard through the leaves of the branches overhead," Tuggle remembers. "But there was no wind. It turned out to be the sound of hundreds of bullets being fired at us." The men quickly sought other cover. Officer Ralph Ray received a gunshot wound to his left arm when rioters fired on the car he was driving.

For several hours Sergeant Tuggle was in charge of a team of forty patrol officers. The police department's strategy was repeatedly to advance, engage the rioters, make arrests, then retreat.

Early in what became a very long evening, Tuggle and Ramos approached an underpass where they witnessed a large crowd scattering. Then they discovered a casualty of the riots: an unconscious homeless man, bleeding profusely and lying lifelessly in the street. A group was kicking and beating the man. There was no doubt in the officers' minds that he was going to be beaten to death.

Tuggle and Ramos ran over to him, fighting off the thugs. The man wasn't moving. They positioned themselves to protect both sides of him, and then they became the focus of the rioters' wrath. Ramos remembers thinking he'd been shot when he took a blow to the head that knocked him to the ground. He felt a warm liquid flowing rapidly down his neck.

"That moment seemed to last forever. Shots were being fired, and you could hear the impact before you heard the *bang*. At first I felt shock, then fear because I thought I was gonna die. Then I realized that I'd been cracked in the head with a large beer bottle. That's when the fear turned to anger."

To further protect the beaten man, Tuggle leaned over his body, using his own body to shield the man from sniper fire. "We couldn't shoot back," Ramos recollects. "One guy came out on his porch with a baby in his arms and shot at us. We just couldn't shoot back." Ramos used the butt of his shotgun to keep rioters away. Though he was armed with a 9-mm pistol, Tuggle held his fire as did Ramos.

Rioters who'd been kept in one area suddenly surged toward Tuggle and Ramos. As he continued to protect the beaten, bloodied man from the crowd, Tuggle was repeatedly struck with clubs and rocks. Despite repeated physical attacks, which included truckloads of men and women firing at them, Tuggle refused to leave the man to seek protective cover for himself, but instead managed to call for an ambulance, which arrived in less than fifteen minutes to take the still-unconscious victim to a nearby hospital. Luckily, Tuggle suffered only cuts and bruises from the blows he'd received.

Tuggle continued to lead the other officers through the crisis. Small battles erupted in various sections of the contained area. Using false alarms, the rioters attempted to lure the officers and firefighters into situations where they could be ambushed. Then real fires erupted, but sniper fire prevented firefighters from putting out many of them; the firefighters, who were not trained to deal with gunshots, couldn't do their jobs without police escorts. Under Tuggle's direction, the police used fire extinguishers to help save a substation while under attack by gunfire, rocks, and bottles. When firefighters were forced to flee a burning shopping center, Tuggle and his men moved in, but they too were driven back by gunfire. Like Ramos, a firefighter reported seeing people using small children as shields so that the police wouldn't return their gunfire. Eventually Tuggle and his men secured the shopping area, clearing it of looters; the body of one individual would be found inside the next day. Due to the snipers, the officers had to clear the projects, where couches and chairs had been set aflame.

"I recognized probably sixty percent of the guys in the streets as gang-bangers I'd known when I was on gang patrol. *I knew these guys.* I couldn't believe they were tearing up their community," Ramos laments, disbelief and disappointment still in his voice.

Ramos recalls seeing SWAT team member Mike Nunez standing at the ready, posted to guard the officers who were trying to rest between skirmishes. "We all went through the whole gamut of emotions. It had been a terribly long day, and it was close to midnight. And here's Mike Nunez guarding us. Nobody could talk to him while he was at his post. The strict discipline was incredible."

As Tuggle led his antiriot squad of officers into the smoky, fire-engulfed streets, he repeatedly exposed himself to numerous snipers as he rallied the officers to hold the line against the rioters. Following his courageous actions, Tuggle's officers reestablished their skirmish line as they fought to gain back control of the streets even while hundreds of rounds of gunfire were being fired at them.

The riots caused an estimated $12 million in damages. Thirty-seven people were injured but, remarkably, only one died that night. A total of eighty adults were arrested that evening along with eight juveniles, who were taken to a juvenile detention center. Not wanting to get caught unprepared again, Metro Police geared up for more violence to break out after the second Rodney King verdict, purchasing special riot gear and accelerating its training for crowd control and riots. Community leaders and government officials worked together to try to address the specific problems that had been simmering in the predominantly African-American area of Las Vegas where the unrest occurred.

Sheriff Jerry Keller has worked for Clark County for thirty-two years, the last seven as the county's elected sheriff. Over the years he's watched the city change as it has grown. He now oversees a department with over 4,000 employees, 2,000 of which are police officers, 650 corrections officers, and the balance in administration. He considers himself extremely lucky to have such a terrific group of people working for him. "Rory Tuggle and Andy Ramos used their bodies to protect an indigent who was being beaten to death," the sheriff proudly told me. "Every citizen has equal rights in Clark County."

Sergeant Tuggle showed by his example that he was a leader who was able to rally his men to take back the streets of the city, thus preventing the civil unrest from spreading into the greater Las Vegas area.

"And Andy was my partner and right-hand man that entire shift," Tuggle reiterates.

Sergeant Rory Tuggle and Officer Andy Ramos each received a Unit Citation for Valorous Conduct. Because they didn't give up ground while being shot at, pelted with bottles, and hit with rocks as they battled to save a fallen civilian, the Medal of Valor was presented to both men from their department. It's the highest honor the department bestows.

For his leadership under fire and courageous actions that saved lives and helped limit property damage, thirty-four-year-old Sergeant Tuggle received the International Association of Chiefs of Police/*PARADE Magazine* Police Officer of the Year Award in 1993. Tuggle wrote that the award was the highlight of his career. He also used the award and the press that accompanied it as an opportunity to thank the leadership of his police department and encourage citizens everywhere to express their support for the law enforcement agencies in their communities. He remarked that the kind cards and letters he received from all over the country should remind all cops why they do their jobs every day.

What does Tuggle think about the riot in hindsight? "I wish that people would take responsibility for their actions. Blaming criminal behavior on a cause doesn't make the perpetrator any less of a criminal. In many cases, our society doesn't allow police officers to do their jobs until it's too late."

Now in his early forties and the father of two daughters, Tuggle is the supervisor for the Community Oriented Policing Office out of the department's Southeast Area Command. His office works with local government, other jurisdictions, and community resources to find long-term solutions to chronic problems. For six years he was a K-9 officer. He and his partner, Cigan, placed first in three of five events at the 1998 Las Vegas Police K-9 Trials, taking Area Search, Building Search, and Tactical Obedience. He hopes to continue his police work for many years to come.

Andy Ramos still recalls the events of that day as shocking and unbelievable. He is now working undercover in vice after being with the department for fourteen years as a regular police officer and a cadet for three years. He's married with one daughter.

Neither Tuggle nor Ramos knows what became of the homeless man they saved that day.

CAPTAIN WAYNE LONGO AND DETECTIVE FRED SWANSON

Idaho State Police

"Deadly Epidemic"

Captain Wayne Longo   Detective Fred Swanson

Methamphetamine represents the fastest-growing drug threat in America today. "Meth" is a dangerous, unpredictable drug that can be lethal. Also known as speed, ice, and crystal, meth is a potent central nervous system stimulant like cocaine. Meth can be smoked, snorted, injected, or taken orally, and its appearance varies depending on how it is used. Usually it's a white, odorless, bitter-tasting powder that dissolves easily in water.

Methamphetamine use produces an increase in blood pressure, body temperature, and rate of breathing while it dilates the pupils. The drug produces temporary hyperactivity, euphoria, a sense of increased energy, and tremors. High doses or chronic use has been associated with increased nervousness, irritability, and paranoia. Users who are under the influence of the drug and in a paranoid state often become violent. Many recorded attempted murders and homicides have involved perpetrators high on meth. Because withdrawal from high doses produces severe depression, it has led to many recorded suicides and cases of self-inflicted wounds.

Chronic use produces a psychosis similar to schizophrenia and is characterized by paranoia, picking at the skin, self-absorption, and auditory and visual hallucinations. During "tweaking," the most dangerous stage in a binge cycle, abusers are irritable and paranoid because they haven't slept in three to fifteen days. Despite their intense craving for more meth at this stage, no dosage will recreate the euphoric high, which frustrates the user and leads to unpredictability and a potential for violence.

Unlike heroin and cocaine, methamphetamine is one drug that users can manufacture themselves. Formulas for making meth are easy to find on the Internet, and the components are readily available from chemical wholesale houses or foreign sources. Although Mexican crime groups produce most of the meth distributed in the United States in "super labs" in California and Mexico, setting up a meth lab doesn't require a college-educated chemist. In fact, more than 90 percent of the suspects arrested for "cooking" meth aren't chemists, which makes it easy to understand why there are so many explosions and fires in the homes, trailers, or motel rooms housing illegal labs.

Even though the amount of meth produced by mom-and-pop labs is small compared with the output of super labs, their proliferation throughout the country has created supersize headaches for law enforcement. In 1993 the Drug Enforcement Agency (DEA) seized 218 methamphetamine labs. In 1999 the DEA alone seized over 2,000 labs, while federal, state, and local law enforcement officers combined seized over 7,000 labs.

Law enforcement faces extreme danger whenever it attempts to close a meth laboratory and arrest the workers inside. The chemicals used to manufacture meth are highly explosive and flammable. And because prison terms can be lengthy for those caught making meth, the labs are often booby-trapped. A police officer opening a door might face a 12-gauge shotgun rigged to go off automatically or might trip a wire that releases an exotic animal like a lion or a cheetah. Meth manufacturers have been known to build elaborate escape tunnels; as they escape undetected, they blow up the laboratory—and any evidence—with a remote control device.

Clandestine meth laboratories are a substantial health and safety threat to their communities. Not only are the hazardous chemicals involved often disposed of improperly, creating environmental problems that require expensive cleanup, but fires, explosions, and toxic gas are a constant threat to the general public. These risks are of no concern to the operators of small labs, however, who spend as little as a thousand dollars for chemicals that will generate ten thousand dollars in methamphetamine.

Forty-two-year-old Jack James Jansen's meth laboratory in Coeur d'Alene, Idaho, was closed down when he was arrested in 1998 for manufacturing methamphetamine. His manufacturing equipment and chemicals were taken into custody as evidence. He ran a small lab, but he had been armed when he was arrested and owned a pit bull that had been trained to attack. When Jansen posted bail, he walked out of jail and apparently right back into the lucrative world of meth production.

On the morning of December 7, 1999, Detectives Paul Berger and Guy Schensky from the Idaho State Police were conducting surveillance on a Coeur d'Alene residence where, according to informants, Jansen had set up another meth lab while awaiting trial. If Jansen was arrested again, there would be no bail and a long term in prison.

The house was in a typical residential area: children walked by on their way to nearby schools and, just four hundred feet away, a day-care center nestled among the other homes. Around 8 A.M., as the detectives watched, someone opened a window of the house to throw something out. When the fluid hit the ground, a white cloud dispensed a strong chemical odor. The familiar odor of ammonia confirmed that at least one constituent of meth was in the house. Dumping a hazardous chemical gave the detectives the probable cause they needed to obtain a search warrant.

Before the raid, detectives briefed law enforcement personnel and the fire department. The whiteboard in the meeting room resembled a page from a football team's playbook. This was not a game, however; the consequences could be deadly if the play wasn't executed exactly as planned. The Coeur d'Alene Fire Department would be positioned a block away, and an ambulance would be standing by. Law enforcement would cover all the building's exits.

Around 10:30 A.M., a team of detectives and Captain Wayne Longo approached the house and announced that they had a search warrant. Suddenly a fire started inside, producing a thick, acrid black smoke. Police later reported that the suspect had set chemicals on fire in an attempt to destroy evidence of his crime. The officers broke down the back door to find a twenty-three-year-old Coeur d'Alene woman and a thirty-one-year-old woman from Hayden Lake, Idaho, asleep in the living room. The officers had to shake the women aggressively to awaken them. As the flames increased, Captain Longo and Detectives Berger and Schensky removed the two women from the house. According to Longo, the women were not especially cooperative with the police on the scene. They stated that Jansen wasn't inside.

Within seconds the fire department arrived to discover noxious black smoke filling the house. Shortly, the west end of the residence was totally engulfed in the blaze, with flames rising as high as forty feet. The situation was dangerous not only for law enforcement officers and firefighters but for the public as well. Full of flammable chemicals, the burning house could explode at any moment. The roof could collapse, trapping people inside. The suspect himself presented a potential danger; at any moment he might fire upon anyone close by. Though the two women insisted that the suspect was not in the house, the detectives knew he was.

Longo and Detective Fred Swanson, who'd been on surveillance during the briefing, decided to enter the residence as police backup to protect the firefighters. Longo donned protective gear and a self-contained breathing apparatus (SCBA) as did Swanson, who had been a volunteer firefighter with the Moscow (Idaho) Volunteer Fire Department from 1982 to 1985. Fire itself didn't concern Swanson, "but explosions and toxic chemicals are always a concern," he told me. Other law enforcement officers evacuated a four-block area surrounding the house. The preschool was evacuated while the elementary school was shut down with the children locked inside for their safety.

With their guns drawn, Longo and Swanson entered through the back door, crawling from room to room as they searched for Jansen on the main floor. When they didn't find him, they searched the second floor of the two-story home, but the suspect was nowhere to be found. As the men were heading toward the door, they noticed a small wooden door that appeared to lead to a root cellar or basement area. When they opened the door, they directed their weapons at several loose cinder blocks under the stairs. Someone was hiding in the crawl space.

Swanson recalls, "I cautiously looked into the hole and saw Jansen lying against the block wall to my right. It appeared he was unconscious at that time. I told Captain Longo that we had found him. Captain Longo went to the bottom of the stairs and called for the fire department's help and returned to my location. The captain returned as I was yelling at Jansen to come out of the crawl space—I knew we would not be able to go into the crawl space and pull him out; there was not enough room for that. After several yells at Jansen, I finally saw his foot move."

"Come out of there. We're your only hope to get out," Longo yelled.

But the figure in the basement refused. Obviously there was no time for a lengthy negotiation, but the officers managed to coax the man from his hiding place, and as he crept toward them on his hands and knees, they grabbed him. The search was finally over, and the safety of the outside world was within reach.

Then Swanson heard the alarm from his breathing apparatus. "The first time I was really concerned was when my SCBA started ringing, giving me a warning that I was running out of air," he recalls. He and Longo raced to escape with their suspect. Though firefighters had extinguished the fire by this time, every space in the house had filled with thick chemical smoke.

"I can't breathe," Jansen muttered, and suddenly he lost consciousness. His heart had stopped beating. At great personal peril, the officers remained with the suspect until they could lift him up the stairs to safety with the help of firefighters. Once outside, emergency personnel administered CPR on Jansen. Swanson's air supply ran out just as he hit the outside door.

"We felt pretty good to save this guy even though we went there to arrest him," Longo told me. What he always wants is for "everybody to go home, for nobody to get hurt."

The police found a stolen 12-gauge shotgun in the house. The house itself had been rented from a couple in Cataldo, Idaho.

Jansen would spend five days in intensive care at Kootenai Medical Center. After three months in jail, he posted bond and was out of jail once again. And once again, he set up a meth laboratory. After police had raided his meth labs three times in three years, Jacky Jansen pleaded guilty to one count of attempted drug manufacturing and two counts of attempted drug trafficking. He was sentenced to a minimum mandatory sentence of at least four years in prison.

"Meth is the number one priority the state police focus on," Longo told me. At the time of this particular incident, law enforcement had already discovered some ninety meth labs in Idaho's five northern counties that year, an increase of 125 percent from the previous year. In the year 2000, police reported that four out of every five crimes in Idaho were related to methamphetamine.

When asked why his region has led the state in lab seizures, Captain Longo replied that one, it's a booming area, and two, they're an aggressive squad and very efficient at what they do. "Maybe we've stopped potential disaster every time we raid these things," he hopes. "The guys really feel good when they take these things down." His region is also ahead of the curve on education about the dangers of methamphetamine. Part of the strategy of the state police is to educate the public about meth labs and meth use by speaking to community groups, service organizations, schools, and parent-teacher groups.

The epidemic continues throughout the area, taking down not only the drug users but also the other victims of the drug—those who are abused, assaulted, or abandoned by the users, including the many children whose parents are in jail or dead. Added to these problems is the potential danger to passersby and nearby property from explosions and fires.

Captain Wayne Longo and Detective Fred Swanson took extraordinary measures to rescue Jacky Jansen while putting their own lives at risk. Though any one of us might enter a burning building to save a loved one, a child, or a vulnerable person, how many would come to the rescue of a methamphetamine cook who set his own home on fire? In saving Jansen's life, Captain Longo and Detective Swanson acted courageously and selflessly. They entered a fully engulfed building to protect the members of the Coeur d'Alene Fire Department. Cognizant of the dangers they might face, the two officers knew that they had to find anyone who might still be inside, even if that person was involved in a methamphetamine lab.

In the letter in which he recommended Captain Longo and Detective Swanson for inclusion in this book, Lieutenant Colonel Glenn Ford, deputy director of the Idaho State Police, wrote that they acted above and beyond the call of duty "when they entered the burning house, fully aware of the limitations of the protective gear they wore and knowing the danger of the environment they were entering. As a result of their persistency and dedication to law enforcement, the suspect was dragged from the basement and taken to safety."

At forty-eight, Wayne Longo is a twenty-five-year veteran of the Idaho State Police with sixteen years as supervisor of detectives and two years in charge of the crowd intervention team. Longo makes the majority of public presentations about meth labs, revealing the potential dangers while providing safety tips. He's married with two children.

Detective Swanson became a special agent with the Idaho Bureau of Investigation in 1990 following jobs with the Moscow (Idaho) Police

Department and the Latah County Sheriff's Department. He's been a polygraph examiner since 1993. He has three children ranging in age from twelve to seventeen.

Captain Longo and Detective Swanson received Valor Awards from the Idaho State Police, the agency's highest award, for courageously placing their lives in jeopardy to save the life of another person. The two heroes also put one more meth lab out of business. Who knows how many lives were saved as a result?

★ 17 ★

SERGEANT CRAIG HOGMAN

Clark County (Washington) Sheriff's Office

"Gut Instincts"

As the car in front of me led me through the beautiful tree-lined streets of an almost picture-perfect old neighborhood on a brilliant spring afternoon, I forced myself to imagine the horrific events that had taken place at this tranquil scene. Pulling over to the curb, Sergeant Craig Hogman of the Clark County Sheriff's Office stepped out of his car to tell me that this was where the getaway car had stopped and turned sideways so the shooters inside were in a better position to ambush him. It was readily apparent that the events of that day do not lie deep in his subconscious but are fresh in his mind, ready to surface with a minimum of prompting. The emotion of that day played out on Craig's face and in his words as he described the event to me.

"I think I lost a little bit of my soul, a little bit," Craig admitted.

Hogman was forty-nine when the incident occurred. With the sheriff's office since 1974, he began his law enforcement career as a custody officer (called a "jailer" in those days). He has served as deputy sheriff, detective in the Major Crimes Unit, and sergeant. Those who know Craig attest to his professionalism, his calm nature, his patience, and his compassion. The three young men who rocked this quiet Vancouver, Washington, neighborhood one violent day in 1997 tested all these attributes.

Aaron Ahern, twenty-five, Michael Brock, twenty-four, and Ronald Bianchi, twenty-five, executed a game plan on October 17, 1997, that would ultimately result in two of their deaths. The third would be sentenced to seventy-two years in prison. They had needed money and, more urgently, there was a local drug dealer who wanted to be paid. Ahern and Bianchi feared the dealer would take payment out of their hides if they didn't clear the debt. Their game plan involved setting off a pipe bomb as a diversionary tactic, then robbing a bank. Bianchi, who liked the scheme, talked Brock into it. Ahern would be the bomb maker, and Bianchi would boost three cars for getaway purposes. It would be a breeze, and nobody would be hurt.

This wouldn't be the first time the three had broken the law. In 1992 Aaron Ahern was convicted for burglarizing and stealing cash from an Idaho Burger King restaurant. After serving five months in county jail, he moved to Vancouver, Washington, where his probation officer lost track of him. He then began using methamphetamine and frequently used marijuana. Although he could be personable, there was something dark, almost evil about him, according to his brother John. Even as a child, he'd talked about robbing banks.

Michael J. Brock, or "Crazy Mike," as Bianchi called him, was originally from Anchorage, Alaska. Brock had been convicted of attempted second-degree robbery in Clark County. His probation officer repeatedly cited him for not reporting in as ordered, failing to notify the probation department of his changes of address, and not paying back the $7,104 he stole from his robbery victim.

Ronald Jay Bianchi, a junior high school dropout, was twice convicted of auto theft in eastern Washington. During one of those arrests, the police found syringes and other drug paraphernalia in the car along with a heavily drugged Bianchi. Like Brock, Bianchi didn't report to his probation officer and didn't make restitution to his victims or pay court costs.

Bianchi's girlfriend Rachel Shannon Barnes, twenty-two, was five months pregnant with his child. She had left home seven years earlier and had no arrests prior to October 1997. She would later be accused of helping to rob a home and steal a gun that was used in the bank robbery. She would also be accused of helping to case the bank and disposing of the sawed-off shotgun barrels.

"That was an interesting day for me," Vicki Hogman, Craig's wife, said in what I consider to be one of the biggest understatements I've ever heard.

Vicki had always accepted Craig's job for what it was; she'd been raised by a father who was in law enforcement. According to Craig, "She doesn't say anything. We don't talk about it, but I know every day is difficult for her."

On that day, Craig had come home to invite Vicki to lunch. As she described it, "He gave me a kiss and said, 'I'll see you in a half hour,' and I started to cry. And he gave me a hug and said, 'Oh, Vic, get over this.' But I was very sad and I didn't know why. I had decided to go for a walk because I couldn't pull myself out of it. A lady, one of my neighbors, stood and watched me coming forward. As I got closer, she said, 'You look very sad today. Are you all right?' I walked over to her and I started to cry, and I said, 'I don't know, but I'm feeling very sad and I don't know why.' " As Craig said, "This is a woman's intuition."

The crime spree started around 10:30 A.M. with an explosion in a forty-foot container behind the Kmart on Andresen Road in Vancouver. The three men used a stolen 1982 Chevy Camaro to get to the site, then ditched it for a 1987 Chrysler LeBaron. Three minutes later, at the scene, the fire department determined there was no smoke and no fire. Almost an hour later, at 11:43 A.M., the Alcohol, Tobacco and Firearms (ATF) agents were on their way to investigate.

At 11:05 A.M., 9-1-1 was alerted to an armed robbery at Wells Fargo Bank, Vancouver Mall Branch. Then at 11:18 A.M., three armed robbers in ski masks, trench coats, and gloves entered a Seafirst Bank on Mill Plain Boulevard and held everyone in the bank at gunpoint. The first man into the bank was armed with an SKS 7.62-mm assault rifle. The second carried a sawed-off shotgun under each arm. The third held a .22-caliber Ruger semiautomatic pistol and a shotgun.

Two calls from Seafirst Bank were made to 9-1-1 minutes after the robbers left the building. The bank manager made the first call, stating that less than several thousand dollars had been taken from three tellers' drawers and that one teller had given the robbers a dye pack that would explode shortly. A distraught teller made the second call. An eyewitness called 9-1-1 to report that the bank had been robbed and the robbers were driving a maroon Chrysler with the license plate TRE 455. Two of the bank robbers were in the front seat and one was in the backseat. All three had rifles and were wearing black ski masks. The Vancouver Police Department and Clark County Sheriff's Office dispatched vehicles to the bank, and all units were told to be on the lookout for the three robbers and their vehicle. The police dispatcher also notified the FBI.

Reports of the robbers continued to come in to 9-1-1. One witness reported that he saw one of the robbers change the Chrysler's license plate to TTH 353. Another described what two of the holdup men were wearing: one was in dark blue pants and a light blue shirt, the other in a flannel jacket in earth-tone colors and high-laced combat boots. What no one knew was that the robbers had switched getaway cars again, exchanging the Chrysler, which was later found running with its windshield wipers going, for a stolen 1966 Mustang.

Around 11:20 A.M., Sergeant Hogman was headed home for lunch, but he'd been following the activity involving the explosion and armed bank robbery on his police radio. He noticed a black Mustang with three passengers, and his gut instinct told him to follow it.

Though he was only following them at about thirty miles per hour in an unmarked Ford, he decided to back off a little because he didn't want to confront them until he had backup. But the driver became aware that he was being followed and sped up.

Sergeant Hogman called the dispatcher to give his location and say he was in pursuit of the black Mustang. Then Ahern opened fire with a semi-automatic rifle from the window of the right front seat. From the backseat, Brock fired at Hogman through the rear window. Hogman calmly called dispatch to give his position and request backup. To protect himself, he used the dashboard of his car for cover but stayed in pursuit. He might have been out of sight, but he was certainly not out of harm's way.

Even though he was almost lying down on the front seat, the sergeant somehow managed to keep an eye on the road and stay behind the black Mustang. He listened to the bullets blast through his windshield and rip through the driver's seat where he had been sitting just moments before. One bullet punctured the radiator, sending steam everywhere. Another bullet struck his radar unit. But the determined policeman kept driving.

Twice the driver of the Mustang put enough distance between the Mustang and the unmarked police car to park their vehicle in the street at an angle in failed attempts to ambush Hogman. But Hogman continued his pursuit.

Even though he was under siege, the sergeant didn't want to return fire during the chase because of his concern about stray bullets in the neighborhood. He'd pursued the men past houses, passing cars, an active construction site with workmen, a church, and a school. He knew that if these guys were bold enough to try to kill a police officer, they would certainly kill anyone who was unfortunate enough to get in their way.

For the first time in his career, Hogman was in a gun battle with no protective vest, no immediate backup, and a shot-up, nearly worthless vehicle for cover. It would later be estimated that sixty rounds of ammunition had been fired at him. Yet somehow he remained remarkably calm, radioing his speed and location regularly so that other units would know where to go. Later he would say that his faith and his training took over. Perhaps he should also have remembered the two promises he made to Vicki when he first became a police officer: that he would always wear his bulletproof vest and place his own safety before anything else. Perhaps he should have paid attention to Vicki's intuition and stayed home that day. But all he could think about was how to stop these crazed gunmen and protect his community.

As the chase continued through the neighborhood at speeds approaching seventy miles per hour, it crossed paths with Vancouver Police Officers Lawrence Zapata, thirty-three, and Adam Millard, thirty. Both transfers to the area, Zapata had been on the Vancouver force for over two years, while Millard was only on his third shift when the Mustang sped by. Still fleeing the persistent Hogman in his shot-up vehicle, the robbers then opened fire upon the Vancouver Police Department squad car, which turned around to join the pursuit. Ahern tossed a grenade at the cars, but it misfired. Attempting another ambush setup, the Mustang crashed into a tree. Police on the scene would later find an undisclosed amount of cash in the car along with several weapons, a couple of pipe bombs, hollow-point .22-caliber bullets, a grenade pin, spent shotgun shells, and empty beer cans.

When all three men abandoned the car, running down a ravine through a wooded area, the confrontation took a deadly turn. Millard, Zapata, and Hogman arrived on the scene. "Probably as a result of their actions, I'm alive today," Hogman told me. "It was three against three, as opposed to one against three."

Leaving his disabled car, Hogman ran behind a guardrail, which he used for cover. Ahern and Brock continued to fire at the three police officers. Only now did Hogman pull his 9-mm pistol to return their fire. Millard and Zapata also returned fire. Brock and Ahern were fatally wounded at the scene, but Bianchi, the getaway driver, managed to climb out of the ravine and escape.

Despite all his efforts, Hogman still regrets that such a dangerous man escaped into a residential neighborhood. "The fact that I let one of the bad guys that had shown a propensity for violence get out of our containment, and he was running up into a neighborhood, that still bothers me— the fact that I felt I let somebody down."

Hogman got back into his bullet-riddled car and tried to locate Bianchi, but he lost his trail. The Clark County Sheriff's Office and Vancouver Police Department arrived to contain the area and start their manhunt. Aided by helicopter support, approximately fifty officers, including FBI, ATF, Washington State Troopers, K-9 officers, and SWAT teams, joined the search, but Bianchi's trail went cold.

As police officers from around the area converged on the scene, Craig phoned his wife. "Craig called me and said, 'I've been involved in a pursuit, everything's fine, but don't go downstairs and watch television,' which, of course, I immediately did. Right when I turned it on I saw Craig by the police car, and the very first thing I noticed was that he had his vest on *over* his shirt . . . not realizing at the time that he didn't even have his vest on at the time of the shooting." But Craig had been inspecting trucks in a special assignment that morning. Crawling under trucks in a vest is very difficult, so he'd taken his vest off. Miraculously, none of the seven bullets that hit his car harmed Craig, even though three came inside the vehicle.

A couple of hours later, Vancouver Police Officer Ron Rose responded to a tip from someone in a nearby high school who'd seen a suspicious white male running through the school's ball fields. Rose spotted the man on Stapleton Road. When he ran the man's name for warrants, he found an outstanding warrant for a parole violation in Washington, so he arrested the man and booked him into the Clark County Jail. The parole violator turned out to be none other than Ronald Bianchi, who'd given the arresting officer his real name.

"When the prosecutor sat down with myself and the two other officers involved, he asked us what we wanted to do. We pretty much told him that the courts should decide what's fair. Let the jury make that decision. Whatever they decide, we'll accept," Craig told me.

Rachel Barnes was arrested on suspicion of conspiracy to commit robbery. She was later charged with first-degree burglary, as an accomplice to first-degree robbery, and with rendering criminal assistance. Bianchi ended up pleading guilty to thirteen counts in exchange for Barnes's release so that she could care for their new baby, who was born after the robbery. Barnes was granted total and complete immunity from prosecution.

On May 21, 1998, Arthur D. Curtis, the county's prosecuting attorney, and Jeannie M. Bryant, deputy prosecuting attorney, accepted a guilty plea from Bianchi for three counts of robbery in the first degree, two counts of assault in the second degree, three counts of attempted murder in the first degree, three counts of possession of stolen property in the first degree for the three cars he stole, attempting to elude police, and malicious explosion in the second degree for the pipe bomb explosion.

As it turned out, the Wells Fargo Bank robbery was unrelated.

Bianchi was twenty-six when he was sentenced to seventy-two years. He'll probably serve sixty years, which would make him eighty-six when he gets out of prison. He and Barnes were married in the Clark County Jail before he was sentenced, but Barnes filed for divorce only weeks after he was moved from the county jail to state prison.

The coroner has not discussed which officers' bullets caused the deaths of Ahern and Brock. "We don't know to this day," Sergeant Hogman admitted as tears welled in his eyes.

Sergeant Craig Hogman was selected by the National Association of Police Organizations as an Honorable Mention Winner of a TOP COPS Award. He received a Washington State Law Enforcement Medal of Honor, a Certificate of Appreciation from the FBI for Exceptional Service in the Public Interest, a Vancouver Police Department Medal of Valor, a Clark County Sheriff's Medal of Valor Award, and a Sons of the American Revolution Law Enforcement Medal. Most important, he won the love and respect of an entire community. Officers Millard and Zapata also received recognition for their actions, including Medal of Valor Awards from the State of Washington and the Vancouver Police Department. I had the honor of presenting an American Red Cross Real Heroes Award to Sergeant Hogman and Officers Millard and Zapata.

Craig Hogman didn't ask for a new car but waited for his white Ford Crown Victoria to be restored. "I wouldn't have a new car—this one and I have been through a lot together. We work well together, and I plan to keep it," he said.

Vicki Hogman confided that something really good had resulted from the events of October 17, 1997. "Do you know what it made us realize? How many wonderful people there are in this community. There are people to this very day that, after all this time, will come up to Craig and say, 'Thank you for what you did three and a half years ago.' Had that not happened, we would never have been blessed enough to know that or to feel that in our community. We truly feel that the good people in the community are behind you, and they do see the good things that you do, and they do appreciate it."

What does the future hold for Craig Hogman? In a low voice he modestly tells me, "I like it on the street. . . . In my heart I feel good knowing that I'm doing a good job. It's a commitment that I made to public safety. It's what I do well at. And if I can help somebody, then I'll continue to do what I do until I'm ready to walk away from it."

18

DEPUTY RICHARD A. BACH

Waukesha County (Wisconsin) Sheriff's Department

"The Traffic Stop"

More than five thousand police officers have been killed in the line of duty since 1973, according to the National Law Enforcement Memorial Fund. That's an average of one every other day. The horrific number includes state, local, and federal law enforcement.

Police officers know the dangers of law enforcement. Two types of so-called routine calls are often the most troublesome and problematic: the domestic call, because emotional family members may become irrational and violent; and traffic stops, because the motorist or other occupants of a stopped car can be gang members, dope dealers, murderers, escaped convicts, or under the influence of drugs.

Deputy Richard A. Bach knows firsthand the dangers of traffic stops. On one such stop, he was taken hostage at gunpoint when an escaped convict didn't want to go back to prison. Fortunately for Bach, his partner was able to get a clear shot, which saved Bach's life. The escapee died on the scene. Deputy Bach went back to work and continued his regular patrol duties. Two years later, while working alone on the same highway, he experienced an even more traumatic event during a traffic stop: he was shot four times at close range.

Although it can get pretty cold in Wisconsin in March, there was no snow on the road in the early morning of March 3, 1988, only remnants of a previous snowfall on the ground. A little after 4:00 A.M. on Interstate 94, the highway that connects Madison with Milwaukee, a car driven by Dr. Glenn Willett passed Deputy Bach's patrol car at high speed. Bach turned on his siren and emergency lights and pulled the speeding car over.

Unfortunately for Dr. Willett, he did not have his driver's license with him. Deputy Bach informed the doctor that out-of-state drivers without a valid license were required to post a bond to guarantee their court appearance. He asked the doctor to follow him back to a convenience store where Willett could cash traveler's checks to post his bond. Then he could continue on his way to Minnesota with his wife and young child.

Bach pulled onto the highway and the doctor followed. As they pulled out, Bach noticed a third car approaching very slowly behind him. At first the act seemed to be a considerate and friendly gesture: it appeared that the driver wanted to stay back to give the two cars pulling onto the highway ample time. But when Bach did a U-turn across the highway median, the third car followed him. It's illegal to make a U-turn across a median unless you are a police officer or driving an emergency vehicle.

Bach became curious at this point, slowing down so he could get a license plate number and call dispatch to see if the car was stolen or, at least, who the owner was. The slower he went, the slower the two cars behind him went. Finally he pulled over to the shoulder, as did the doctor. The third car passed the two cars on the shoulder, then pulled in front of Bach's patrol car. According to courtroom testimony and police reports, this is what happened next.

The driver, who was alone, exited his vehicle and began walking toward Bach's squad car. Bach exited his vehicle and told the driver three times to stop approaching. The driver, who had his hands in his pockets and appeared agitated, finally complied. Bach patted the driver down and asked for his driver's license. The driver, who said his name was Alfredo H. Camacho, responded to the request for a driver's license by saying, "Me no got."

During Bach's cross-examination at trial, he could not remember whether he had patted Camacho down, but Dr. Willett testified that he had. Contrary to Camacho's story, Dr. Willett also testified that Bach did not use any type of force or threats.

Bach instructed Camacho to return to his vehicle and sit down. Bach then approached Camacho's vehicle to inquire about the spelling of Camacho's name and his date of birth. Upon receiving this information, Bach returned to his squad car and called to verify whether Camacho possessed a valid driver's license. He learned that Camacho did not have a driver's license.

Bach then called for a city squad to assist and take Dr. Willett to post bond. When Officer Charles Moranchek showed up shortly afterward, Dr. Willett left the scene as instructed, following Officer Moranchek. The doctor must have thought this night would never end.

Without drawing his gun, Bach approached Camacho's vehicle on the driver's side. Camacho told Bach that he was looking for his cousin, Trooper Santiago Camacho, so he could give him a gift of tacos.

Trooper Santiago Camacho, who is not related to Alfredo Camacho, would later testify that he had pulled Alfredo Camacho over on February 28, a Sunday, and issued a ticket for speeding and driving without a license. At that time, the defendant commented on Trooper Camacho's gun, saying that he also had a gun. Alfredo Camacho told detectives after he was arrested that he had bought the gun on Monday. He would later testify that he bought the gun because he was angry with Trooper Camacho for giving him a citation; he thought it was unfair for a Hispanic to give another Hispanic a citation. From his own testimony, it appeared that Alfredo Camacho had purchased a gun with the intent to exact retribution for receiving a traffic ticket.

As Deputy Bach leaned toward the open window to speak once again with Camacho, Camacho suddenly spun, grabbed an automatic weapon from under the front seat, and, while smiling, shot Bach four times at close range. One bullet hit Bach's walkie-talkie, two struck his upper chest, and one hit him in the abdomen. Two additional bullets missed their target altogether.

Bach made it back to his squad car and, with his car for cover, shot six rounds through Camacho's back window. The pattern his bullets made was a perfect circle. Several hit the backseat on the driver's side, but the steel framework kept them from hitting Camacho. Bach called dispatch and told them he was hurt and bleeding badly. Anticipating the need for a transfusion, he gave his blood type and said he might need a helicopter for transport to the nearest hospital. Just as he completed his call, much to his amazement he heard the assailant's car start up and saw him drive away from the scene.

Bach was badly wounded but determined not to let Camacho get away, so he followed Camacho at high speed for about a mile. Camacho finally stopped when he saw a second squad car also giving chase.

Shortly afterward, Trooper Santiago Camacho arrived at the scene; he had been dispatched to interpret for Alfredo Camacho. A squad car rushed Bach to the emergency room of a local hospital where the slug in his shoulder was removed. He had lost a great deal of blood, and one of the chest shots had penetrated a lung. Surgeons removed part of his left lung and the bullet in his abdomen in a six-hour surgery. The slug that caused the lung damage was removed from his upper back in a second surgery the next day.

Bach was not wearing a bulletproof vest when he was wounded. At that time, wearing a vest was required only when an officer was on a SWAT team assignment or whenever a police action indicated that firepower might be required; otherwise vests were optional. If deputies wanted to wear a vest, they could—if they personally paid for it. But on a police officer's salary, the four- to five-hundred-dollar investment was hard to make. In any case, the three shots that hit Deputy Bach would have been above and below the vest, according to a sheriff's spokesperson.

After several weeks in the hospital, Bach was discharged and, with no long-term disability, returned to his patrol duties. Promoted to detective a few months later, he has continued to serve and protect the citizens of Waukesha County, Wisconsin.

As a detective, Bach still stops a lot of cars. And he still makes the stops by the book. The biggest change since he was shot, he said, is that "time after time after time, whenever I approach a car, I think, 'Will it happen again?' That's always there. You just don't know."

For his actions that day, Deputy Bach was awarded the American Police Hall of Fame Silver Star for Bravery and their Legion of Valor Award. He also received the Military Order of the Purple Heart National Law Enforcement Citation, the Valor Award from the Wisconsin Professional Police Association, and awards from other state and local organizations. For his community involvement, Bach was recently honored with the Wisconsin Vietnam Veteran Outstanding Achievement Award for his eight-year service as a town board member and his activities on behalf of charitable organizations such as the Make-A-Wish Foundation.

Alfredo Camacho, an illegal alien from Mexico, was found guilty of attempted first-degree murder while armed with a dangerous weapon. He received a twenty-year sentence for attempted murder and a five-year sentence for using a gun. Upon his release from the Wisconsin state prison system, he will be handed over to the Immigration and Naturalization Service for deportation.

As incredible as it may sound, Camacho appealed his conviction on the basis that he shot Deputy Bach in self-defense. Although a state court of appeals ordered a new trial, the Wisconsin Supreme Court upheld his conviction.

Deputy Bach did nothing to warrant being shot except wear the uniform of a police officer. For that, he almost died. This incident perfectly illustrates the dangers our police officers face every day simply by choosing law enforcement as a career. The next time you're stopped for a traffic violation, you may wonder why the officer approaches your car cautiously, asks you to remain inside, and usually stands behind or in front of your door. It's part of their training. They don't know who you are or if you are armed. As Bach's shooting illustrates, when a motorist opens fire on an officer without warning from two feet away, the officer has little chance to protect himself. As Paul E. Bucher, District Attorney for Waukesha County, stated in a letter to me, "The only way Deputy Bach survived was his will to live."

How many lives did Deputy Richard Bach save that fateful morning in which he almost lost his own? If Alfredo Camacho was willing to shoot down a police officer in cold blood over a traffic citation, who would be safe?

I asked Detective Bach's commander to try to pinpoint for me the moment Bach became a hero. Was it when he put on his uniform the day of the hostage situation? Was it when he kept his cool during the hostage situation and tried to talk the escapee out of harming anyone else even while the man pointed a gun at his head? Was it when he returned fire after taking four bullets in an ambush? Or was it when he chased the shooter after being shot multiple times?

The commander's one-word response spoke volumes: "Yes."

19

OFFICERS JAMES ANGLEMIER AND LARRY ROBERTS

Salem (Oregon) Police Department

"Resisting Arrest"

Officer James Anglemier   Officer Larry Roberts

When Salem (Oregon) Police Department Officers Larry Roberts and James Anglemier of the SWAT team were called into action one February evening, neither could have imagined that a simple floodlight would put their lives at risk.

The concept of SWAT teams grew out of several sniping incidents against civilians and police officers around the country in the late 1960s. A few years later, the Los Angeles Police Department (LAPD) created these heavily armed teams for quick response to action by subversive groups and other criminals. The teams were and continue to be very successful in quelling crime.

A good example is the now infamous Bank of America armed robbery in North Hollywood, California, where two men covered head to foot with pieced-together Kevlar armor and armed with high-power automatic weaponry robbed the bank and dared law enforcement to stop them. The robbers thought they were untouchable and invincible. In spite of hundreds of rounds fired on both sides, only two deaths occurred: both the armed robbers. In spite of many injuries, not one police officer or civilian was killed. SWAT teams everywhere earned well-deserved recognition thanks to the LAPD's quick, decisive, and brave actions.

According to a study by Peter Kraska, professor of police studies at Eastern Kentucky University, the number of paramilitary police call-outs increased tenfold between 1980 and 1995. The tactical buildup has been fueled by fattened drug-war budgets and gifts of equipment to local police departments from the Department of Defense, according to journalist and author Christian Parenti. There is also increased recognition that lives can be saved by using these highly specialized teams to deal with extreme policing actions.

It's not fair or smart to use police academy-trained officers to deal with heavily armed and military-trained terrorists, or drug lords who give standing orders to their henchmen to shoot anyone who approaches their warehouses, growing fields, or manufacturing facilities. On occasion, a SWAT team may be called in against a heavily armed gunman holding hostages. The SWAT team usually has negotiators who will first attempt to talk the gunman into surrendering. If all else fails, a sharpshooter or a power takeover may be the strategy used, depending upon the circumstances.

SWAT teams are also used to serve high-risk warrants. Today, as much as 85 percent of SWAT call-outs are for serving no-knock warrants, according to Kraska.

Officers James Anglemier and Larry Roberts were part of an eight-man SWAT team assigned to serve a no-knock warrant on a suspect believed to be heavily armed and trafficking in large quantities of drugs. When the team assembled at 6:50 P.M. on February 10, 1986, each man was outfitted in a black military-style camouflage uniform. Both the uniforms and the black baseball-style caps they wore were emblazoned with the Salem Police Department emblem. Each man wore two Kevlar armor vests. The heavier, outer tactical vest carried handcuffs, a field first-aid kit, doorstops and jambs, flash-bang devices, a length of rope—anything that might be needed. The lighter vest had less stopping power and was worn underneath the uniform.

Sergeant Bill Kohlmeyer briefed the team on the suspect, Kelly Ray Kaighin, age twenty-six. Kaighin lived in a trailer in a rural area of southeast Salem. The team was shown a photograph of Kaighin and studied a diagram of the trailer, which was accessible for drive-up entry only by a driveway that crossed a narrow bridge between two ponds. The team would have to access the site on foot because Kaighin was known to block the driveway when he did any type of drug dealing.

From intelligence reports and three consecutive days of site reconnaissance, police believed that Kaighin was heavily armed, heavily into drug trafficking, and extremely paranoid. The intelligence unit reported that Kaighin had made statements that he would shoot it out with anybody who tried to get into his house during any drug transactions, even with the police; that he always came to the door with a .44 magnum revolver, which was always cocked and loaded somewhere near the front door; and that he had a shotgun and numerous other weapons throughout the house. Police had reports that he had been observed firing automatic weapons in the backyard.

Officer Roberts had been on numerous assignments, and this one followed the usual procedure. He was assigned the "key," an eighty-pound battering ram with which he would hit the front door to gain access. He was to be third into the trailer after Officer Anglemier as "point," and Sergeant Kohlmeyer, the team leader. Once inside, Roberts was to provide security.

After the briefing, the team loaded into the SWAT van. They parked off Highway 22, about half a mile from Kaighin's home on Southeast 71st Avenue. A Marion County Medic Unit was on standby.

The team set out through a field of Christmas trees at about 7:20 P.M., advancing through the trees for about twenty minutes. The rolling hills and soft soil made it slow going for men carrying heavy loads. From a hill they observed a vehicle leaving the residence and saw that the three vehicles previously observed there were parked near the barn. The team moved to the edge of Kaighin's backyard. They checked their weapons, making sure their holsters and magazines were intact. A light came on inside the trailer in a room with red curtains. No exterior lights were on.

Officers Leon Colas and Rick Hubbard went to their positions at the rear while the other six men moved along the front of the trailer, staying low as they passed under the window. They didn't see anyone and did not know how many were inside. Officer Anglemier went onto the deck, followed by Kohlmeyer and Roberts. Roberts later said, "I didn't check the guys behind me; I know they were there."

What happened next occurred in a matter of three seconds. Anglemier tried the outer door and whispered, "It's glass and it's locked." He heard someone approaching the door. Then a floodlight came on over the porch, illuminating the men there. Anglemier jerked the screen door open, and Roberts hit the inside door, yelling, "Police." All the officers were yelling repeatedly, "Police," "Police officers," and "Police with a warrant." They knew they were exposed—they'd lost the element of surprise. They wanted Kaighin to know exactly who they were.

Officer Roberts heard a shot and saw a muzzle flash fired from inside on the right. "I knew I was hit," he said. "I dropped the key, drew my weapon, and fired at the flash. I tried to fire two more times, but my gun went *click, click,* and couldn't fire." He'd never had trouble with his weapon before.

Roberts went flying backward. "It was like my feet came out from underneath me," he said. "I was still on the porch. I was on my rear end, maybe my back, I don't recall. I used another magazine to reload and covered the windows to make sure no hostile fire came from that direction."

Officer Anglemier had grabbed Roberts with his right hand and pulled him out of the line of fire. Kaighin fired at Anglemier as he was leaning against the screen door to keep it open; Anglemier then fired once with his left hand in the direction of the muzzle flashes, using his .45-caliber submachine gun set on semiautomatic mode. Kaighin again fired at Anglemier, who fired once more. Anglemier heard someone fall to the floor. There were no more shots. He did not hear or see anyone inside the trailer except Kaighin.

At the same time Officer Anglemier fired, Officer Robert Hartley was shooting at the front door with his .45-caliber service pistol. Officer John Hoffmeister knocked out the porch light as the gunfire ended. No more shots were fired.

Still outside the trailer, Anglemier used his flashlight and saw Kaighin lying on the floor with a weapon beside him. Anglemier continued to announce that they were the police, that they had a warrant. When told to come out, Kaighin crawled out on his hands and knees. There the police handcuffed him, and Hartley gave him first aid for the wound in his left upper thigh. The ambulance arrived in about a minute.

Shot in the lower right arm, Roberts had received first aid from Corporal Dan Cary. He was taken to the hospital, where he was treated and released.

When Anglemier swung the door all the way open, he saw a woman, later identified as Kaighin's wife, sitting on a couch facing the door. She was holding an infant, and a young girl sat beside her. She followed instructions and didn't seem upset. The children were quiet.

Only three officers had fired their weapons.

The subsequent search of the residence turned up forty pounds of marijuana, three-quarters of a pound of cocaine, twelve hundred Valium capsules, twenty-eight firearms of various kinds, and thirteen thousand dollars in cash.

Two years later, Officer Anglemier testified at Kaighin's sentencing hearing:

> I've thought a lot about this; how we put the plan together, and I don't think I would change anything on the execution of how we did the search warrant. There's no doubt in my mind that after Mr. Kaighin fired the first round there was a slight break in the gunfire when I was moving Officer Roberts behind me. And I was standing directly in the doorway totally exposed to Mr. Kaighin under a 300-watt or more flood lamp and he continued to fire. There's no doubt in my mind what his intention was to do was to kill me. . . .
>
> He continued to fire, and that's why he was shot, in order to stop that. I firmly believe had this warrant execution been done by normal street patrol officers, more officers either would have been wounded or even killed. Mr. Kaighin definitely did not want to go to jail, did not want to have that search warrant executed, and he made the decision to have a gunfight.

In 1988 Kelly Ray Kaighin was sentenced by the state of Oregon to ten years for assault in the second degree and five years for attempted assault in the second degree. Judge Richard Barber stated that Kaighin was "definitely a danger to the community" and that he "need[ed] to be separated from it for a lengthy period of time." The fifteen-year sentence was to run concurrently with the fifteen-year sentence Kaighin was already serving in federal prison on drug charges.

After the incident Officer Larry Roberts was awarded the Medal of Valor by the Oregon Peace Officers Association and received a Merit Award from the Salem Police Department, which also recently awarded him a Purple Heart retroactive to the incident (since the department didn't award Purple Hearts until 2001). Roberts, now a detective working in narcotics, served on the SWAT team for nearly nine years.

Officer Anglemier was awarded a Medal of Honor by the Oregon

Peace Officers Association and another by the Salem Police Department. He moved up to SWAT team leader and served for thirteen years. In 1992 he was recognized by the Salem Fire Department for his courage and self-lessness in rescuing a young woman from a burning apartment; for his actions, he received a Medal of Valor from the Salem Police Department "For Distinguished Service in the Face of Extreme Threat to Personal Safety." In 1993 the Salem Police Department presented him with a Life-saving Award for his actions in preventing a woman from jumping into the Willamette River in an attempt to take her own life. Now a sergeant, Anglemier works drugs and vice in the street crimes unit.

"The whole thing about SWAT is to make it as peaceful as possible," Anglemier said. He reviewed his missions before he left the SWAT team, and in the eighteen where deadly force would have been authorized, no guns were fired at all. "When you have experience," he said, "you develop a sixth sense about how to plan. You learn how to put yourself in the mind-set of the criminal," as in the Kaighin incident.

To Anglemier, the three-second event on 71st Avenue seems as if it happened yesterday. "It makes you realize you have to pay attention to details," he said. "You want to train harder than you think you need to per-form in the field so that you react and don't freeze up and have to think about what you're doing."

"SWAT tactics change with the times," Officer Roberts added.

There have been significant improvements in the SWAT team since the Kaighin incident, Anglemier informed me. The body armor has improved immensely; a ballistic Kevlar helmet protects the head, and a hood of fire-resistant Nomex protects officers from flash fire and gives them "psycho-logical protection." When a criminal sees a figure all in black except for the eyes, he freezes for a few seconds. The officer gains three to five sec-onds of advantage, enough to gain control of the situation. Plus, more non-lethal options are available, such as beanbag ammunition.

The presence of the SWAT team has a trickle-down effect that is benefi-cial to the department; training regular police officers in tactics helps them handle situations better. In Salem, the SWAT unit has gained increased support from the department *and* the community. Salem has more inci-dents resolved peacefully and far fewer where gunfire is necessary.

But perhaps the most telling recognition comes from the prison popu-lation. Guards from the five prisons in the Salem area tell Anglemier that they hear prisoners say, "Regular officers are okay, but don't be messing with the SWAT team."

20

OFFICER JOHN JOSEPH WILBUR

Pittsburgh (Pennsylvania) Police Bureau

"The Ring"

At about 1:15 A.M. on Wednesday morning, June 26, 1996, Officer John Joseph Wilbur, three years on the force, was about two hours into his shift. He was on patrol by himself in Shadyside, a neighborhood in the East End of Pittsburgh, when a woman in a car flagged him down and told him that a suspicious car was sitting at the traffic light at Fifth and Shady Avenues—suspicious because the light had turned green twice and the car hadn't moved. She had driven around the car, which was a gold Honda Accord, and saw two men slumped over in the front seat. Following procedure, Wilbur called for backup, then reported, "This looks very suspicious. I think I may have two car thieves here."

Seven minutes passed before any other communication about the car came in.

After Officer Scott Green arrived to back him up, Wilbur approached the driver's side of the car. The driver and front seat passenger, who both wore industrial-type gloves despite the warmth of the summer night, were still slumped over. What appeared to be a screwdriver lay on the front seat. Wilbur tapped on the driver's window, waking him up.

At that moment, Wilbur noticed movement in the backseat and opened the rear door, where he found a young man also wearing gloves. The driver, who was later identified as twenty-two-year-old James Mitchell, Jr., began moving his hand, so Officer Green pulled his weapon, ordering Mitchell and the young male passenger in the front seat to put their hands on the dashboard, which they did.

Wilbur saw the young man in the backseat put something he suspected to be drugs into his mouth and ordered him to "spit it out." Wilbur reached into the backseat, but during the ensuing confrontation, the driver pulled away, and the car door suddenly closed on Wilbur's left hand. His wedding ring was firmly lodged in the door mechanism, trapping him. Mitchell, the driver of the car, stepped on the gas, narrowly missing Officer Green, and began accelerating down Fifth Street. Still caught by his wedding ring, Wilbur was unable to pull free of the car door.

"Emergency! Emergency!" Green radioed. For seconds Wilbur ran alongside the accelerating car, then managed somehow to crawl onto the trunk. A witness would later report seeing the car weaving back and forth in an S-pattern, apparently trying to free itself of the unwanted cargo. After some fifteen seconds, Green reported, "My partner's on the roof. The car took off on us. He was [unintelligible] on the roof. Shots fired. Shots fired."

Detective Tom Foley had come onto the scene just as the vehicle took off with Wilbur. Foley, who became the lead car in the wild chase that followed, called in on the radio: "They're dragging an officer. Fifth Avenue toward Hamilton. They're flying."

Wilbur was only able to stay on the trunk for about eight seconds before falling off. As the car accelerated to speeds up to seventy miles per hour, he bounced on his buttocks along the road, his hand still caught in the door. Using his feet, he tried to arch his buttocks off the ground. As his equipment and clothing were being torn off, he remembers thinking, "This really hurts." Uppermost in his thoughts were his wife, family, and friends.

The 9-1-1 tapes would show that other officers reported seeing Wilbur dragged down the street. Pursuing officers watched helplessly—Wilbur was in the line of fire.

Knowing that he was going to die if he didn't do something, Wilbur found the strength to reach with his right hand and remove his twenty-shot, 9-mm semiautomatic weapon from its holster. "I think my will to live forced me to use my weapon," Wilbur told me. He arched on his side and began firing into the vehicle, but the car continued to move down the street at a high speed. *Preservation* is the word he used when he described his response to me, saying that he knew when he hit the ground he had to do something. "Shooting was the only alternative I could come up with."

"I was afraid at Fifth and Penn I was going to get T-balled by another car at the intersection, just slamming into me and killing me," Wilbur later testified. He was losing strength but got off another shot. He heard the bullet ricochet off a trestle just before his ring pulled free of his hand and he finally rolled free of the car. His wedding band remained in the car.

"Eventually, my wedding band cut through my finger from the stress of holding me between the door and the frame. It peeled the skin back on my finger like a banana till my finger was small enough that it slipped through the ring. When I came free of the car, I thought my finger was gone. I didn't have enough nerve to look," he recalled.

Officer Wilbur had been dragged almost a mile. As he lay in the street before the police and paramedics arrived, he heard a woman screaming, "There's a dead cop in the street! There's a dead cop in the street!" Wilbur was rushed to Presbyterian University Hospital for emergency surgery. The EMS crew had to tell him several times that his finger was still there; he kept saying, "It's gone."

Meanwhile, officers chased but lost the speeding vehicle; twenty minutes after the car sped away leaving Wilbur lying in the street, police discovered the abandoned gold Honda, which indeed was a stolen vehicle. They found twenty-year-old Maurice Hall, the front-seat passenger, and backseat passenger Craig Guest, nineteen, still inside the car, dead from multiple gunshot wounds. Also inside the car: a .45-caliber semiautomatic handgun with a laser sight. An autopsy would reveal crack cocaine under Guest's tongue. Guest and Hall had extensive arrest records dating from the ages of fourteen and fifteen, respectively.

An intense manhunt began for the driver, who had fled the scene. No one had positively identified him, but one detective knew that Guest and Hall hung out with suspected gang member James Mitchell, Jr., and that Hall and Mitchell had twice been arrested together in 1995. Blood on the driver's seat and door along with a bullet hole in the driver's headrest indicated that he had been wounded.

Then, the morning after the incident, a police informant phoned the detectives to report a robbery; a family member had identified one of the robbers as "Lett." The police knew that "Lett" was one of the nicknames used by Mitchell. Another way the police could identify the robber: he had a bullet sticking out of his head. Within twenty-four hours of the incident, detectives had a warrant for Mitchell. When they went to Mitchell's house, they found a bloody towel on top of a garbage can outside the door. Inside, they found a bloodstained pillowcase. The blood on those items matched the blood found in the car. But they didn't find Mitchell.

On July 3, a little over a week after the incident, Mayor Tom Murphy called a peace rally in support of the police and Wilbur, who is white, after hearing complaints that the shooting deaths of Guest and Hall, both African-American, were racially motivated. According to Paul Muschick's article in the *Pittsburgh Tribune-Review* of July 4, 1996, Murphy said he was "overwhelmed with anger . . . when it was reported that some were speculating Officer Wilbur's actions may have been racially motivated" when "the facts pointed to an officer who was doing his job and ended up fighting for his life." John's wife, Terry, tearfully told the gathering of more than two thousand people that the entire city, not just her husband, needed time to heal.

Thirteen days after the incident, after acting on tips and searching Mitchell's known hangouts, detectives arrested him at a friend's apartment and charged him with attempted homicide, aggravated assault, criminal conspiracy, auto theft, receiving stolen property, and a firearms violation. He was unable to make bond because of two outstanding warrants: one on gun charges and another for fleeing. Before being sent to jail, Mitchell's head wound was treated at a hospital. Wilbur's bullet had cracked his skull when it entered the back of his head and emerged from the top. Remarkably, no brain damage had occurred.

Mitchell's arrest on July 9, 1996, came on the same day that Officer Wilbur was released from Presbyterian University Hospital. Wilbur had a concussion, a severely mangled hand, and a broken leg. The other leg was almost burned to the bone from being scraped on the road; numerous skin grafts were needed to replace the scraped-off skin. A toe and part of a foot were amputated; his right ankle, which was totally shattered, had to be reconstructed. Doctors weren't even sure that he'd be able to walk again. He still faced three months of bedrest before he could begin physical therapy.

When I spoke to Wilbur, he told me that he had become depressed after the incident and was diagnosed with post-traumatic stress disorder (PTSD). Brought on by severely disturbing, violent events, PTSD is a condition in which painful memories can strike at any time. The experience can be like reliving the original event. Thankfully, Wilbur no longer suffers from the disorder.

Coroner Cyril H. Wecht scheduled an open inquest, which is typically done when police are involved in fatal shootings, for August 20, 1996. Ten witnesses and Officer Wilbur, who was in a wheelchair, testified during the two-day inquest. The five eyewitnesses—three motorists and two police officers—corroborated the account of the events given by Wilbur.

As if Wilbur and his wife had not gone through enough already, four of the six jurors on the coroner's jury decided that charges should be brought against Officer Wilbur. However, the jury verdict was only a recommendation to Allegheny County District Attorney Bob Colville, who declared, "The law is clear. Anybody being dragged at seventy-one miles per hour down the street for almost a mile has and should have the right to protect himself against those people." He concluded that the two men had lost their lives because of their actions and the actions of the driver, which almost resulted in a policeman's death. The coroner also disagreed with the jury's verdict.

In August 1997 Allegheny County Judge David Cercone sentenced James Mitchell, Jr. to eight to sixteen years in prison. He told Mitchell that the nature of the offense and his history of violence against the police made him "a danger to society" who deserved a severe sentence. Mitchell's record showed that he had previously run over an officer's foot while trying to elude police. Mitchell apologized to the families of Hall, Guest, and Officer Wilbur before he was taken back to his cell to await another trial. On July 10, 1998, twenty-four-year-old James Mitchell, Jr. was given a mandatory life sentence without parole for the murder of Tyrell Hinton, twenty, in a drive-by shooting in April 1996. Judge David Cashman decided that Mitchell must complete the prior sentence of eight to sixteen years before serving the life sentence.

Seven and a half months after the incident, Wilbur returned to duty as a detective at the Zone 6 police station in Squirrel Hill. During a September 1997 ceremony in which Mayor Murphy presented Detective John Wilbur with a Purple Heart, Murphy said, "This is an opportunity for us to recognize officers who have performed beyond the call of duty, officers who in some cases have put their lives at risk to protect the citizens of Pittsburgh."

In October 1997 Detective Wilbur was awarded a TOP COPS Award by the National Association of Police Organizations, which annually recognizes the top officers involved in acts of heroism. Earlier in the day, Wilbur had visited the White House along with the seventeen other TOP COPS from across the United States and met with President Clinton.

Commander Edward Kelly, Wilbur's boss, had nominated him for the national award. Kelly wrote in part, "Officer Wilbur demonstrated great courage and professionalism when thrust into this crisis situation. He didn't submit to the intended outcome, but fought with all he had to stop the vehicle and stay alive."

On March 13, 2001, U.S. District Court Judge Donald J. Lee, stating that Officer Wilbur's conduct was clearly objectively reasonable, dismissed a federal lawsuit against Wilbur and the city of Pittsburgh brought by the parents of Craig Guest.

With all that he's been through, John J. Wilbur is glad to be alive. "I'm really happy to still be here," he says. Married with two children, he currently works with the FBI on cybercrime. Completely recovered, he admits, "I feel pretty good." And what about his wedding ring? It's still being held as evidence.

"At some point, I do hope to get it back," Wilbur said. Then he confided that his wife had made him replace it. "She told me, 'You're not walking around with no wedding ring on.'"

On August 2, 2001, Wilbur was one of the police officers who were credited with making Pittsburgh a safer city. At the city's first public presentation of the Pittsburgh Police Bureau Officer of the Year awards, John Wilbur was honored as 1997 Officer of the Year.

21

OFFICER PAUL HOLLAND

Boca Raton (Florida) Police Services Department

"Risky Pursuit"

One of the most controversial issues in law enforcement today is that of high-speed police chases. According to an article by Corporal Clyde Eisenberg and Corporal Cynthia Fitzpatrick of the Hillsborough County Sheriff's Office in Tampa, Florida, in the *FBI Law Enforcement Bulletin*, "Forty percent of all law enforcement pursuits end in collision, and approximately 290 pursuit-related deaths occur each year." High-speed police pursuits were a subject of debate even as far back as 1922, when New York City patrolman Frank Mondo, a distinguished veteran officer, was killed while chasing a speeding vehicle.

Pursuit is the riskiest of all police operations, according to Deborah Amos on ABCNEWS.com. In her article, she quotes former New York Police Chief Louis Anamone's statement that more officers receive injuries from vehicle accidents than from gunshots. In general, officers have only seconds to decide whether or not to chase a suspect, who could be armed and dangerous or might be merely a panicked traffic violator.

Police departments all over the country are starting to adopt rules about high-speed chases. The Florida Highway Patrol and police departments in New Jersey and Kansas now prohibit hot pursuit except in the case of a dangerous felon. Some law enforcement agencies are using retractable, hollow steel spikes that can be deployed ahead of the suspect's vehicle and remotely activated. The spikes penetrate the tires, releasing air and stopping the car safely. Departments around the country emphasize proper training in skills and procedures regarding pursuits.

Late in the morning of February 1, 2000, Officer Paul Holland of the Boca Raton Police Services Department became involved in a high-speed pursuit that went through four cities and two counties, resulting in a shoot-out with the suspect. But this story actually began on November 12, 1999, when Boca Raton Police Officer Sam Tatum was checking on a suspicious young man in a white Toyota parked in a Holiday Inn parking lot. While fleeing the scene, the suspect reversed his vehicle, knocked Tatum down, and ran over both his legs.

On November 28, 1999, around 1:30 A.M., Florida Atlantic University (FAU) Police Sergeant Keith Totten noticed a white Toyota with its lights on. It appeared to be occupied. Fifteen minutes later he noticed that the lights were off. When Totten turned on his driver's side alley light and approached, a young male who'd been sleeping under a blanket sat up in the passenger seat, appearing nervous to the officer. When Totten asked him for identification, the man rolled up the passenger side window and jumped into the driver's seat. Totten moved to the front of the vehicle, but the man began to accelerate toward him, so he jumped to one side to avoid being hit, then struck the passenger side of the windshield with his flashlight, shattering the windshield. The driver then fled the scene, almost hitting another campus vehicle driven by Officer Robert Gaumond. Gaumond, followed by Totten and Officer Robert Schroder, pursued the car, but when it got onto southbound Interstate 95, Totten terminated the pursuit and the officers returned to campus to make a report. The driver was not identified by Totten, but the similarity of the incidents along with the description of the vehicle and suspect led police to believe it was the same person who ran over Officer Tatum's legs.

On January 17, 18, and 19, 2000, while Boca Raton Police Officer Gary Winterstein was monitoring an area of Spanish River Boulevard due to a number of auto burglaries, he noticed a white Toyota Corolla. He took note of the car because the man in the car was slumped in the seat for extended periods of time. The passenger side of the front windshield was cracked, and the Toyota's tag was registered to a Pontiac. After Winterstein arrested the suspected auto burglar a couple of days later, he happened to run into Captain Dennis O'Hara of the FAU Police Department in a restaurant. During their conversation, Winterstein told O'Hara about the auto burglaries and the suspicious white Toyota Corolla. O'Hara then told Winterstein about the incident involving Sergeant Totten.

On February 1, 2000, O'Hara drove by a white Toyota Corolla on Spanish River Boulevard. Because the plates on the car matched the partial license tag that Totten had recorded at the November incident and the car had a cracked windshield, he called the Boca Raton Police Services Department, which dispatched police officers to the scene. Officer Winterstein, who'd heard the call on his radio, also responded.

When Winterstein approached the suspect at about 10:30 A.M., the driver saw him and took off in his vehicle. The chase, which would last about thirty-five minutes, started on Spanish River Boulevard near North Ocean Boulevard. The white Toyota headed west on Spanish River Boulevard. At the intersection with Federal Highway, the suspect collided with two cars as he forced his way between them while they were stopped at the light. He turned onto Federal Highway, then continued south.

Officer Paul Holland was traveling east on Spanish River Boulevard listening to his police radio when he heard Winterstein attempt to stop the car. When Winterstein passed him going west, Holland made a U-turn, joined the pursuit, and followed the Toyota south on Federal Highway. When Winterstein had to slow down due to a truck in his path, Holland took the lead. The two officers were following the white Toyota as it turned right onto Glades Road.

Sergeant Robert Rutter had been traveling southbound on Dixie Highway near the scene of the chase. After the white Toyota turned south onto Dixie Highway with Holland behind it, Rutter caught up to Holland and the chase continued.

Boca Raton Police Services Department policy states that "only two Boca Raton units should be directed to engage in pursuing the suspect." When Lieutenant James Mackey broadcast that only Holland and Rutter were to continue pursuing the white Toyota Corolla, Winterstein dropped his pursuit shortly after getting onto Dixie Highway. After running a red light on Dixie Highway, the suspect turned east on NE 2nd, then south at Federal Highway, with Holland and Rutter still in pursuit.

The intersection of Federal Highway and Sample Road was congested with traffic. As the suspect approached the busy intersection, he collided with a car, then drove up onto the sidewalk, barely missing a pedestrian. He continued driving down the sidewalk until he reached the intersection, where he turned right onto Sample. Officers Holland and Rutter slowed down to approximately thirty miles per hour as they approached the intersection, then cut through a gas station to make the right turn. One officer, witnessing Holland and Rutter proceed so slowly through the intersection, thought the chase was over.

The Toyota led the two police cars west on Sample to I-95, where the suspect entered the southbound entrance ramp. But instead of merging into the southbound traffic, the suspect took a sharp left turn and drove in the breakdown lane against oncoming traffic, causing another car to spin out of control as it swerved to avoid a head-on collision.

Officer Holland reported that he followed the suspect onto the ramp, pulled over, and stopped to see if the suspect was going to abandon his car. But Holland saw the white Toyota continue driving against the flow of traffic in the breakdown lane. Witnesses would later report that the Toyota appeared to be going at least ninety miles per hour. When Holland broadcast that the suspect was traveling the wrong way on I-95, Captain Daniel Alexander directed the units to stop the pursuit. Holland acknowledged the order and turned off his overhead lights. Rutter didn't see the suspect after he entered I-95.

Unable to turn around safely because of a sharp drop-off, Holland drove slowly north in the breakdown lane until he could exit at SW 10th, the same exit that witnesses said the white Toyota had taken. From radio broadcasts, Holland was able to keep track of the suspect's position.

Caught in traffic on SW 10th, Captain Alexander observed the white Toyota heading west on SW 10th, then north onto Powerline Road. Holland kept proceeding in the direction the suspect was taking. As the suspect approached W. Palmetto Park Road, he turned around and headed south. Then he drove through a shopping plaza before entering W. Palmetto Park Road heading westbound in the eastbound lanes. He turned north onto Palmetto Circle until he picked up Powerline again. As he approached the intersection of Glades Road, traffic was stopped at a signal, and cars were backed up. Again the suspect turned his vehicle around, reversed his direction, and traveled southbound in the northbound lanes of the street.

Sergeant Norman Floyd, who was approaching the suspect, was passing a truck that obstructed his view when his car collided with the white Toyota. The Toyota went over the curb, ending up in the grass, where it appeared to come to a stop.

Officers Paul Holland and Alan Cook pulled up in separate vehicles. Cook parked on the road's edge west of the Toyota, while Holland stopped on the grass south of the suspect's white car. Both officers thought the pursuit was over. Then the Toyota suddenly lurched forward, hitting Cook's vehicle. As Cook struggled to get out of his car, Holland quickly left his vehicle to take a position in front of the Toyota.

Sergeant Floyd had pulled up in the meantime, and he approached the suspect on the passenger side. Holland ordered the suspect to show his hands. Even though both officers had their guns drawn, the suspect leaned over, reaching into the passenger side of his car, and sat up holding a silver 9-mm automatic handgun.

Floyd yelled, "Gun . . . gun . . . gun!"

The suspect pointed his weapon directly at Officer Cook, who was still trapped in his vehicle. Because his fellow officer was in imminent danger, Officer Holland fired at the driver through the Toyota's windshield. The man then aimed his gun at Holland and began shooting at him. The shoot-out continued until the suspect's weapon fell. Although Fire Rescue arrived shortly after the shooting, thirty-one-year-old Deerfield Beach resident Mark Edward Lewis was pronounced dead at the scene.

Officer Winterstein had decided to pursue Lewis because he had reason to believe that he was involved in the incidents against Officer Tatum and FAU Police Sergeant Totten; then Lewis fled the police, which is a felony. The Boca Raton Police Services Department deemed that the decision to pursue Lewis and the pursuit itself were within departmental guidelines. The Palm Beach County Sheriff's Office, the Office of the State Attorney, and the Boca Raton Police Services Department's Internal Affairs Unit reviewed the shooting incident and declared that the use of deadly force was justified given Mark Lewis's actions.

Lewis was no stranger to crime. In 1996 he was charged with carrying a concealed weapon and illegal possession of cocaine, marijuana, and narcotics equipment. He was given two years' probation. Half a year later he was again arrested on the same charges, plus the additional charge of resisting an officer without violence. In 1997 he was charged with burglary with assault or battery after he broke into his estranged wife's house. He also served six months in state prison for violating his parole and was released in February 1999. In the ten years prior to his death, he had a dozen traffic citations as well as a suspended license. After the chase, Officer Tatum publicly identified Lewis as the man who had run over his legs in November.

Interviews with Lewis's friends revealed that he had violent tendencies toward the police. And the white Toyota he was driving was one that a friend had rented from Hertz. Lewis had borrowed the car but never returned it.

In July 2000 when the position of director of the Police Athletic League became vacant, Paul Holland applied for and was selected for the job, having worked with children prior to becoming a police officer. He became a dedicated director and successful fund-raiser, and his exemplary record, extraordinary valor in the chase incident, and work in community policing and juvenile programs earned him the 2000 Boca Raton Police Officer of the Year Award. Chief of Police Andrew Scott III called Holland "the 'total' or 'complete' police officer" whose "dedication to training and discipline as a member of the SWAT team led to his ability to act when necessary to save the life of a fellow officer."

Holland received the Distinguished Law Officer of the Year Award from the *Palm Beach Post* newspaper. For his brave actions, his department presented him with the Medal of Valor Award on July 15, 2001.

22

OFFICER MICHAEL PRESLEY

Shreveport (Louisiana) Police Department

"Making the World a Safe Place"

The idea of police patrolling on bikes is not a new one. Bicycles were commonly used in New York City to control traffic from 1895 to about 1934 when they were replaced by motorcycles and cars. The first modern use of the bicycle for police patrols may have been in San Jose, California, where two officers who cycled to work started a squad in 1979. In New York City, about nine hundred cops were riding bikes on the job by the late 1990s. With over two thousand bicycle units now deployed in the United States, the use of bicycles by police officers has grown in popularity.

One of the best-known places for bicycle cops is Seattle, Washington, where traffic-clogged streets and the construction of an underground bus tunnel turned inner-city streets into a nightmare for police in the 1980s. Their four-man "Adam Squad" started in 1987 was immediately successful—so successful, in fact, that other cities requested their advice about bicycles, training, clothing, and even what sunglasses to use.

It is easy to see why bicycles are so effective in certain situations.

Besides being cost-effective (ten to fifteen officers can be outfitted for the cost of one patrol car), officers on bikes travel faster than officers on foot; they can get through traffic more easily than cars and can get into areas inaccessible to cars; and they have the advantage of stealth, often blending in with the crowd. In addition, officers who ride bikes are more approachable than officers in cars—people tend to talk to them more. Public reaction to officers on bikes has been favorable, while bike officers tend to have better morale and health than officers who patrol in cars.

Shreveport, Louisiana, population 200,000, is one of over two hundred cities in the United States that have bike officers. The Shreveport Police Department has a total of fifteen to twenty bike officers, most of whom patrol the downtown area. The bike patrols operate year-round both day and night on specially designed 21-speed mountain bikes with slick street tires. The bicycles are equipped with numerous reflectors, an emergency flashing light, and saddlebags containing traffic tickets, incident reports, and other forms. Officers wear bright yellow shirts and carry radios on their weapon belts; on days where there is rain, ice, or even the occasional snowstorm, they dress in Gore-Tex suits.

Officers Michael Presley and his partner of three years, Matthew Reardon, patrol District 18, the downtown area, on their bicycles at night. Within a ten-block area next to the Red River, the downtown area has a convention center, two casinos, several museums, and numerous bars and restaurants. Officer Presley told me that this beat is fairly quiet most of the time; there is an occasional stolen car or arrest for disorderly conduct. In the last six years, there have been only three shootings. The most frequently reported crimes are thefts and vehicle break-ins. The officers are on a first-name basis with business owners. Thanks to good police work, there are no prostitutes working the riverfront area, and if there are drug deals being made, they are not being made in the streets or parking lots in District 18. The officers on bike patrol cover a smaller area than those in patrol cars, and because they are actually on the streets, they seem to feel the pulse of what's happening in the area.

That's probably why, on April 14, 2000, around 3:15 A.M., Officers Presley and Reardon were able to respond immediately when they heard shots being fired just half a block away from where they were talking to the owner of Studio 54, a riverfront club.

Both officers jumped on their bikes and pedaled as fast as they could to a crowd standing in front of Lacy's Nightclub. As Presley stopped, dropping his bike across the street from the crowd, he saw a gunman raise his right hand and fire three shots into the crowd. Twenty-six-year-old Rodrigues Rusley had left the club and was walking to his car when he was hit in the side by a bullet. Police described Rusley as an innocent bystander. Those who knew him were shocked at his death by gunshot, commenting that he had spent most of his life fighting sickle cell anemia.

People were running and screaming, but miraculously no one else was injured or killed.

As he drew his gun, Officer Presley ordered the gunman to drop his weapon. According to Presley, the man, later identified as Eric Persley, twenty-four, ran to a 2000 Mercedes, jumped into the left side of the back-seat, and yelled to twenty-one-year-old Calvin James Mitchell, who was at the wheel, to take off; Mitchell hit the accelerator, letting the forward momentum of the Mercedes close Persley's door.

Because he was unable to get a clear shot—people were everywhere— Officer Presley didn't fire his gun, but he got back on his bike, preparing to follow the shooter and his accomplice. According to Presley, the driver, who could have used any one of the street's four lanes, chose the lane he was in. He rolled out of the way as the car attempted to run him over.

Presley quickly got up, drew his weapon, and saw that the car was now heading for his partner, Officer Reardon. It was clear now that, to avoid being hit, the officers were going to have to shoot.

With the department since 1994, Presley told me that his training kicked in as he "accessed the backdrop," determining where his bullet would go if he missed his target. His two greatest concerns: that the bystanders lingering in the area might be hit and that he and Reardon might hit each other in the crossfire. He decided to fire at the low end of the side window.

"We were taught in the police academy to shoot to kill. If we pull our weapon out of the holster, it better be for the purpose of saving our own life or the life of another. When I pulled my weapon on April 14, 2000, I intended to kill the suspect. I also knew that I was protecting my own life and other lives as well as my partner's."

Both officers opened fire.

According to Officer Presley, as the driver allegedly again tried to run him over, Presley and the passenger exchanged shots. Then Officer Reardon hit his target, shooting Mitchell in the nose and shoulder. The car abruptly stopped; the wounded man couldn't park the car or open the door. The officers pulled both men from the car and cuffed them on the ground. Eric Persley was not wounded in the exchange of shots.

Mitchell was taken to Louisiana State University Hospital-Shreveport, but his injuries were not life-threatening. Days later he was booked into Caddo Correctional Center on a charge of attempted first-degree murder. Persley was charged with second-degree homicide.

Detectives found two handguns and spent shell casings in the Mercedes. Suspects Mitchell and Persley had been in Lacy's earlier that morning, according to witnesses. After arguing with someone, they left briefly. Upon their return, they allegedly opened fire outside the club. It is not known if they were aiming at someone in particular or shooting at random. According to Officer Presley, there was speculation that it was a drug deal gone bad, but no one knows for sure.

The grand jury indicted Calvin Mitchell and Eric Persley for second-degree murder. Persley was released four days after Rusley was killed; out on bond awaiting a hearing, he was seriously wounded in a shooting that killed two people in November 2000. Mitchell and Persley await trial as of this writing.

After the shooting and murder attempts on Presley's life, he went back to the police station and called his wife of ten years, Linda. He told her not to worry because he was all right, but he asked her not to let their eight-year-old son see the 6 A.M. news on TV as it might scare him.

That afternoon when Presley picked up his son at school he learned that his son had heard about the incident. He told his son that he was not proud of what had happened and it didn't make him happy. "I told him that I do my job to protect people and make the world a safe place for children to grow up."

Presley told me that it takes about seventy-two hours to wind down from a high-stress situation. That's why most police departments give officers at least three days off after an officer-involved shooting. As Presley told me, however, "A shooting affects an officer's entire life." He said that an officer might begin to worry more about what can happen on the job or question whether he would hesitate the next time . . . and perhaps an innocent bystander might be hit. "You never really know how a police officer will react until it actually happens."

Presley told me, "I hope there won't be a next time, but I'm confident that I will do what I was trained to do. I know I can count on Matthew Reardon and that Matthew can certainly count on me."

Officers Michael Presley and Matthew Reardon were both awarded the Police Medal of Valor for their actions and courage. Sergeant M. C. Jaudon's recommendation states that "Officer M. Reardon placed himself in harm's way between suspects and innocent bystanders. Officer M. Reardon was located in the middle of an intersection with no cover whatsoever available. Officer M. Presley placed himself in front of a moving vehicle to provide cover for Officer Reardon. Officer Presley was also in the middle of an intersection with no available cover. Both Officers acted courageously with no regard for their own personal safety, but for the safety of the hundreds of bystanders in the immediate area, preventing any additional injuries or death."

In addition, they each received a Department Commendation Award, given only when an officer puts his or her personal safety and well-being at stake.

Officer Presley has been in the National Guard for fourteen years. A platoon sergeant, he told me that going to war was a "tremendous possibility" following the terrorist attacks of September 11, 2001. When we spoke last, he was waiting to be called for duty.

23

OFFICER PETER REYNOLDS

Miami (Florida) Police Department

"Exactly the Same Way"

An estimated thirty-six million women in the United States have experienced violence as either a child or an adult, according to an article in the
May/June 2001 edition of *Women's Health Issues* published by the Jacobs
Institute of Women's Health. Sexual abuse is one of the most invisible
forms of violence because the crime is often carried out by a person of
trust, such as a father, brother, grandfather, uncle, or stepfather. If the
crime is even reported, many times the rights of the child are sacrificed to
protect the abuser or the family's name. Family should be equated with
love, safety, and security, and home should be a sanctuary but, for many
women and girls, it's not. All too often the violence turns into a cycle of
abuse that continues throughout the woman's life.

The health consequences of domestic and sexual violence against
women are long-term and pervasive, as UNICEF's May 2000 *Innocenti
Digest* article entitled "Domestic Violence against Women and Girls"
points out. The consequences range from injury, unwanted pregnancy,

and permanent disabilities to psychological outcomes such as depression, fear, sexual dysfunction, and post-traumatic stress disorder. In the worst cases, the outcome is murder or suicide.

One young woman eighteen years old tried to escape the abuse she alleges took place by moving out of the home she shared with her father, forty-four-year-old Lionel Boursiquot. But the young woman moved only a few blocks from her father, and she would learn the hard way that she hadn't gotten him out of her life. She would escape dying for her decision only with the help of Peter Reynolds, a brave Miami police officer.

On Monday, October 30, 2000, the woman had finished working in the day-care center at Miami-Dade Community College's Wolfson Campus. As she left the facility around 8:15 P.M., her father allegedly confronted her. The campus was busy at that time of night, with night students arriving and commuters heading off toward Interstate 95. Witnesses later told police that they heard the father and daughter arguing as they made their way down the street.

Officer Peter Reynolds had just finished studying for a promotional exam at Wolfson. His study session came after his regular shift, so he was still in uniform. He had just started driving home in his marked police car when a citizen flagged him down. She described seeing an African-American female being beaten and dragged down the street by an African-American male.

Officer Reynolds, who was officially off duty, quickly got a description of the man from the witness, then drove north on NE First Avenue. At the intersection of Fifth, he saw a man who matched the description. He stopped his car about two car lengths away from the man and got out.

As Officer Reynolds approached, he called out to get the man's attention. The woman, who was being held by the suspect, looked relieved that a police officer was on the scene. She broke free of the man's grasp and began running toward Officer Reynolds. Behind her, Lionel Boursiquot allegedly raised his gun and began firing, shooting her three times, twice in the back and once in the arm. She fell to the curb.

"I was scared," Officer Reynolds candidly told me during a phone conversation. "I was thinking, 'Oh, God, he's killed her. Oh, God, I am being shot at. Run for cover. Call for backup. Don't freeze up, or that man is going to kill me.' "

But Officer Reynolds's instincts and training as a cop took over. As Boursiquot allegedly was firing at his daughter, Reynolds pulled his gun and, in a low crouch, ran for cover behind a red pickup truck. Boursiquot allegedly began firing at Reynolds as well as his daughter, so Reynolds returned fire. During the exchange of gunfire, a bullet pierced a car door, hitting an innocent female bystander who was being dropped off by her husband to attend an evening class. Investigators later concluded that the suspect had hit the woman, since they were able to account for all of Reynolds's bullets.

As Boursiquot fled the scene, Reynolds's initial reaction was to chase after him but, realizing that two people were injured, he turned to help the victims instead. He positioned himself so that he could shield them from further harm in case the shooter returned. While he was administering CPR and rendering first aid to the shooting victims, he was also keeping watch for the shooter. He requested an ambulance and provided a good description of the assailant to the dispatcher.

Police cordoned off the section of campus where the shootings had occurred, while K-9 units searched for the suspect. Unfortunately, the suspect eluded the manhunt, although local television stations ran his photo on the news that night. Throughout the night and the next morning, police patrolled the city with a photo of the suspect, who was said to be armed and dangerous.

As police searched for Boursiquot, he was in an area of Miami known as Little Haiti. He was reported to have been staggering around, and he finally collapsed in front of a house on North Miami Avenue a little before noon. The fire-rescue crew that responded to a 9-1-1 call called an ambulance after checking out the man's condition. He had apparently swallowed chlorine in an attempt to commit suicide; also, his left foot was bleeding since one of Officer Reynolds's bullets had shot off one of his toes. But the paramedics didn't know that this was the man the Miami Police Department was hunting. En route to the hospital, Boursiquot allegedly told them that he had done something terrible and didn't know how he could live with himself.

One of the bystanders watching the paramedics treat Boursiquot was Mr. Danis Georges, a Citizen on Patrol. The function of Citizens on Patrol is to observe and report suspicious circumstances and criminal violations within their neighborhoods. Georges recognized Boursiquot from seeing his photo on television, so he contacted the Miami police. As a result of Georges's tip, the police caught up to the suspect at the North Shore Medical Center emergency room and arrested him for attempted first-degree murder. He was subsequently transferred to Jackson Memorial Hospital— the same hospital where his daughter was still in critical condition.

The young woman is still undergoing therapy and has not returned to work as of this writing. The bullet that hit a bystander entered the woman's thigh, then exited it. She was treated at the hospital and released the following day.

According to Assistant State Attorney John Lindeman, Lionel Boursiquot, who has no criminal history, made a full confession in Creole after being charged with attempted first-degree murder, armed kidnapping, and sexual battery on a minor. The state is asking for three life sentences. The case is still pending and no trial date has been set as of this writing.

During the investigation after the shooting, police found a suicide tape reportedly recorded by Boursiquot. The man on the tape declares that he is going to shoot his daughter twelve times in the mouth for telling the police that he sexually abused her on several occasions. According to Officer Reynolds, the suspect also said that he was not only going to kill his daughter but also somebody important, maybe a cop. According to a November 1, 2000, article in the *Miami Herald,* the daughter had "told investigators about an incestuous relationship she ended." The same article reported that a police spokesperson stated the daughter had moved out when she became "tired of the abuse," but the police would neither confirm nor deny that the abuse was sexual. The Miami Police Department could not comment officially on this issue since the case hadn't gone to trial.

It was lucky for the young woman that Officer Reynolds was there on October 30. Thanks to his quick response, police training, and thirteen years' experience as a cop, he protected not only Boursiquot's daughter but an innocent bystander. And because he was there to handle the situation, other lives may have been saved as well.

I asked Reynolds if there was anything he would have done differently that night. "If I had to do it again, I would do it exactly the same way," he said.

Officer Reynolds received the Medal of Honor from the city of Miami. It's awarded by the chief of police in the name of the citizens of Miami to a member of the department who shows conspicuous gallantry and courage at the risk of his or her own life, above and beyond the call of duty while engaged in armed conflict or in the face of extreme danger. Sergeant Faith Williams, Model City supervisor, nominated Reynolds for "his outstanding performance while engaged in a violent armed conflict, and for displaying such heroism in the face of extreme danger."

Officer Reynolds now patrols the Liberty City area. He told me, "I don't think patrol cops are recognized enough. Although other departments may get credit for solving crimes, the cops on the street are the backbone of every department."

But don't call this patrol officer a hero to his face. Reynolds would probably respond as he did to me: "I simply enjoy helping and working with people."

24

SERGEANT JAMES McMULLIN

Chicago (Illinois) Police Department

"In an Orderly and Swift Manner"

"I love the street," Sergeant James "Moon" McMullin exclaims. In his thirty-one years with the Chicago Police Department, he has watched his 18th District go from a poor area with high crime rates to a revitalized urban-growth area with new buildings and expensive homes. I myself was raised on the near North Side of Chicago, so I know firsthand that things could get pretty tough there.

Sergeant McMullin was on routine patrol the morning of October 30, 1998. He'd learned a long time ago to appreciate those rare moments when he wasn't called into service as he patrolled the streets. Some shifts would move nonstop from traffic accidents, domestic disturbance calls, and drug deals in the streets to robberies and occasional shootings. This morning would be far from quiet or routine.

New construction was going up near the Thomas Flannery Senior Homes located at 1507 North Clybourn Avenue. Around 11:00 A.M., a backhoe operator punctured a twenty-four-inch natural gas main at a town house development. A twenty-four-inch main is the largest gas main in Chicago; most are eight to twelve inches. First the operator heard a loud noise like air escaping from a collapsing balloon. Because natural gas is invisible to the human eye, a dye is infused into the gas to make it visible, so the operator could then see gas skyrocketing over a hundred feet into the air. He jumped off the backhoe and ran to call Peoples Gas Light & Coke Co. to close the massive main. Gas was filling the air so quickly that the possibility of a gas explosion was increasing exponentially.

In placing the call for assistance, the police dispatcher unfortunately gave the wrong address. One officer in the area replied that she'd head over to the scene, and McMullin, just a few blocks south of the development, responded to the call saying he'd provide backup. McMullin was driving toward the incorrect location when he heard an explosion. He stopped his vehicle, stepped out, and heard a tremendous roar.

"At first I thought it was a jet plane crashing," he told me. He drove toward the noise, and within seconds he was the first officer on the scene. In describing the chaos, he said, "People were running in every direction." The natural gas was shooting hundreds of feet into the air.

McMullin called in an Emergency Plan One, which was a call to send seven units for assistance and traffic control. He would later up the response level to an Emergency Plan Two—send help from all available districts.

McMullin had three things running through his mind as he ran from his car toward the seniors' residence: First, because it was a cold, overcast day, he was concerned that the static electricity in the air might ignite the gas. Second, he recalled an incident six years earlier just a mile away in which a gas explosion killed four people. Third, he wondered how he was going to evacuate the high-rise building.

When I asked McMullin how he felt as the rescue began unfolding, he replied, "You don't think—you just rely upon your training and react. You react in an orderly and swift manner. We knew if that gas caught fire, we were in for serious trouble."

The sergeant ran from apartment to apartment, knocking on every door and shouting for people to get out. The officer who'd initially responded but had been sent to the wrong address soon joined him. They moved methodically from floor to floor. McMullin carried invalids who couldn't walk from the building.

By now several other police officers had arrived to help with the rescue effort. Because the elevators had been shut down to prevent sparks from igniting the gas, McMullin and the other officers had to carry some of the senior citizens down twelve, thirteen, and fourteen flights of stairs. They transported one elderly lady to safety in her wheelchair. Knowing that the gas could be ignited at any moment, they all worked as fast as they could.

The building's head engineer stopped McMullin before he could complete the evacuation to tell him that the residence was connected underground to another residence also occupied by senior citizens. The two buildings shared a boiler room.

The officers completely evacuated the fourteen-story building in twenty minutes. In all, eighty-five residents, most in their late seventies and early eighties, were rescued. One officer was treated for chest pain as the exhausted officers caught their breaths. Then, as they stood between the evacuated building and the still-occupied residence, the gas burst into flames. Speculation has it that the explosion was caused by the pilot light of a stove; an elderly woman on the eighth floor in building two apparently had her window open.

"The explosion literally lifted all of us off the ground," McMullin told me.

Flames were shooting two hundred feet into the air, and as the officers watched, the wind carried the flames right into the second building. McMullin was concerned that some of the elderly might become disoriented or want to stay in their apartments out of fear. He didn't think he had another twenty minutes to get them to safety.

With no time to lose, he set his second evacuation into motion by dividing the police rescuers into two teams. He sent half the officers to the top floor of the second building and the other half to the ground floor; the two teams would work their way toward the middle floors. Armed with sledgehammers, they first knocked and yelled at each apartment door; if no one responded, they used the sledgehammers to break down the door. Officers knocked down between forty and fifty doors in the second building. Each unit was searched and cleared before the officers would proceed to another apartment. If they found someone who wasn't ambulatory, they'd carry the person down the stairs and out to safety as fast as they could. The police also escorted to safety two people who became disoriented in all the confusion.

The huge blast was heard three miles from its source, causing 9-1-1 boards to light up. Firefighters, police officers, and other city workers from around Chicago showed up to assist. Firefighters worked to contain the flames, which had engulfed the building above the eighth floor, as police continued to rescue the occupants. Anticipating the worst, the coroner's office set up a makeshift morgue in a YMCA gym several blocks from the scene. Dozens of body bags lay in waiting.

In less time than it took to empty the first seniors' home, the second was completely evacuated of its eighty-four occupants. Remarkably, there were no casualties. The residents from both buildings were given temporary housing nearby. It took the firefighters until 1:25 P.M. to extinguish the fire after they'd been able to contain it to the top six floors. McMullin was treated for heat exhaustion, as were three of his fellow officers and five firefighters.

For his bravery and courage in averting a potentially disastrous situation, Sergeant James McMullin received a TOP COPS Award from the National Association of Police Organizations in 1999. He also received their coveted Citizen's Choice Award. The Illinois Commerce Commission, the agency that regulates the gas companies, presented a lifesaving award to the sergeant for his actions on October 30, 1998. The Emerald Society of Illinois named him Police Officer of the Year. McMullin still insists he shouldn't be singled out for his actions that day.

Today, McMullin is chairman of the Chicago Police Sergeants Association, which boasts thirteen hundred sergeants as members. He and Monica, his wife of thirty-six years, have two sons: a thirty-year-old who works for the Chicago Water District, and a twenty-six-year-old who is a tradesman, a tile setter.

During my interview with Sergeant McMullin, he told me that one of the most interesting cases he had worked on during his long career with the Chicago Police Department was when he was still new to the job. Assailants had pulled up alongside five rival gang members, jumped out of their car with guns drawn, and made the five lie facedown on the sidewalk. The shooters then fired a single round into each head, killing all five. Abandoning their car, they then fled the scene, leaving five bodies on the sidewalk.

Officer McMullin, a rookie, was ordered to wait for a tow truck after the bodies were taken away. The car would be impounded as evidence. First the fingerprint experts showed up and dusted the car. Next, detectives examined the car for evidence. As McMullin and his partner continued to wait for the tow truck, they saw a vehicle registration application in the car. None of the other police officers had noticed it.

Taking initiative, McMullin and his partner drove to the address on the application after the tow truck took away the vehicle. The occupant at the address said that he had nothing to do with the hit but knew who did. He took the two police officers to an apartment across the street from where the car had been parked. Three suspects ran onto the roof as the officers approached the apartment. "We chased them as they jumped from one roof to the next, and we caught all three of them," McMullin recalled. The shooters were sentenced to life in prison.

Sergeant McMullin has earned 230 honorable mentions and six department commendations during his distinguished career, as well as the respect of his fellow officers. However, it's the love of the job—of the street—that keeps him motivated. If he had his way, he would patrol Chicago's near North Side for *another* thirty-one years.

25

OFFICERS MARK COTA AND
DENNIS O'MAHONY

San Francisco (California) Police Department

"The Tenderloin"

Officer Mark Cota

Officer Dennis O'Mahony

San Francisco is truly one of the great American cities. It is also one of the most eclectic. To describe the community as multicultural doesn't scratch the surface of the neighborhood complexities. It is the music of Aaron Copeland, Leonard Bernstein, Jerry Garcia, and Grace Slick all rolled into one. It's the artwork of Norman Rockwell, painted by Picasso, and framed by Andy Warhol. How would you describe that to an outsider? You can't always understand it, but you can always appreciate it. Some people see the town as strange, others as brilliant.

Without debate, San Francisco is a place of great culture, with its celebrated theaters, ballet, philharmonic, and world-class museums. But it is also a place of great variance with few peers in America. There is only one Haight Ashbury, just as there is only one Greenwich Village. In "The City" as locals like to call it, on one side of the street a tuxedoed couple can step from a limousine to enter a great hall, while on the other a prostitute plies her trade. The incongruities are enormous.

And then there's the Tenderloin.

For the uninitiated, the word *tenderloin* generally refers to a district in any city that is largely devoted to vice. San Francisco's Tenderloin has been more notorious than most, and its roots lie in the famed Barbary Coast. In *A La California: Sketch of Life in the Golden State,* Colonel Albert S. Evans described the sordidness of old San Francisco around 1871:

> Every city on earth has its special sink of vice, crime and degradation, its running ulcer or moral cancer, which it would fain hide from the gaze of mankind. London has its St. Giles, New York its Five Points, and each of the other Atlantic and Western Cities its peculiar plague spot and curse; it is even asserted that there are certain localities in Chicago where vice prevails to a greater extent, and life, virtue and property are less secure than in others. San Franciscans will not yield the palm of superiority to anything to be found elsewhere in the world. Speak of the deeper depth, the lower hell, the maelstrom of vice and iniquity—from whence those who once fairly enter escape no more forever—and they will point triumphantly to the Barbary Coast, strewn from end to end with the wrecks of humanity, and challenge you to match it anywhere outside of the lake of fire and brimstone.

What would the good colonel have written had he visited the Haight during the summer of love?

Today, the Tenderloin is certainly more civilized than its cousin of old. But it is diverse to be sure. Now there is a strange mix among the high-rise buildings near the financial district. There are many fine hotels and museums, professional buildings, and government offices. Yet within a short distance there are strip clubs, bars, panhandlers, fortune-tellers, streetwalkers, and drug dealers. Thus, for the police, the Tenderloin has often been considered the most crime-ridden beat in town. So when leaders in the community and in government decided to make a change, the Tenderloin became the focus of a citywide cleanup effort. Police officers assigned to the Tenderloin joined forces with community organizations to take on the crime problems and address the quality-of-life concerns. In 1997 Willie Brown, the city's flamboyant mayor, held a televised press conference in Boedekker Park to promote this agenda.

Officers Mark Cota and Dennis O'Mahony were among many young and energetic officers brought in to help clean up the district. On the late afternoon of Friday, January 15, 1998, the officers were patrolling around Boedekker Park in the center of the Tenderloin's highest crime area. While it was very cold outside and the clouds were threatening, it wasn't raining. The rush hour traffic was heavy, and pedestrians filled the sidewalks, making their way home for the weekend. It was a typical end of the business week in the city of San Francisco, and traffic had come to a halt near the Tenderloin.

Close friends, Cota and O'Mahony had been partners for three years in the elite TTF, or Tenderloin Task Force. Working a radio car in the district, the two were very, very good. As one thought something, the other spoke it. As one advanced, the other provided cover. They were more than just partners and close friends—they were a team that acted and moved as one. Very active, they were routinely commended for the excellent felony arrests they made. On this Friday afternoon in the middle of what seemed to be a routine shift, they were making small talk about the issues of the day. But as they kibbitzed, a few blocks away a crime was taking place.

At about 5:15 P.M., Buford White entered the Bank of America at 33 New Montgomery Street near San Francisco's financial district. White was a convicted bank robber who was wanted by the FBI and police for questioning in four other takeover bank robberies in the East Bay and San Francisco areas. He reportedly bragged about how he'd like to "shoot it out with the cops" someday and promised he wasn't going back to the joint.

To commit his robberies, White usually wore a ski mask and latex gloves. He carried a .357 magnum revolver and lots of ammo. That afternoon he walked into the bank and shouted, "Everyone hit the floor!" All the customers waiting in the bank dropped down. When the employees inside a back office heard the commotion, one quietly dialed 9-1-1. Speaking softly to the dispatchers, the unidentified voice whispered that a bank robbery was in progress. San Francisco Police Department dispatchers immediately put out a radio broadcast: "Any area unit: a 211 bank robbery in progress at the Tenderloin Bank of America." Officers Cota and O'Mahony realized they were just a few blocks away and decided to "buy the call." Traffic was stop-and-go as they attempted to reach the scene, however, and their frustrations would begin to build as the incident became more serious by the second.

Inside the bank, White gathered cash from each of the teller stations. Then things spun out of control. A young man inside the bank, afraid that White was going to shoot them anyway, decided to try to subdue the gunman. The twenty-six-year-old attempted to tackle White and wrestle away the .357. White wasn't fazed. He quickly overpowered him then shot him twice, point-blank, in the face. With shots ringing out in the background, witnesses on the telephone with police dispatchers frantically described the gruesome details. An updated broadcast to responding officers advised, "All units on the Bank of America 211: This is now a takeover robbery, shots fired, at least one victim is down." For the responding units, it didn't get any more serious than that. With sirens blaring, Cota stepped on the gas, driving down side streets to avoid the stopped traffic.

White collected the cash and ran out of the bank, carrying with him some "bait money," cash that can be identified later because the bank's operations officers have prerecorded the serial numbers. As he fled, officers responding to the robbery were given updates on the suspect's last known location. By now, Cota and O'Mahony had pulled onto 4th Street and were headed toward Mission. They were receiving a broadcast of the robbery suspect's description from the dispatcher, who advised, "Suspect is male, black, six foot, two hundred pounds, wearing a black leather jacket, a dark-colored watch cap, and a stocking or netting on his face to disguise his appearance." Witness updates were pouring in from people calling on their cell phones as they watched the gunman flee down the street. As some brave witnesses kept White in sight, they advised the police that he was shedding his clothing as he ran. The officers could feel the tension over the airwaves as the updates were broadcast. The dispatchers had just listened to the sound of a man being shot, yet they never lost their composure. They were cut from the same cloth as the two officers who were now moving into harm's way.

Officer Cota pulled onto New Montgomery following behind several other radio cars. The police cars began pulling over; officers were going out on foot into the area. Cota decided to drive farther down the street past the bank to Mission Street. O'Mahony thought this might put them in front of the robbery suspect or at least establish a wider perimeter to aid in the search.

As Officers Cota and O'Mahony approached 1st Street and Mission, they observed a man carrying a black jacket talking on a cell phone. The man, glancing around as though looking for the police, appeared upset or very tense. Once he made eye contact with the officers he began waving frantically toward another individual wearing an overcoat and a black watch cap who was walking in front of him. Both officers instinctively knew this had to be the suspect. When a second witness pointed toward the same man, the officers were sure.

Cota pulled over, and he and O'Mahony took off on foot after the suspect. Realizing that the police were behind him, White picked up the
pace. But it appeared that he wasn't just trying to get away—he was heading to a spot where he had a tactical advantage over the officers. Though
Cota and O'Mahony were aware that White was drawing them away from
other officers and backup, they continued to follow.

Then Cota saw White's face. Cota said, "I thought I knew the guy from
a prior contact. For a split second I wondered if this was the same man,
because those encounters had been pretty cooperative and low-key."

Although the hesitation was slight, the suspect took advantage of it,
quickly moving away. He turned, then crouched down and in an instant
sprang back up and opened fire on Officer Cota. The first shot from the
.357 ripped through Cota's right knee. He felt the heat from the bullet,
and he was conscious of his bone shattering as he was knocked to the
ground. The searing pain momentarily stunned him, but he wasn't out of
the fight. He pulled himself up from the street and returned fire.

With Cota shot, White turned his attention toward O'Mahony, firing
four or five rounds at the officer. The bullets tore into O'Mahony, shattering his ankle and foot.

O'Mahony remembers, "I was knocked to the pavement but was still
able to return fire. White moved toward a nearby parking lot, and at gunpoint he tried carjacking a sport utility vehicle from two women who happened by." Fortunately, White was unsuccessful.

Despite his shattered anklebone, O'Mahony got up and tried to run
over to the parking lot, but the extreme pain dropped him to the pavement. "The pain was unbelievable, and I tried to move, but my leg just
gave out." When White saw O'Mahony falter, he opened fire on him
again. During this second volley of fire, White missed with each shot. Still
exposed, O'Mahony fired four more shots, forcing White back around a
car. The suppression fire by O'Mahony forced White to move directly into
Officer Cota's view.

There is an old line in police work describing a serious officer safety
concern: "If you can see the suspect, he can probably see you too." As
soon as White saw Cota, he opened fire.

Cota reacted by returning fire, again and again. He never let up on his
attack, nor did O'Mahony. They kept shooting, reloading, and shooting
again to keep White immobilized. Both officers were clearly disabled by
gunshot wounds, but they never eased up. They crawled along the sidewalk and the gutter trying to get a better shot at White.

As Officer O'Mahony got closer, White ran around the car to get cover and began shooting indiscriminately down the crowded street. In the Friday night rush hour traffic, it was pandemonium. As backup officers ran to the scene, they were high-stepping over people who were lying on the sidewalks or hiding in the gutter trying to avoid being shot by White. White then started shooting at every officer on the scene.

White continued to reload and shoot; his desire for a gun battle with the police was definitely being fulfilled. Both officers had now emptied their Beretta 9-mms and were reloading. Cota recalled, "I hunkered down next to a curb and used a telephone pole for cover. The rounds were going off all around both me and Dennis. I had burned through eleven rounds, and I knew I was in trouble." The officers both realized that this suspect wasn't going to surrender.

According to Officer Cota, "I knew White was going to kill us or be killed, and even though it sounds strange now, I forced myself to slow down and think. I had to calm down. I needed to get a hold of myself and settle my emotions so we could survive this gun battle. This whole situation was just so unreal." Cota knew he had to find a tactical advantage even though he was seriously wounded and pinned down by White's sporadic gunfire. No one was near enough to offer any assistance. Cota was essentially the point of the spear, and the suppression fire by O'Mahony had forced White back into Cota's gun sights.

Then, Cota said, "My training took over. We're always taught to keep up our will to survive and to never quit under pressure. I just followed what we were taught." As his will to survive became palpable, his response was automatic. Even though he remained under fire, Cota took slow, careful aim until he got the suspect back into his sights. Once White came into view, Cota slowly fired eleven more rounds at the gunman. Just as he was doing this, two other officers got into position to help. They rushed to Cota's side and began to drag him to safety. As the officers moved, White again rose up to fire at the police, shooting and moving to prevent the officers from closing in on him or getting a clear shot. He kept rolling over and over on the pavement to keep from getting hit by the gunfire. One of the worst running gun battles in San Francisco's history didn't look as if it was going to end anytime soon.

At last Officer Jesse Serna was able to get in a position of tactical advantage. He used parked cars, telephone poles—whatever cover he could find on the street. He took careful aim, then fired seven times at White. Suddenly it was over, and White was down. Unbelievably, he was still alive and struggled with the police as they rushed to take him into custody. In the end, suspect Buford White had been shot twenty-four times, two times directly in the head. Yet he didn't stop fighting or shooting at the police until he finally collapsed. He died on the way to the hospital.

Both wounded officers were immediately transported to San Francisco General Hospital where they underwent emergency surgery. True to their character, they successfully went through recovery and rehab, returning to duty in about eight months. Back on patrol in the Tenderloin, they're still partners, just as they've been now for over five years.

The death toll resulting from White's rampage didn't end with his own death. On the evening the shooting occurred, the department's Special Operations Group (SOG) was asked to assist with the area search and field investigation. During the initial stages of the investigation, officers on the scene weren't sure if there were any additional suspects. They worked diligently to determine that Buford White acted alone. The SOG commanding officer, Captain George "Jake" Stasko, spent hours working late into the night as inspectors sorted out the chaotic scene. When he finally went off duty, he drove the long distance to his home on the other side of the bay. Along the way, he evidently fell asleep at the wheel. Captain Stasko died when his car ran off the road and crashed.

Officers Cota and O'Mahony faced peril few officers hear about, let alone experience. They were both seriously wounded in a running gun battle, yet they stayed the course. They refused to give up or to give in, somehow maintaining their will to survive despite the odds. The men remembered the obligations of their sworn and solemn oath to preserve, protect, and defend. In doing so, they also showed the world why as partners they're among the best of the best.

Officer Mark Cota and Officer Dennis O'Mahony performed in an exemplary manner under extreme circumstances. Their actions were clearly above and beyond the call of duty. While many of San Francisco's finest exhibited courage beyond measure, the performance of these two officers was exceptional. They demonstrated their commitment to excellence, their physical and moral courage, and their fidelity to their profession. Their selfless acts of bravery and uncommon valor were in the highest traditions of the law enforcement service and the San Francisco Police Department. In 1998 they received the San Francisco Police Department's Medal of Valor and, in January 1999, they were honored as the California Robbery Investigators Association Officers of the Year.

26

POLICE HEROES OF THE
WORLD TRADE CENTER DISASTER

"The Deadliest Day in the
History of American Law Enforcement"

From that first awful moment on September 11, I have been so very aware that I have been standing in the company of heroes. They will be kept alive in our minds and hearts forever.

—LEWIS EISENBERG,
CHAIRMAN OF THE PORT AUTHORITY,
AT THE MEMORIAL SERVICE FOR PORT AUTHORITY STAFF

While thousands of terrified people ran from the Twin Towers on September 11, 2001, after two commercial jets crashed into them, firefighters, rescue workers, New York City Police Department (NYPD) and Port Authority police officers, and other government workers rushed to the scene. Not all of them were called to the scene; many came because they knew they could help save lives.

Unable to use the elevators, many raced up the stairs to help the injured, to assist those in wheelchairs, and to guide those who'd lost their way as visibility became increasingly difficult. Many also stayed on the ground, shielding people from the horror outside and helping them find the exits. One officer shot out the windows to relieve the bottleneck at the revolving doors, saving hundreds of people by her actions. Another gave strength by his calm demeanor, reassuring those who were in shock from what they'd experienced and what they'd witnessed.

About twenty-eight hundred people in the World Trade Center—including hundreds of firefighters, police officers, rescue workers, and others—died on September 11. But despite the fatalities, this may also have been the greatest rescue effort in American history. When the attack began, *USA Today* estimated that five to seven thousand people were in each tower. They had less than two hours to evacuate the buildings. This number does not include the several thousand more who were streaming toward the buildings on foot, on Port Authority Trans-Hudson (PATH) and subway trains, or walking through the World Trade Center mall. These people were diverted to safety by Port Authority personnel. *USA Today*'s December 19, 2001, article by Dennis Cauchon reports that 99 percent of those people who could get out—namely, those below where the planes crashed—did.

When Port Authority Police Captain Anthony Whitaker called for a full alert, two hundred Port Authority officers were there within ten minutes. The Fire Department's Engine 10 and Ladder 10 on Liberty Street were the first to arrive, followed by the NYPD's Emergency Service Unit (ESU) Truck 1. After that, hundreds of workers were called in or volunteered to assist in rescue efforts, including officers assigned to protect the courts. FBI Agent Leonard Hatton, who was on his way to the office, came to help. U.S. Secret Service Master Special Officer Craig J. Miller was also among the lost.

Most of the details of these heroes' stories will never be told. The courageous men and women who perished on that fateful day took the details of how they died with them. But whatever else they did, they resisted the natural flight response and chose to help save lives. As Martin Glynn, a trader at Eurobrokers who'd been on the eighty-fourth floor of Tower Two, said in the New York *Daily News,* "Heroism is not only running into flames. It's doing your job in the face of horror."

Those involved in the rescue effort were stationed in different ladder companies, precincts, transit districts, and ESUs. Some were ending their shifts or off duty, but all had one thing in common: a strong sense of duty. Their wives, children, friends, and colleagues were not surprised to learn that they were there; helping people was what they did.

I was originally scheduled to meet with my publisher about *Police Heroes* two weeks after September 11. I kept that appointment. Seeing Ground Zero with my own eyes was almost as hard as the interviews I conducted later with some of the families and friends of police officers who were lost in the tragedy. I couldn't shake from my mind the images of the burning buildings, of officers in uniform and in civilian clothes converging from many different locations to lend a hand and help save lives. My mind raced with visions of men and women running up the stairs toward danger while still lending support and strength to those who were descending and with thoughts of their efforts to protect people at all costs, shielding civilians from flying debris when the buildings collapsed.

I don't think it's possible to see Ground Zero and not shed tears for the lost.

To all the Port Authority police officers, NYPD police officers, firefighters, federal workers, and emergency rescue workers whose stories perished with them on September 11, 2001, I simply want to say you will never be forgotten. Your watch is over. All Americans will honor your good names, your devotion to duty, and your heroism for all time.

SPECIAL AGENT LEONARD HATTON
Federal Bureau of Investigation

Jerry Savnik, Supervisory Special Agent in the FBI's New York Field Office, was not surprised when he first learned that Special Agent Leonard Hatton was missing at the World Trade Center.

In 1993 Special Agent Hatton had been officially assigned to assist in the investigation of the bombing of the World Trade Center, but this time it was different. He was driving to his New York FBI office when he heard what happened on his radio. He turned his car around and drove directly to the World Trade Center. He first went to a nearby hotel and radioed information about the damage back to his New York office. But after the hijacked jet hit Tower Two, he went into the tower to lead people out of the smoke-filled building. After Special Agent Hatton (known as "Lenny") helped a man out of Tower Two, he went back inside and was never seen again.

Lenny was a volunteer firefighter in his hometown of Ridgefield Park, New Jersey. A great investigator throughout his distinguished career, he worked on the FBI's New York Task Force, the first multi-agency task force in the United States. He also worked as a bomb technician and did forensic work, such as on the 1993 bombing of the World Trade Center and on TWA Flight 800 that crashed off Long Island in 1996. In 1993 he joined the Joint Bank Robbery Task Force, investigating more than eight hundred bank robbery cases during his career.

Lenny loved his work and was good at it. He had great people skills that helped him gain the confidence of crooks. A great interrogator, Lenny had a reputation for getting clean, usable confessions. His only fault, according to a fellow agent, was his inability to tell a joke. Oftentimes after telling a joke, Lenny was the only one laughing. But his heart was always in the right place.

During his career, Lenny received twenty-nine Letters of Commendation, three incentive awards, and three quality step increases, which are accelerated promotions determined by the special agent in charge.

At his funeral, FBI Director Robert Mueller III and the assistant director in charge of the New York FBI office Barry Mawn honored their fallen agent and emphasized his determination and heroism. Over a thousand friends, family, and fellow officers attended his funeral.

Many fine FBI agents have lost their lives in service to our country. While at Quantico, Virginia, to speak to FBI agents at their training facility, I noticed a board in the main hallway with photos of slain FBI agents. This was on my third visit, and I remember thinking that no new agents had been added during the time I had been providing workshops for the FBI. I'm confident that the Bureau's latest hero agent, Leonard Hatton, will be prominently displayed in this place of honor.

NEW YORK CITY POLICE DEPARTMENT

The NYPD is the largest municipal police department in the United States. With over forty thousand officers in seventy-six precincts, it is responsible for the five boroughs of New York City.

SERGEANT JOHN COUGHLIN
ESU Truck 4, Bronx

When the call came for help at the Twin Towers, Sergeant John Coughlin and Officer Stephen Driscoll rushed there in ESU Truck 4. After a brief pause to shake hands with Mayor Giuliani and Police Commissioner Kerik on West Street, they started up the stairs of Tower Two (South Tower). Neither one returned.

Kerik remembers that he told Coughlin to be careful. "He was the last cop I spoke to before the tower came down," he told the New York *Daily News*.

Coughlin, forty-three, loved rescue work. In fact, just to stay in "cop heaven" he never even took the lieutenant's test. But his first priority in life was his family: Patty, his wife of twenty years, and their three daughters, teenagers Erin and Tara and six-year-old Kayla. Despite his dedication to work, he never missed a sports practice, dance recital, or music lesson. They went parasailing, to amusement parks, and whitewater rafting.

He was not only dedicated to his own children. He always spent one week of his vacation each year sorting, wrapping, and delivering gifts for the Marine Corps' Toys for Tots program. He was also a volunteer firefighter in Pomona, New York, where he lived, and he participated in the Member Assistance Program that helps police officers in crisis situations.

Coughlin was in the Marines from 1976 to 1979. He joined the NYPD in January 1983. He was promoted to sergeant in 1988. He served the Housing Department's Police Service Area (PSA) 5, PSA 8, and the Housing Bureau before he transferred to the ESU in May 1995.

NYPD Commissioner Bernard Kerik attended the memorial mass for Coughlin. Kerik had met Coughlin for the first time on August 25, 2000, when he rushed home after his wife called to tell him his one-year-old daughter, Celine, was choking and unable to breathe. Though his wife had called 9-1-1, Kerik requested help from the NYPD and came home to find his infant daughter safe and sound in Coughlin's arms. "He was a true hero," Kerik said of Coughlin, as reported by *The Journal News*. "He showed that heroism on August 25, and he showed it again on September 11."

SERGEANT MICHAEL CURTIN
ESU Truck 2, Manhattan

Sergeant Michael Curtin started the day by bringing his wife, Helga, coffee in bed. He sent flowers to her at work and planned to make dinner for her in the evening. It was her birthday: September 11. He went to work and was last seen helping carry someone from the North Tower just before it collapsed.

Curtin was born in Liberty, New York, and grew up on Long Island. He enlisted in the U.S. Marine Corps shortly after he graduated from high school in 1975 and was called to active duty for the next twelve years. He and his wife met while serving in the U.S. Marines. During Operation

Desert Storm, Curtin was a gunnery sergeant on the front lines of battle. He retired as a sergeant major in 2001. He received a B.S. in Police Sciences from the State University of New York.

Curtin joined the NYPD in January 1988 and was promoted to sergeant in December 1995. He served in Field Training Unit (FTU) 13, the 75th and 113th Precincts, and ESU Squads 7 and 8 before he transferred to Truck 2 in March 1998. Always prepared, on slow days he drilled his squad on old skills and taught new ones.

Sergeant Curtin was no stranger to terrorism. He was one of the fifty-six cops, firefighters, paramedics, and doctors who were sent to help victims after the Oklahoma City bombing. He was also heavily involved in the relief and rescue efforts during the 1993 World Trade Center bombing. In 1999 he saved construction workers who were trapped after a floor collapsed during demolition of the old New York Coliseum. He received one Commendation, four Meritorious Police Duty Awards, and twelve Excellent Police Duty Medals while with the NYPD.

A resident of Medford, New York, he is survived by his wife and three daughters, Jennifer, fifteen, Erika, thirteen, and Heather, eleven.

OFFICER JOHN D'ALLARA
ESU Truck 2, Manhattan

John D'Allara, an eighteen-year veteran of the NYPD, was used to dangerous rescues. In 1995 he was part of a rescue effort to save a thirteen-year-old boy who'd fallen eight stories down an elevator shaft. In 1997, after a scaffold collapsed, he rappelled under the 59th Street Bridge to save workers dangling 130 feet in the air. So when the call came on September 11, he was quick to respond.

Part of a close-knit family, D'Allara, forty-seven, who grew up in Manhattan and the Bronx, is survived by his wife, Carol, his sons John, seven, and Nicholas, three, his twin brother, Daniel, and his parents.

After earning his bachelor's and master's degrees in Physical Education from Lehman College in the Bronx, D'Allara taught high school, first at Park West High School in Manhattan, then at Roosevelt High School in the Bronx. But he had always wanted to be a police officer and joined the NYPD in July 1983. After beginning his career on patrol in Neighborhood Stabilization Unit (NSU) 7, he served in the Patrol Borough Bronx Task Force, the 46th Precinct, and ESU 3 before he transferred to ESU 2 in

July 2001. He had received three Commendations, sixteen Meritorious Police Duty Awards, and twenty-five Excellent Police Duty Departmental Medals.

OFFICER VINCENT DANZ
ESU Truck 3, Bronx

The funeral for Officer Vincent G. Danz, thirty-eight, at St. Kilian Roman Catholic Church of Farmingdale, New York, on October 5, 2001, was the first service for an NYPD officer lost in the World Trade Center attacks. The standing-room-only crowd of mourners included Mayor Giuliani, who said that Danz "was truly a hero who protected freedom and democracy," and Police Commissioner Bernard Kerik, who said that Danz had been courageous throughout his entire career.

As reported in the *New York Times,* Felix Danz said of his brother: "He was a special breed. . . . He wasn't boastful. . . . He loved his work and the guys that he worked with. They would die for one another. I think that goes globally for the NYPD. My brother and his partner went into the Trade Center without any questions. They knew what to do and how to do it. Unfortunately, this thing was bigger than either of them."

Angela Danz, Vincent's wife and the mother of their three daughters, said she would never forget the message her husband left for her on their answering machine on September 11. "Hon, it's 9:50 and I'm at the World Trade Center. I'm up in the building. Say a prayer that we get some of these people out. I'm okay, but say a prayer for me. I love you." Danz had originally been scheduled for the 4 P.M. to 12 P.M. shift but switched so he could attend engineering school. He was in the North Tower when it collapsed.

A fourteen-year veteran of the force, Danz grew up in Jackson Heights, Queens, the youngest of nine children. After moving to Southampton, Long Island, as a teen, he was Angela's "personal tour guide" when she came to the United States from Ireland to work as an au pair in 1987. Danz served in the U.S. Marine Reserves as a communication specialist and in the Coast Guard Reserves as a marine safety technician. He joined the NYPD in January 1987. He served in the Housing Department's PSA 9, PSA 4, and the Housing Bureau before he transferred to ESU 3. He received three Commendations, two Meritorious Police Duty Awards, and two Excellent Police Duty Medals.

An avid fan of the New York Rangers and the Mets, he also loved hockey so much that he started PSA 9's floor hockey team.

OFFICER JEROME DOMINGUEZ
ESU Truck 3, Bronx

On September 11, Officer Jerome Dominguez, thirty-seven, was climbing the stairs in the North Tower when it collapsed, according to reports from colleagues.

Officer Dominguez grew up in the Pelham section of the Bronx. He graduated from Mount St. Michael Academy in the Bronx and joined the NYPD in July 1985. He served in FTU 7, the 42nd Precinct, the Highway District, and Highway Unit 1 before joining ESU. He transferred to ESU 3 in October 1999. While he was an officer with the NYPD, Dominguez also served in the U.S. Air Force Reserve where he was a highly decorated member of the 105th Security Police Force.

He was committed to his job both on and off duty. At the risk of his own life, he saved the life of a fellow officer while they were diving off the coast of Long Island. During a 1999 trip to Texas for Air Force training, he rescued more than a dozen children from an overturned bus before flames broke out. According to his family, he even carried tools in his car that would help extricate victims at accident scenes. He had received one Commendation and three Excellent Police Duty Medals from the NYPD.

A firearms enthusiast and instructor, the West Islip, New York, resident competed in numerous shooting matches. He also enjoyed scuba diving and riding his Harley-Davidson with his wife, Jessica.

OFFICER STEPHEN DRISCOLL
ESU Truck 4, Bronx

The last time Officer Stephen Driscoll, thirty-eight, was seen, he was on the twentieth floor of the South Tower—and going up. His wife, Ann, said she wasn't surprised that he was running toward danger. "He wouldn't have stopped until he reached the top, making sure everyone was out safe," she said. Ann knew him very well, having met him when they were teenagers. They were married eighteen years. Their son, Barry, is now fifteen.

Driscoll and his six siblings grew up in the Bronx. A veteran of the U.S.

Navy, Driscoll joined the NYPD in January 1992, serving in the Midtown South precinct. He also served in the Street Crime Unit before joining ESU. He transferred to ESU 4 in August 1998. He had received five Meritorious Police Duty Awards and fifteen Excellent Police Duty Medals. A member of the New York Shields, he also served as color guard in the NYPD Emerald Society Pipes and Drums. He loved sailing and living by the water.

At the Memorial Service at St. James the Apostle Church in Carmel, New York, Officer Kevin Donohue told several thousand mourners that Driscoll was known as the "mayor of emergency service."

OFFICER MARK ELLIS
Transit District 4, Manhattan

Officer Mark Ellis and his partner, Ramon Suarez, were at their post at the Delancey Street subway station on September 11. When the call for help came, the officers commandeered a taxi to the Twin Towers. Ellis and Suarez were separated while trying to rescue people, and both perished. During the Christmas Eve service for Ellis, according to the New York *Daily News,* Mayor Giuliani said that, while Ellis gave his life, he "helped unify this country in a way we've never been unified before."

At twenty-six, Ellis was the youngest New York City police officer killed on September 11. Ellis graduated from the Police Academy in 1998. He received four Excellent Police Duty Medals. The Secret Service had recently accepted him as a candidate.

Ellis grew up in Huntington Station, New York, and had one sister. He received a Bachelor of Arts degree in Criminal Justice from the State University of New York, Farmingdale in 1999. He was engaged to be married to his longtime girlfriend, Stephanie Porzio. He was an avid outdoorsman and enjoyed snowboarding, riding bikes, and fishing.

OFFICER ROBERT FAZIO
13th Precinct, Manhattan

Officers Robert Fazio and Moira Smith of the 13th Precinct were on their regular tour on the morning of September 11 when they saw the first plane hit the Twin Towers. Officer Smith called in the information. They first headed to the nearby precinct to interview witnesses but were last seen at the site of the World Trade Center.

Fazio was known for his love of fast machines—cars and motorcycles—according to his sister, Carol Lovaro. As reported in *Newsday*, she said it was not unusual for him to help a stranded motorist or change the brakes on a neighbor's car. Though he went out of his way to help others, he never asked for help.

Fazio, forty-one, grew up in South Hempstead, New York, and lived in Freeport on Long Island to be close to his other passion, boating. He joined the NYPD in July 1984. Before he transferred to the 13th Precinct in June 2000, he had served NSU 18, Patrol Borough Manhattan South, the Property Clerk, and the Technical Assistance Response Unit and had been a community officer in the 13th Precinct. He had received one Meritorious Police Duty Award and three Excellent Police Duty Medals. He was enrolled at St. Joseph's College where he was taking classes in criminal justice and law enforcement.

His January 9, 2002, funeral in Rockville Centre, New York, was attended by hundreds of fellow officers. According to the New York *Daily News*, Police Commissioner Raymond Kelly said, "Your son was put on this earth to save lives, even if it meant risking his own. He had an outstanding record. He was a peacemaker who was called home too soon. He served the people of New York and America. We can never replace him."

SERGEANT RODNEY GILLIS
ESU Truck 8, Brooklyn

It was 8 A.M., the end of his shift. Officer Rodney Gillis was talking to fellow officers when the call came in about the Twin Towers. He and other ESU officers, including his former high school teacher, Officer D'Allara, were first on the scene. The last message he left was on the answering machine of his grandmother and best friend, Annie Gilliam. As reported by *Newsday*, he told her he was in the World Trade Center and was all right. He asked his grandmother to tell his mother he was all right and said he'd talk to her later.

Raised in Brooklyn, Gillis had a degree in criminal justice. He joined the department in 1988 and was promoted to sergeant in 1997. He was well respected by the men in his unit, and they were thrilled when he became their boss. He loved working overnight and was called "a true warrior" by his former supervisor, retired Lieutenant Richard Green. He kept his men loose with his deadpan sense of humor. He served in FTU 12, the 77th and 79th Precincts, and ESU Squads 3 and 4 before transferring to his present command, ESU 8, in May 1999. He had received one Commendation, two Meritorious Police Duty Awards, and seven Excellent Police Duty Medals.

Gillis had Emergency Medical Technician (EMT) certification and was trained in scuba diving and emergency psychology. He was also trained to deal with hazardous materials. He was devoted to his three children, Jonique, fourteen, Alessia, seven, and Rodney II, six.

OFFICER RONALD KLOEPFER
ESU Truck 7, Brooklyn

Officer Ronald Kloepfer, thirty-nine, was remembered as "a true American hero" during a ninety-minute memorial service that nearly nine thousand cops attended. Among those at the service were family members, including his wife, Dawn, daughters Jamie and Taylor, his son, Casey, and six siblings.

I had the privilege of speaking to his brother Michael, who told me that Ronny, as he was known in the family, "was always looking to help people" and was "the straightest guy I ever knew." He would not want to be known as a hero but rather as a good father and husband, Michael said.

Officer Kloepfer joined the NYPD in January 1983. He served in NSU 18 and the 73rd Precinct before transferring to his present command, ESU 7, in 1988. In 1993 Ronny rappelled down the Twin Towers looking for clues about the bombing. He also helped pull survivors out of the water after a plane went off a La Guardia runway. He was awarded one Commendation, two Meritorious Police Duty Awards, and six Excellent Police Duty Medals. Officer Kloepfer was known in his unit for his big heart. His favorite expression was, "When people need help, they call a cop. When cops need help, they call ESU."

Kloepfer followed family tradition on Sunday when he attended New York Jets games with his brothers. During the last Jets game that Michael watched with his brother, Ronny told him that he loved his job and had no interest in a desk job or retiring. Besides skiing and hunting, his true passion was lacrosse. In 1997, with the help of the Patrolmen's Benevolent Association, he established the first NYPD lacrosse team. Their practices two to three times a week for two hours at a time paid off when they won two championships.

When I asked Michael how his brother should be remembered, he said, "Ronny is a true American hero, a great father, and he was a great police officer."

OFFICER THOMAS LANGONE
ESU Truck 10, Queens

Officer Thomas Langone fulfilled a dream to save lives when he became a police officer with the NYPD. He came from a background of volunteer firefighters, nurses, and former ambulance company volunteers. It was only natural that Tommy would become a cop and Peter, his brother, a firefighter. Peter was also lost on September 11.

"This is what they do for a living," his sister Joanne Ciborowski said, as reported by *Newsday*. "They live it, they breathe it, they love it. It's what they've always done, both of them."

Officer Langone, thirty-nine, was one of the department's twenty snipers and was able to hit a target at a thousand yards. He was also a leading instructor for emergency service training and wrote a how-to manual about rescuing people who threaten to jump off buildings or bridges. Both Langone brothers were at the 1990 crash of Avianca Flight 52 in Cove Neck, Long Island, as well as the World Trade Center bombing in 1993. Officer Langone was sent to Oklahoma City for a week after that bombing for search and rescue.

The Langone family, two boys and two girls, grew up in Roslyn Heights, New York. At age twenty-four Officer Langone became one of the youngest chiefs the fire department had. According to *Newsday*, Fire Chief Alan Schwalberg credited him with helping to establish Roslyn, New York's emergency medical service, which now handles about eight hundred ambulance calls a year. Langone was 2nd Assistant Chief with the Roslyn Rescue Fire Company and was the department's training officer. He was lead ESU instructor at the Nassau County Fire Academy. He was working toward a bachelor's degree in Empire State College's distance learning program. His goal was to teach after he retired from the department.

Langone joined the NYPD in July 1984. He served in NSU 15, and the 45th and 103rd Precincts, before joining ESU. He transferred to

ESU 10 in July 1991. He had received four Commendations, nine Meritorious Police Duty Awards, and twenty-nine Excellent Police Duty Medals.

Officer Langone had been married to JoAnn for fifteen years. They had two children, Caitlin, twelve, and Brian, ten.

On the morning of September 11, Officer Langone was riding back to his unit. After hearing the news, he suited up, collected equipment, and went to the World Trade Center. He was last seen on a twentieth floor stairway in the South Tower.

During the memorial service, Police Commissioner Bernard Kerik said, "Whenever disaster struck, the Langone family came to the rescue."

OFFICER JAMES LEAHY
6th Precinct, Manhattan

Officer James Leahy, thirty-eight, was only twelve when his father, whom he idolized, was shot dead during a robbery. His mother said that it was a turning point in influencing his decision to become an officer. He joined the NYPD in January 1992 and worked in the 6th Precinct.

Leahy's last message to his wife on September 11 was left on their answering machine: "I'm on the twentieth floor helping people get out. I'm OK. Tell the boys. . . . I'll call you back later." His partner, Victor Laguer, who was rescuing people in the underground mall, last saw Leahy going up the stairs of the North Tower with firefighters. After the South Tower collapsed, Leahy radioed from the North Tower saying that he and the others wouldn't leave the people they were trying to rescue. Not long after, the North Tower fell.

Leahy had been married to his childhood sweetheart, Marcela, for nineteen years. He was close to his three boys, James, Jr., eighteen, Danny, thirteen, and John, six. The oldest of five children, he grew up on Staten Island.

One of Leahy's favorite holidays was Halloween, when he would dress up and go trick-or-treating with his sons; he also dressed up to look like a prop on the lawn to startle unsuspecting trick-or-treaters. He played football in high school and became an avid fan of the Pittsburgh Steelers. He attended Walsh College in Ohio.

Leahy had been working his usual shift in downtown Manhattan when he saw the first plane hit. He and his partner quickly made the mile-long trip to the World Trade Center. They blew out a tire on the patrol car and ran into the shopping mall between the two towers where they found people running over each other trying to get away from the smoke.

Leahy and four firefighters ran into the North Tower carrying oxygen tanks, while Laguer and two Port Authority cops pulled people onto the street through the South Tower. After their third trip, the South Tower shook from the impact of the second plane. When Laguer radioed to Leahy, telling him to get out of the North Tower because another plane had hit, Leahy said, "We'll be all right."

As Laguer and the Port Authority officers started back to the South Tower, they heard a rumble and the South Tower collapsed. Laguer dove under a van for safety. When he heard Leahy radioing him, Laguer told him the tower had fallen. As the North Tower collapsed, Laguer heard Leahy yelling, "Victor! Victor!" over the radio.

"It was complete terror. I don't know how my heart didn't stop. *Hero* isn't a big enough word to describe Jimmy," Laguer said at the memorial service for Leahy, as reported by the *New York Post*.

OFFICER BRIAN McDONNELL
ESU Truck 1, Manhattan

For a man who always put others first, it is not surprising that Officer Brian McDonnell, thirty-eight, was one of the first to respond to the World Trade Center disaster. He was last seen going into the South Tower, according to the *New York Times*.

Officer McDonnell received an associate's degree in Criminal Justice from the State University of New York, Farmingdale. He served with the Army 82nd Airborne for three years before he joined the NYPD. He served in NSU 3, the 106th and 110th Precincts, the Narcotics Division, and the Patrol Borough Queens South Task Force before transferring to ESU 1.

McDonnell was a rookie cop in 1987 when he went on a blind date with Maggie, who later became his wife. On Valentine's Day only two months later, he gave her an Irish claddagh ring—a traditional Irish wedding band. They were engaged in June and married a year later. They have two children, Katie, eight, and Thomas, three.

During his fifteen years with the NYPD, McDonnell talked people out of committing suicide and pulled individuals who were drowning out of the East River. But the story that made headlines was when he freed a cat that was stuck in a car engine in May 2001. For all his courageous actions, he was not decorated because he never wrote himself up for a Commendation.

His dream was to be in the ESU, which he joined in 2000. According to his wife, he'd said a few weeks before the attack that if he died now, he would die a happy man because he'd accomplished all his dreams.

OFFICER JOHN PERRY
40th Precinct, Bronx

On the morning of September 11, 2001, Officer John Perry, who was off duty, went to police headquarters at One Police Plaza to file retirement papers. When he heard the explosions at the World Trade Center, he and a friend, Captain Tim Pearson, raced there to help. Perry helped hundreds of people escape before assisting a woman who'd fainted. The woman escaped, but Perry did not.

Perry, the son of a New York State Department of Mental Health psychiatrist, grew up in Seaford, New York. He was a first lieutenant in the New York State Guard. He received a bachelor's degree from Stony Brook College and a law degree from NYU Law School. He spoke numerous languages, including Russian, Spanish, and Swedish. He was a board member of the Nassau County chapter of the New York Civil Liberties Union (NYCLU) and worked on former NYCLU head Norman Siegel's campaign for public advocate. He collected bulletproof vests from retired officers to give to officers in Moscow, Russia. Once a week he was a volunteer at the Kings County Society for the Prevention of Cruelty to Children. He was also an extra in TV shows and movies.

Officer Perry joined the NYPD in August 1993. He served in the Central Park Precinct, the Manhattan Traffic Task Force, and the Department Advocates Office before transferring to the 40th Precinct in April 2001.

Perry's mother, Patricia, said that Perry always wanted to be a police officer. But after nine years, he had decided to leave the force and use his legal training in private practice.

Patricia said that on September 11 her son did what any cop would do.

"That's what they do: they run in and help people during their time in need," the *New York Post* reported.

OFFICER GLEN PETTIT
Police Academy, Manhattan

Officer Glen Pettit was not only a wonderful storyteller and a history buff, he was a talented photographer and cameraman. The thirty-year-old worked as a freelance still photographer and cablevision cameraman before becoming an officer in the video unit of the NYPD, making training and promotional videos. A volunteer firefighter since the age of sixteen, he continued to be a volunteer with the West Sayville (New York) Fire Department and also worked for News 12 Long Island.

On September 11, Officer Pettit was on his way to the World Trade Center with his partner, Scott Nicholson. The South Tower had already collapsed, and they were walking toward the North Tower when the girders of the building began to give way. The men fled the avalanche of debris, but Pettit disappeared in the dust and ash.

One of six children, Pettit grew up in Bay Shore, New York. He received a B.A. in Communications from New York Tech College. Pettit joined the NYPD in December 1997 and began his career on patrol in the 10th Precinct. He was transferred to the Police Academy in July 2000 and assigned to the video unit.

As reported by *Newsday*, Pettit's sister, Deirdre Kroupa, said Pettit's colleagues from work have told her how kind he was and that he had advanced to the video unit two years faster than normal because of his talent.

An ardent videographer, he was seen at countless NYPD emergency scenes capturing video images of his fellow officers. His expertise led to opportunities to freelance for the *New York Times* and *Newsday*.

DETECTIVE CLAUDE RICHARDS
Bomb Squad, Manhattan

Detective Claude Richards made his colleagues feel safe, according to Detective Daniel McNally, who'd been with Richards since their days at the Police Academy in 1983.

Detective Richards, forty-six, worked on the Bomb Squad for fifteen years and put 100 percent of himself into the job. As the bomb squad's intelligence coordinator, he even spent his off-duty hours planning his next workday. A native of Bethpage, New York, he was the sixth of seven children. He received a bachelor's degree from New York University. He served in the Army as an Airborne Ranger and was a member of the elite Presidential Honor Guard in Washington.

Richards joined the NYPD in January 1983 and began his career in NSU 14. He was promoted to detective investigator in July 1989 and detective 2nd grade in December 2000. He also served in the 6th Precinct and the Arson and Explosion Division before transferring to the Bomb Squad in October 1997. He had received one Commendation, two Meritorious Police Duty Awards, and three Excellent Police Duty Medals. In 1996 he volunteered and served one year with a United Nations peacekeeping force in Bosnia disarming land mines and other bombs. He loved to travel and was a martial arts enthusiast.

On September 11, Detective Richards was killed while searching for survivors in the World Trade Center's Building 6 when the North Tower collapsed. The other officers with him, Officer John D'Allara and Sergeant Michael Curtin, were also killed; Daniel McNally was injured.

Richards was unmarried with no children.

SERGEANT TIMOTHY ROY
Bus Squad, Manhattan

More than three thousand people attended the November 30, 2001, memorial service at St. William the Abbott Roman Catholic Church in Seaford, New York, for Sergeant Timothy Roy.

When Roy heard about the World Trade Center disaster while on his way to traffic court, he ran to assist his colleagues. He was last seen helping a burn victim in Building 5.

At thirty-six, Roy was a sixteen-year veteran of the NYPD. He is survived by his wife, Stacey, and their three children. He was the youngest of eight growing up in Massapequa Park, New York. His father was an FDNY 1st Grade firefighter. Two of his brothers are retired 1st Grade FDNY firefighters; one is an active 1st Grade firefighter; and one brother is a retired housing police officer.

Roy started out as a beat cop in Brooklyn in July 1985. He served in NSU 13 and was promoted to sergeant in March 1991. He also served in the 68th, 71st, and 73rd Precincts before transferring to the Bus Unit in November 1995. He had received five Meritorious Police Duty Awards and twenty-two Excellent Police Duty Medals. Roy's awards include a unit citation for work done during the Crown Heights riot in 1991.

Roy had a passion for golf. He loved the outdoors and taking the family on vacations as often as he could.

OFFICER MOIRA SMITH
13th Precinct, Manhattan

Officer Moira Smith, thirty-eight, the first New York City police officer to report that a plane had crashed into the Twin Towers, was on patrol the morning of September 11. She and her partner, Officer Robert Fazio, brought victims and witnesses to the 13th Precinct, then went to the WTC. While helping to evacuate the South Tower, Smith prevented a logjam by looking people in the eye and calmly ordering them to keep moving and to not look outside. She was photographed leading a man away from the South Tower and was last heard from between the third and fifth floors.

Her husband, Officer James Smith, who is assigned to the Police Academy, told the *New York Post*, "She never got scared, never." Since joining the NYPD in July 1988, she had served in the Transit Bureau and Transit Districts 2, 4, and 30 before transferring to the 13th Precinct in March 1996. She was the recipient of two Excellent Police Duty Medals.

Officer Smith grew up in Bay Ridge, Brooklyn, and attended Niagara University in upstate New York. She met her husband when they both served in Transit District 4. An avid sports fan who loved to travel, she was devoted to her two-year-old daughter, Patricia.

On February 13, 2002, a new NY Waterway East River high-speed ferry was christened "The Moira Smith" to honor Moira and all the officers who died on September 11. On what would have been her thirty-ninth birthday, February 14, 2002, more than ten thousand police officers lined up outside St. Patrick's Cathedral to pay their respects. She was also named "Woman of the Year" by the Policewoman's Endowment Association and *Glamour* and *Ms.* magazines.

OFFICER RAMON SUAREZ
Transit District 4, Manhattan

Officer Ramon Suarez said good-bye to his wife, Carmen, at 6:30 A.M. on September 11. The forty-five-year-old father of three and grandfather of one left his Delancey Street subway post with his partner, Officer Mark Ellis. Together, these Transit District officers commandeered a taxi to the Twin Towers. Once there, they separated. Suarez was photographed as he rescued a distraught woman from a building that was going to collapse. After the photo was taken, Suarez rushed into the South Tower and was never seen again.

Suarez joined the NYPD in January 1987. An Excellent Police Duty Medal recipient, he served in the Transit Bureau, Transit District 4, the Transit Borough Manhattan Task Force, and the Highway District before transferring back to Transit District 4 in March 2000.

One of four children, Suarez grew up in East Harlem. He had a nine-year-old daughter, Jillian, with his wife, Carmen. He also had two grown children from his first marriage: Sophia, twenty-six, and Ray, Jr., twenty-five. He graduated from the Manhattan School of Graphic Arts and Design and had nearly completed a Bachelor of Arts degree from Pace University.

Suarez was a staunch advocate of physical fitness and received numerous trophies and awards for his expertise in karate. A runner, he coached track at Jillian's elementary school.

At Suarez's memorial service, Mayor Giuliani said that Suarez showed tremendous valor and will "forever live in history," according to the *New York Post*.

OFFICER PAUL TALTY
ESU Truck 10, Queens

Officer Paul Talty, forty, was probably thinking about his new daughter, Kelly, born August 18, when he went to work on Tuesday morning, September 11. He and his wife were building an addition onto their Wantagh, New York, house to accommodate their growing family.

Officer Talty grew up in Rockville Centre, New York, and Brooklyn with his five siblings. He worked for years as an electrician and received his Bachelor of Arts degree in Sociology from Queens College.

Talty joined the NYPD in August 1993 because he wanted a job with more security. He served in the 108th Precinct before transferring to ESU 10 in October 1999. He received a police medal in 2000 for rescuing a toddler who was wedged between a building and a shipping container.

He and his wife, Barbara, have three children: Paul, Jr., twelve, Lauren, nine, and Kelly. A former track star, Talty loved the outdoors and enjoyed vacationing in Florida every year.

OFFICER SANTOS VALENTIN
ESU Truck 7, Brooklyn

Officer Santos Valentin, forty, answered the call for help on September 11 and never returned. At his memorial service, more than a thousand police officers came to pay their final respects to him. His partner, Sergeant Richard Kemmler, said in a *Newsday* article that Valentin loved the job so much that he used his own money to buy equipment, such as special boots or gloves.

Officer Valentin began his career with the NYPD in January 1984. He served in NSU 4, the 19th Precinct, the Street Crime Unit, and ESUs 4 and 8 before transferring to ESU 7 in March 1996. He had received two Commendations, five Meritorious Police Duty Awards, and four Excellent Police Duty Medals.

Officer Valentin, known as "Papo," was one of five children. His sister Denise is an NYPD sergeant. He had an associate's degree from the Academy of Aeronautics. A sharpshooter who was trained in counterterrorism tactics, he loved fishing, white-water rafting, camping, and playing golf.

DETECTIVE JOSEPH VIGIANO
ESU Truck 2, Manhattan

Detective Joseph Vigiano, thirty-four, one of the city's most highly decorated officers, was singled out by Police Commissioner Bernard Kerik in April 2001 for a promotion to detective second grade—an almost unheard-of honor for an ESU cop.

The last sighting of Vigiano was in the North Tower, helping a fireman on the third floor. Kathy Vigiano, his wife, herself an NYPD officer and mother to their children, Joseph, eight, James, six, and John, four months, was not surprised that he remained in the building to help.

"Everyone knows Joe was a great cop. But not everyone knows he was an even better father," Kathy said of Vigiano, as reported in the *New York Post*. At the funeral, their oldest son, Joe, read a eulogy for his dad, who was supposed to become a Cub Scout master for Joe's troop on Tuesday, September 11.

Detective Vigiano joined the NYPD in April 1987 and worked on patrol in FTU 16. He was promoted to detective investigator in January 1992. He served in the 73rd and 75th Precincts and ESU 7 before his transfer in April 2001 to ESU 2 as detective second grade. He had received the Police Combat Cross, the Medal for Merit, two Honorable Mentions, three Commendations, seven Meritorious Police Duty Awards, and twenty-one Excellent Police Duty Medals.

Detective Vigiano was a volunteer firefighter. He was also the Deer Park, New York, fire commissioner for several years. In his free time, he traveled around the United States lecturing to other law enforcement agencies on tactics.

One of Vigiano's three brothers, John, a firefighter, was also lost in the World Trade Center attack. When President George W. Bush came to New York City on September 14 to meet with some of the relatives of the missing, Vigiano's father, John, a retired FDNY captain, was among those present. Not long after, Detective Vigiano's shield was presented to Queen Elizabeth to thank the British people for their support during and after the World Trade Center tragedy.

OFFICER WALTER WEAVER
ESU Truck 3, Bronx

Officer Walter Weaver loved the outdoors and animals. He and his girlfriend, Shannon Faulkner, had just moved into a new home where there was plenty of room for their pets, including two dogs, turtles, birds, and an iguana. Weaver had also rescued a dog that had been abandoned. After nursing him back to health, Midnight, a shepherd-Doberman mix, became ESU Truck 3's mascot. Midnight was on hand during the memorial Mass in Hicksville, New York, riding in a vintage 1930s Emergency Service truck.

Officer Weaver, thirty, joined the NYPD in June 1992 and was with the 47th Precinct before joining ESU Truck 3. He had received one Commendation and six Excellent Police Duty Medals. While on patrol in the 47th Precinct, he helped deliver two babies.

Officer Weaver is survived by his parents and his brothers, Brian and Michael.

NEW YORK STATE OFFICE OF COURT ADMINISTRATION COURT OFFICERS

Court officers are dedicated to keeping order in the courts and protecting those who participate in court proceedings. In a place where emotions often run high, these defenders of the justice system are a vital link to keeping safe not only persons who are on trial but the juries, judges, attorneys, and witnesses. Some prisoners may see the court as their last opportunity to escape; the court officers are the ones charged with making sure those accused do not escape. Always on guard, they are trained to defuse potentially dangerous situations and respond accordingly.

New York state has about three thousand court officers statewide, with close to two thousand assigned to New York City alone. The officers go through a rigorous nine-week training program in their own academy, which is staffed by fifteen instructors. In addition, the officers are required to attend in-service training.

On September 11, the commanding officer at the Manhattan Supreme Court's Criminal Division asked for the assistance of medically trained officers. These men and women came running to help from various locations: the training academy on Williams Street, the courthouses at 100 and 111 Centre Street, and the commuter train. The ones who got there early helped clear out the floors in the North Tower, going as high as the fifty-first floor until they were ordered out after the collapse of the South Tower. Others made their way into Building 5, where they treated the injured until the building collapsed.

Helen Dachtler, who had survived the 1993 World Trade Center bombing, was at her job on the sixty-fifth floor of the South Tower when the first plane hit the North Tower. She called her daughter, who was on the fifty-ninth floor, advising her to leave. After telling her coworkers to leave the building and calling her husband to tell him she was leaving and that she loved him, she heard a noise and saw a 767 heading directly at her. She saw the pilot's hands on the controls before he pulled back on the stick and crashed the plane above her. She was knocked out of the office into the hallway next to the stairwell.

With the help of a coworker, Helen was able to make it to the street. Near a hotel, she collapsed with chest pains. Moments later, the South Tower began to fall. She thought she would be trampled by the panicked people fleeing around her. Then she heard the voice of Court Officer Andy Scagnelli.

Scagnelli had gone with Captain William Harry Thompson when the captain told him and the other Supreme Court officers at the Williams Street training academy that he was going to help with the rescue effort. Just the day before, Scagnelli had completed the lifesaving portion of his in-service training. He first helped evacuate the lobby, getting three injured people out, calling their loved ones, then assisting at the newly set up triage center at the corner of Liberty and Church Streets. When the South Tower began to crumble, he took shelter in a nearby building, then saw an injured man and Helen in the street. He got both of them into the building, saving their lives.

While Andy Scagnelli was assuring them they were safe, he was privately thinking that all three of them would die. But he was able to lead them to a safe area a couple blocks away, where he gave them water, called their loved ones, and advised them to start walking north. Then he went back to the site.

Andy Scagnelli survived, but two of his fellow officers—Thomas Jurgens and Mitchel Wallace—and academy instructor Thompson did not make it. Scagnelli insists that they are the real heroes.

In the days just after the tragedy, employees at the Supreme Court set up a shrine to the missing court officers. The sign in the midst of the flowers and flags read, "Missing But Not Forgotten." During a September 21 vigil, an emotional Chief Judge Judith Kaye addressed hundreds of court employees and officials. "Our court officers are the truest, the noblest, every single day of the week, and they proved it in the very best of times and in the worst of times," she told the group.

On November 5, 2001, the families of the three court officers accepted on behalf of their loved ones the Albert L. Gelb Man of the Year Award, the State Court Officers Association's highest honor.

SENIOR COURT OFFICER THOMAS JURGENS
Manhattan Supreme Court, Criminal Division

Senior Court Officer Thomas Jurgens, affectionately known as "Tommy at the Ready," and Court Officer Joseph Ranauro were patrolling the Manhattan Supreme Court building at 100 Centre Street on September 11 when the first plane hit. Jurgens retrieved a medical emergency kit, then joined nine other court officers who sped to the scene in a jury van.

Once at the site, Jurgens went to the lower concourse level of Building 5 to help with the badly burned victims. He was lost when the South Tower collapsed.

Officer Jurgens was a four-year veteran of the court. The twenty-six-year-old newlywed, who'd been trained as a Army combat medic, had met his wife, Joan, when he was a volunteer firefighter. "Any kind of crisis, he would always be the first one to respond," she told *Newsday*. In an interview, Chief Jewel Williams, who is now first deputy chief of public safety for the New York State Office of Court Administration, said that Jurgens "greeted everyone with a big smile. He was enthusiastic about his job."

CAPTAIN WILLIAM HARRY THOMPSON
Court Officer Academy

When Captain William Harry Thompson responded to the call for medical help on September 11, he'd been conducting in-service training at the court officers' academy on Williams Street. He raced over to the World Trade Center to help.

While some of his colleagues who'd arrived there earlier were clearing out the floors, Thompson joined Jurgens, Wallace, and others in the lower concourse level of Building 5. He and Court Officer Pat Maiorino were yards apart when the South Tower collapsed, crushing one side of Building 5. Maiorino was thrown twenty to thirty feet and survived. Thompson, Mitchel Wallace, and Tommy Jurgens, who were on the other side, did not survive.

Thompson, fifty-one, was a twenty-seven-year veteran officer respected for his dedication and professionalism as an instructor. In his role as captain, he was in charge of protecting the judges. "He was a spit-and-polish kind of guy and an imposing figure," Chief Jewel Williams said. "But he was a gentle giant. People were comfortable with him—you could talk about anything with him." His healthy diet and habit of always taking the stairs to his teaching position on the twelfth floor kept him in shape. After taking recruits for a run and stair climb, he would be the only one who wasn't breathing hard.

Thompson was the father of grown-up sons and the sole support of his widowed mother. Michael Thompson, one of Harry Thompson's sons, told the *Miami Herald* that, for a second, he was angry because his father did not run for safety; then he realized that his father "did what was in his heart."

SENIOR COURT OFFICER MITCHEL WALLACE
Manhattan Supreme Court, Criminal Division

Senior Court Officer Mitchel Wallace, thirty-four, was walking to work from the subway with his medical bag on September 11. He wasn't in his uniform yet but recognized his help was needed and raced over to the World Trade Center. Wallace, Thompson, and Jurgens were helping out injured people who were in the basement of Building 5 when the South Tower collapsed. He was to be married to Noreen McDonough in October 2001.

Wallace was thrilled when he received a promotion to Supreme Court officer, according to what his colleagues and superiors told Chief Jewel Williams. In May 2001, he received an honor from New York State Chief Judge Judith Kaye for saving the life of a man who went into cardiac arrest on the Long Island Rail Road.

Wallace's seven-year-old nephew, Logan Miller, who was close to his uncle, was chosen by Mayor Giuliani to ring a handheld bell during a special ceremony to honor those who died at the World Trade Center. The ceremony was in Times Square at 6 P.M. on New Year's Eve, 2001. The new crystal ball that brought in the new year was engraved with the names of the NYPD, FDNY, Port Authority, and EMS workers and the names of all the countries that lost citizens on September 11.

Leonard Hatton

John Coughlin

Michael Curtin

John D'Allara

Vincent Danz

Jerome Dominguez

Stephen Driscoll

Mark Ellis

Robert Fazio

Rodney Gillis

Ronald Kloepfer

Thomas Langone

James Leahy

Brian McDonnell

John Perry

Glen Pettit

Claude Richards

Timothy Roy

Moira Smith

Ramon Suarez

Paul Talty

Santos Valentin

Joseph Vigiano

Walter Weaver

Thomas Jurgens

William Harry Thompson

Mitchel Wallace

PORT AUTHORITY OF NEW YORK
AND NEW JERSEY

Ronald Shiftan served as deputy executive director of the Port Authority of New York and New Jersey from 1998 to 2002. Following the attack on the World Trade Center on September 11, 2001, he also served as the Port Authority's acting executive director. For *Police Heroes* he was kind enough to write down his thoughts about the impact on the Port Authority of the terrorist attack on the World Trade Center:

By now, there may not be a person on the earth who has not seen photographs of the destruction of the World Trade Center. For most, the buildings were an elegant symbol of America, an icon of the New York skyline. For the men and women of the Port Authority of New York and New Jersey, however, the Twin Towers represented so much more. The Port Authority had conceived of the towers and built them. Port Authority staff cleaned them and cared for them. The Port Authority Police protected them, as well as the fifty thousand people who passed through the World Trade Center each day to work, to shop, or simply to marvel at an incomparable symbol of the American spirit.

Most of us knew the buildings as well as we knew our homes or apartments. This, after all, was where we spent most of our time, eight, ten, or twelve hours each working day. For us, the attack on the World Trade Center was more than an attack on America, or on New York City. It was an attack on us. It was personal.

The Port Authority Police responded from all over the Port District, a region of about fifteen hundred square miles centered on the Statue of Liberty. They came from their posts at the bridges and tunnels spanning the Hudson River, from the Port Authority Bus Terminal in midtown Manhattan, and from the Port Authority's vast marine terminals on Staten Island and in New Jersey. They raced in from Kennedy, LaGuardia, and Newark Airports and from Port Authority police headquarters in Jersey City. They rushed in from their homes throughout the region. They came by car, by taxicab, and by bus. They arrived in organized groups, and one by one.

Together with firefighters, EMS workers, and members of the NYPD, our men and women ran into the buildings as the two thousand civilian Port Authority staff that worked in the Twin Towers streamed out. They climbed the stairs to seek out those of us who might be trapped, or not able to descend on our own. They stayed with their injured friends as the buildings literally came down around them.

Their response was not the result of their training or experience. It was the response of mothers and fathers, brothers and sisters, to family members in distress.

To all those who came to our aid, we are forever in your debt. We owe you our lives.

To those who have not come home, we say with conviction that you continue to live on in our hearts and memories. May your families and friends find peace in knowing that the rescue effort at the World Trade Center will be remembered as the most successful in history, with over twenty-five thousand people successfully evacuated.

The Port Authority Police Department is the nation's twenty-sixth largest law enforcement agency. A total of thirty-seven Port Authority officers and one K-9 officer were lost on September 11. This loss—just over 2.5 percent of the fourteen hundred in the force—was the largest loss of police officers in a single event in the history of American law enforcement, according to the head of the Port Authority Police Benevolent Association, Gus Danese. In the eighty years before September 11, only seven Port Authority officers had been lost in the line of duty.

Among those who lost their lives were Police Director Fred Morrone, more than half of the ESU, and the commanding officer of the Port Authority Police Academy. Nineteen reported in at the roll call at 7 A.M. on September 11 in the Jersey City, New Jersey, headquarters. Thirteen of those men were dead just four hours later. The fifteen-member Port Authority Emerald Society Pipes and Drums band lost most of their drum section with the deaths of Liam Callahan, Steve Huczko, and Richard Rodriguez. The band played at the memorial services for the lost.

OFFICER CHRISTOPHER AMOROSO
Tactical Response Bureau, World Trade Center

Officer Christopher Amoroso, twenty-nine, a Port Authority officer who was trained in special tactics and fire control, played an active role in the rescue effort at the World Trade Center. After leading a number of people to safety from the lower levels, he collected oxygen packs and hard hats and was last seen entering the North Tower.

Officer Amoroso was born in Rockville Centre, New York, but grew up in North Bergen, New Jersey. He had four brothers and two sisters. He attended St. John's University, then worked for Consolidated Dairies as a route manager until entering the Port Authority Police Academy in August 1999. He graduated in January 2000. According to his father, he had waited five and a half years to get into the academy.

A fan of the New York Yankees, Amoroso enjoyed playing hockey, football, and baseball. He was also fascinated by history, and two of his favorite activities were playing with his daughter, Sophia Rose, and watching the History Channel. He and his wife, Jaime, lived in Huguenot on Staten Island.

On November 28, 2001, Amoroso and another Port Authority officer who died in the World Trade Center attack, Robert Cirri, were honored by their alma mater, North Bergen High School. Amoroso graduated in 1990 and Cirri in 1980. The sixteen American flags that hung in front of the school were each given to family members after the service. The flagpole was adorned by red, white, and blue ribbons. Etched into a small stone monument at the base of the flagpole are an American flag, the Twin Towers, the names of Amoroso and Cirri, their years of graduation, a dedication to all who suffered from the attack, and the following inscription: "In memory of the North Bergen High School graduates who perished in the line of duty at the World Trade Center on September 11, 2001."

OFFICER MAURICE BARRY
ESU, Newark (New Jersey) PATH Station

Officer Maurice "Moe" Barry, forty-eight, was assigned to the PATH commuter train system in Newark, New Jersey, but when he learned of the terrorist attack, he rushed there from Jersey City to be one of the first on the scene. He was last seen in the North Tower where he was trying to reach trapped workers on the upper floors.

His wife, Marianne, said Moe wasn't happy unless he was helping people. His twenty-year-old son, Jon, remembers that his dad bought season tickets for the Philadelphia Eagles for the two of them because Jon is a fan. They attended the games together—even though Moe was a Giants fan. When his younger son, now eighteen, once said he wanted a Volkswagen van, his dad found one on the Internet and drove him to South Carolina to pick it up.

Officer Barry worked for the Port Authority as an engineering supervisor responsible for train repairs. He then joined the Port Authority police in 1985. His career and life clearly demonstrate his dedication to the job. He was involved in rescue work during a LaGuardia Airport plane crash. He also rushed to the scene of the 1993 World Trade Center bombing. He once climbed a bridge to retrieve the body of a person who'd been electrocuted. During Hurricane Floyd, he rescued a woman from her home by boat.

Officer Barry was born on an Air Force base in Tampa, Florida, and raised in Jersey City, New Jersey, the eldest of four brothers. Barry and his wife lived in Rutherford, New Jersey. Barry was known for taking delight in others' joys. He went out of his way to make his friends and family happy. He was always doing things for others, such as clearing their driveways with his snow blower.

Officer Barry was a Rutherford Ambulance Corps volunteer, a past Port Authority Police Benevolent Association delegate, and a former Boy Scout leader.

OFFICER LIAM CALLAHAN
ESU, Journal Square (New Jersey) PATH Station

Officer Liam Callahan, forty-four, of the Port Authority ESU was called to the World Trade Center on September 11—one day before his twentieth wedding anniversary—and never returned. His wife, Joan, said that after he'd received the call for help, he phoned home to ask about the kids. What started out like a regular day for Joan Callahan became a nightmare.

A veteran with over twenty years of service, Callahan once saved the life of a man who tried to jump off a roof of the Port Authority Bus Terminal. He won a Valor Award in 1993 for rescuing disabled people during the World Trade Center bombing.

An Irishman who was proud of his heritage, he was a drum sergeant for the Port Authority Emerald Society Pipes and Drums band. He and Joan had four children: Brian, seventeen; Bridget, fourteen; Ellen, thirteen;

and James, eleven. A frequent volunteer at the children's schools, he was often a chaperone on cafeteria lunch duty. An active member of St. Cecilia Church of Rockaway, he was well known for the pancakes he cooked at church functions.

LIEUTENANT ROBERT CIRRI
Port Authority Police Academy, Jersey City (New Jersey)

On September 11, Lieutenant Robert Cirri was in his Jersey City office when the first plane hit the Twin Towers. He drove his car through the Holland Tunnel to help. When he was a couple blocks away, he called his wife, Eileen, at work to tell her he couldn't watch people running out of the building, that he had to help. He called her again to tell her that he and Captain Kathy Mazza were rerouting people who had been heading into a fire. They were on the twenty-eighth floor. When the call came to evacuate after the collapse of the South Tower, Lieutenant Cirri and Captain Mazza were helping a woman down the stairs. They were in the lobby of the North Tower when it collapsed.

Cirri, thirty-nine, served the Port Authority for over fifteen years. He was an executive officer at the academy, where he trained others, and had received his promotion to lieutenant in 2000. On weekends he worked part-time as a paramedic at Hackensack University Medical Center. His ham radio operation, which started as a hobby, was used to help people when he joined the Jersey Coastal Emergency Services, a nonprofit organization that monitors emergency airwaves.

Lieutenant Cirri is survived by his wife, two children—Robert, Jr., seventeen, and Jessica, thirteen—and three stepchildren, Bianca, fifteen, Francesca, thirteen, and Kara, eleven. On the memorial service program, each of his children wrote a tribute to him. His name also appears on a monument at the base of the flagpole at North Bergen High School from which he graduated in 1980.

OFFICER CLINTON DAVIS
World Trade Center

Port Authority Officer Clinton Davis, thirty-eight, enjoyed people and music, according to his sister, Sandra Davis. He always had his karaoke equipment at parties or celebrations so he could display his singing talent. "He was always one to lift your spirits," Port Authority Officer Louis Solivan said, as reported in the New York *Daily News*.

But on September 11, he was in the North Tower working at ground level when it collapsed. His body was found on the stairs next to a close friend, Port Authority Officer Uhuru Houston.

Davis grew up in Queens, New York. He joined the Air Force in 1981 and was stationed in Austin, Texas. He left active duty in the late eighties and returned to New York City. A Massapequa, New York, resident, he is survived by his three children, Clinton, Jr., seventeen, Priscilla, twelve, and Julian, nine.

OFFICER DONALD FOREMAN
Holland Tunnel

Officer Donald Foreman, fifty-three, a captain's clerk at the Holland Tunnel, was ordered to report to Tower Two (South Tower) Command Center on September 11. His companion of seventeen years, Cheryl Cooper-Foreman, said his habit was to let his family know he was okay. That call was the last time they spoke.

Foreman grew up in Richmond Hills, Queens. He had six brothers and three sisters. He joined the Port Authority Police Department in 1971 after working for five years as a postal worker. Early in his career he worked as a traffic officer. He spent many of his years at the Port Authority working as a captain's clerk for fifteen consecutive captains.

Officer Foreman was a vegetarian and an avid *Star Trek* fan; he also coached basketball and was the director of Immaculate Conception School's sports program. He volunteered at a homeless shelter near the Holland Tunnel along with his colleagues and friends Walter McNeil and Nathaniel Webb. McNeil and Webb are also among the lost.

He has one son, Marcus, and two stepdaughters, Cacia and Tia Walker.

OFFICER GREGG FROEHNER
ESU, Journal Square (New Jersey) PATH Station

Officer Gregg Froehner, forty-six, had specialized training in numerous rescue areas. He was on hand in 1993 during the World Trade Center bombing. A year ago, he was there when an out-of-control elevator with a dozen passengers slammed into a tower's ceiling. And he was at the World Trade Center on September 11. This time he never made it out.

Froehner started working for the Port Authority in 1979. He completed a counterterrorism course on toxic and biological agents in 1995. He was also a handyman who fixed equipment in the field. Port Authority Police Sergeant John Gilburn, who knew Froehner for more than two decades, said that he was one of those guys everyone wanted to have around.

Froehner loved to play golf and spend time with his family—his wife, Mary, and their children, teenagers Meghan, Heather, and Matthew, and ten-year-old Kathleen.

OFFICER THOMAS GORMAN
ESU, Journal Square (New Jersey) PATH Station

Officer Thomas Gorman, forty-one, was one of the first to respond to the call for help at the World Trade Center. An officer in the ESU, he died during the rescue effort.

Officer Gorman had worked for the Port Authority at Newark Airport and at the Port Authority Bus Terminal before he was assigned to the Journal Square PATH station in Jersey City. Before he joined the Port Authority, he worked at the Bayonne Fire Department as a firefighter.

While Gorman loved being a public safety officer, he lived for his family. He and Barbara, his wife of eighteen years, had three children: Laura, Patrick, and Bridget. He was a loyal Giants fan and also coached a basketball team and Little League baseball. Gorman enjoyed cooking and often had a candlelight dinner ready for Barbara when she came home from her job as a nurse. "He was just a very genuine person," she told *Newsday*. "He told you what he thought, what he felt. But he would do whatever he could for you, and do his best. He was a man who worked hard but also knew how to enjoy life."

OFFICER UHURU HOUSTON
World Trade Center

In the basement plaza of the World Trade Center on September 11, three Port Authority patrolmen greeted each other. Uhuru Houston and Edward Finnegan, who were working in plain clothes, came over to greet Robert Vargas. Vargas had known Houston for seven years but hadn't seen Finnegan in four years. After a hurried greeting, Vargas watched Officer Houston run up into one of the towers. It would be the last time he saw Houston.

Houston grew up in Brooklyn with his three sisters, one of whom is a police officer. After working in the business world, Houston joined the Port Authority in 1993 and worked at the Port Authority Bus Terminal. He was assigned to the World Trade Center in 1999.

Houston, forty-four, met his wife, Sonya, while they were attending Norfolk State University in Virginia. They married in 1996 and have two children, Hasani, four, and Hannah, one. On September 11, Uhuru, or "Bee" as he was often called, told Sonya in a phone conversation just after the first plane hit the North Tower, "Whatever you do, don't come down here."

OFFICER GEORGE HOWARD
ESU, John F. Kennedy International Airport

September 11 was Officer George Howard's day off, and he was at home instead of at John F. Kennedy (JFK) International Airport where he worked for the ESU of the Port Authority. When he first learned about the attack, he called JFK Airport and was told to report to the World Trade Center. He and a colleague went into the city to lend a hand. His partner, Pete Johnson, was caught in traffic and never made it there.

It probably seemed all too familiar to Howard, who had rushed in to help after the 1993 World Trade Center bombing. He had also been off duty that day. Johnson recalls that not long after that incident, Howard thought someone could ram a plane into the building and contacted the engineers, who told him the buildings could withstand a hit.

Howard was forty-four years old and a sixteen-year veteran of the Port

Authority Police Department. He was also a volunteer captain in the Hicksville (New York) Fire Department and an instructor in the Nassau County Fire Academy. He is survived by his wife, Eleonora, and two sons, Christopher, nineteen, and Robert, thirteen.

Just days after the disaster, his mother, Arlene Howard, gave her son's badge to President George W. Bush during his meeting with relatives of the missing firefighters and cops. Later the President held up the badge as a symbol of the lives lost.

OFFICER STEPHEN HUCZKO
Newark International Airport

Stephen Huczko, forty-four, a fifteen-year veteran of the Port Authority Police, was last seen by his wife, Kathleen, before he went to work on September 11. He, along with colleagues Officer James Parham, Chief James Romito, Lieutenant Robert Cirri, and Captain Kathy Mazza were found buried with a woman they were trying to rescue.

Huczko was born on Staten Island. While studying nursing, he worked as a police officer on the night shift at Newark International Airport. He graduated with a nursing degree from Raritan Valley Community College in Somerville, New Jersey, in 1995.

Huczko was with the Port Authority during the 1993 World Trade Center bombing and the Federal Express plane crash in 1997 in which an MD-11 cargo plane carrying hazardous materials flipped onto its roof and burst into flames at Newark International. All five people aboard the plane climbed to safety.

A bass drummer in the Port Authority Emerald Society Pipes and Drums, Huczko is survived by his wife and four children, Kaitlyn, seventeen, Liam, thirteen, Cullen, seven, and Aiden, five.

INSPECTOR ANTHONY INFANTE, JR.
John F. Kennedy International Airport

On September 11, Inspector Anthony Infante, Jr., was in Jersey City attending a Port Authority meeting. He was one of the many Port Authority officers to rush to Manhattan to aid in the evacuation of the buildings.

As reported by the New York *Daily News*, an e-mail from a survivor to his brother, Andy, said that Inspector Infante was seen in the North Tower going up the stairs. He was calming people down and telling them there was a clear exit to the street. "You could all imagine what a comfort it was to see Anthony in the stairwell and to hear his comforting words," the e-mail said.

Inspector Infante always knew he would be a policeman. He worked for the Newark Police Department, then joined the Port Authority. He worked there for twenty years, eventually becoming a commanding officer for JFK Airport.

He is survived by his wife, Joyce, and their children, Marie, twenty-three, and John Joseph, nineteen. Infante was active in the community, coaching his children's softball and basketball teams, volunteering at a soup kitchen, and teaching at St. Patrick's Church in Chatham, New Jersey. After attending night classes, he earned a bachelor's degree from St. Peter's College in Jersey City and an M.A.E. from Seton Hall University in South Orange, New Jersey.

OFFICER PAUL WILLIAM JURGENS
Rescue Training Center, PAPD Academy

Officer Paul Jurgens, forty-seven, was driving from JFK Airport to Jersey City on the morning of September 11. He was last seen speeding to the World Trade Center to help. A Port Authority officer for twenty-one years, he helped rescue many of the injured during the 1993 bombing at the World Trade Center. In 1992 he was involved in the successful evacuation of 292 passengers from a burning jet that had crashed on takeoff at JFK Airport.

A former Marine Corps corporal, Jurgens joined the Port Authority Police in 1980. His proficiency in rescue work led to a job as instructor at the Port Authority's Rescue Training Center. Jurgens also volunteered for the East Meadow Fire Department and coached Police Athletic League baseball.

He and his wife, Maria, had three children, teenagers Paul and June and nine-year-old Lindsay. The youngest of four siblings, Jurgens loved pulling practical jokes. As reported in the *New York Times* and *New York Post* accounts of the September 29 memorial service for Jurgens, his brother-in-law said he woke up after dozing off one evening after dinner to find the words "Paul Jurgens is my hero" written on his arm. "Now I realize how true that is," he said.

SERGEANT ROBERT KAULFERS
Hoboken (New Jersey) PATH Station

Port Authority Police Sergeant Robert Kaulfers, forty-nine, was at the PATH bureau in Hoboken, New Jersey, when the call came through about the World Trade Center attacks. Reports vary, but it is believed he was last seen at the South Tower.

After graduating from Trenton (New Jersey) State College in 1975, Kaulfers was an investigator for the Bergen County (New Jersey) Prosecutor's Office's Narcotics Task Force. In 1979 he became a facility operations agent. He was promoted to sergeant in January 1996 and was assigned to the bus terminal in New York City and the PATH train.

Kaulfers was known for his wit, his loyalty, and his songwriting and singing talents, which he displayed at fellow officers' retirement parties. According to Port Authority Police Inspector Timothy Norris, Kaulfers was the most popular sergeant on the force. He was married to Luz ("Cookie") for twenty-five years; they'd known each other since they were ten years old. They had two children, Timothy, twenty-two, and Meredith, eighteen.

OFFICER PAUL LASZCZYNSKI
ESU, PATH Station

Officer Paul Laszczynski always wanted to be a police officer. He spent years earning a science degree and even worked in a New Jersey lab, but he jumped at the opportunity to join the Conrail Transit Police. His former wife, Karen, told *The Star-Ledger,* "He liked the idea of helping people and making a difference in their lives, helping them out as best he could in any situation."

Laszczynski was born in Baltimore and raised in Jersey City. He played football in both high school and college and tried out for two professional football teams, the New York Jets and the New York Giants.

During the 1990s he worked at the Port Authority central police pool, then the PATH command in Journal Square (New Jersey). His supervisor for more than a dozen years, Lieutenant Susan Durett, told *The Star-Ledger* that Laszczynski "took tremendous pride in being a member of this police department and was an exemplary cop in every aspect, from the way he dressed to the way he dealt with people."

After the 1993 bombing of the World Trade Center, Officer Laszczynski earned a Fraternal Order of Police Valor Award after helping carry someone down more than seventy flights of stairs. He also climbed the George Washington Bridge more than once to rescue would-be jumpers. He then trained for and became a member of the ESU. He also had a position with the Port Authority's honor guard.

Officer Laszczynski was last heard from somewhere above the twentieth floor of the North Tower where he was assisting victims.

A Paramus, New Jersey, resident, he rode his Harley-Davidson motorcycle with a police group that raises money for children's charities. He is survived by two daughters, Amy, twenty-two, and Jennifer, twenty.

OFFICER DAVID LEMAGNE
Journal Square PATH Station

When word of the September 11 attack came, Officer David Lemagne, twenty-seven, asked if he could respond to the emergency because he had paramedic training. He was last seen at the Twin Towers where he was part of a human chain evacuating the North Tower. He was lost during the collapse of the tower.

Lemagne was known for his sense of humor—he was always the one who told jokes and kept people laughing. He enjoyed cycling and playing softball and had recently traveled to Portugal and the Dominican Republic. He was also known as someone who pushed. "He pushed people to get the grades, to get moving, to get motivated," his sister, Maggie, told the *New York Times*. "He pushed a lot of friends, and they went further in life because of him."

When he was just eleven years old, he joined the Union City Volunteer Ambulance Corps as an Explorer. After receiving his EMT Certification while still in high school, Lemagne entered into service with the Union City Volunteer Ambulance Corps. After he graduated from high school in 1992, he then worked as an EMT for the Jersey City Medical Center and for the University Hospital EMS. In 1994, he received an associate's degree from the University of Medicine and Dentistry of New Jersey and started working as a paramedic for the Jersey City Medical Center. From 1997 to 1998, he returned to his alma mater, Hudson Catholic High School in Jersey City, where he was an assistant coach to the football team and an athletic trainer. He became a Port Authority police officer in August 2000.

OFFICER JOHN LENNON
Court Liaison, Jersey City (New Jersey)

Officer John Lennon was working as a court liaison in Jersey City when he heard about the attack on the World Trade Center and joined in the rescue effort.

Lennon, forty-four, who went by the nickname "Jay," grew up in Brooklyn where he was a star basketball player at Nazareth Regional High School. He graduated from St. Francis College. He and his father coached baseball for the Howell (New Jersey) Central Little League for twelve years. A resident of Howell, Lennon also coached baseball and basketball at a local school for two years.

Lennon had been in the Port Authority's ESU from 1993 until early in 2001. He helped with the recovery effort during the 1993 World Trade Center bombing. During his career, he earned three Excellent Police Duty Citations. He could have retired with twenty years of service two years ago, but he enjoyed work too much to quit.

He is survived by his wife, Patricia, and their four children, Melissa, twenty, John III, eighteen, Kathleen, twelve, and Christopher, ten.

OFFICER JOHN LEVI
Port Authority Bus Terminal

Port Authority Police Officer John Levi was working overtime on September 11 because he liked to have his weekends with his fiancée, Debralee. He called her twice, once when the first plane hit and again when he was in the basement of the World Trade Center searching for evidence.

Before he became a police officer with the Port Authority sixteen years ago, he was a mechanic at the Holland Tunnel. He had recently received a departmental commendation for his role in capturing a shooting suspect who arrived on a bus from Boston.

Levi was a thoughtful person who loved to build. He spent two years building his mother's beauty parlor on the first floor of her Brooklyn house. On September 11, he was just one step away from finishing the remodeling of his childhood home. His mother, Johanna Levi, who is eighty-three years old, and Debralee plan to finish that last step: putting up the wallpaper.

Officer Levi is survived by his children, Dennis and Jennifer, who are both in their twenties, and his granddaughter, Katarina.

OFFICER JAMES F. LYNCH
Emergency Services and Hazardous Material Response, World Trade Center

Officer James Lynch was in the Port Authority's main office at the World Trade Center on September 11. He was there not because he was on duty but because he was dealing with medical forms from a recent knee surgery. He was last seen carrying air tanks and breathing masks up to firefighters.

The forty-seven-year-old was willing to help anyone, according to people who knew him. Officer Lynch was one of six growing up in New Jersey. He was a corrections officer at what is now known as East Jersey State Prison in 1975. He later worked for Conrail, then joined the Port Authority Police in April 1979. During the 1980s, he was in the Coast Guard Reserve and earned an associate's degree in science at Middlesex County (New Jersey) College. His heroic actions during the 1993 bombing at the World Trade Center earned him a group valor citation.

Officer Lynch, an avid fisherman who earned his professional captain's license eleven years ago, was the father of a fifteen-year-old son, James.

CAPTAIN KATHY MAZZA
Port Authority Police Academy, Jersey City (New Jersey)

Captain Kathy Mazza, forty-six, was the first female commanding officer of the Port Authority Police Academy. On September 11, she joined her colleagues at the scene. When there was a bottleneck of people at the revolving doors in the North Tower, she shot out the floor-to-ceiling glass walls on the mezzanine. Her action allowed hundreds of people to escape. She was last seen with Lieutenant Robert Cirri; they were helping carry a woman down the stairs when the building collapsed.

Captain Mazza grew up in Massapequa, New York, with three brothers. After she graduated from Nassau Community College, she was an operating room nurse at two New York hospitals, the Long Island Jewish Hospital in Queens and St. Francis Hospital in Roslyn, New York. In 1987 after ten years of working as a cardiothoracic nurse in the operating room, she enrolled in the Port Authority Police Academy. She patrolled JFK Airport for a year, worked in the central police pool for one year, then returned to JFK Airport for the next six years. She was promoted to sergeant in 1994 and was assigned to the Port Authority Bus Terminal for two years. She was then assigned to the Police Academy for three years and was promoted to lieutenant in December 1998 while at the academy. Her next assignment was the Staten Island Bridges/New Jersey Marine Terminals command. In April 2000 she became one of only two female captains in the Port Authority. There are twelve male captains.

In 1992 she had open-heart surgery to correct a quarter-size hole. A year later, she saved her mother's life by recognizing what her mother's chest pains meant—that her arteries were blocked.

During her career with the Port Authority, she supervised the agency's first-aid programs and certified first responder and EMT training. She also taught emergency medical service programs at the Port Authority Police Academy. In 1999 the Regional Emergency Medical Services Council of New York City named Captain Mazza its Basic Life Support Provider of the Year based on her work on the use of portable heart defibrillators. The training program she initiated in 1997 for six hundred officers to use defibrillators in airports has saved at least thirteen lives.

Captain Mazza was married to Christopher Delosh for sixteen years. Delosh is an NYPD officer serving at the 25th Precinct. At a memorial service for emergency service workers, Mayor Giuliani said of Mazza, as reported by the *New York Post:* "She was a trailblazer with a career that was truly unique. She had an incredible desire to help people. She's an American hero."

OFFICER DONALD McINTYRE
PATH Station

Officer Donald McIntyre, thirty-nine, was outside Two World Trade Center, the South Tower, on September 11, but he and four other officers went back in. McIntyre was last seen on the thirty-second floor and climbing, hoping to find his cousin's husband, John Sherry, a EuroBrokers trader. He had time to call his friend Officer Paul Nunziato and leave him a message that two planes had crashed into the World Trade Center and to call the police desk. Nunziato was already on a bus with thirty other officers heading to the Holland Tunnel.

McIntyre is survived by his wife, Jeannine, and their children, Caitlyn, five, Donald, Jr., three, and a baby girl born in December 2001. A devoted father, he had planned to take the month of December off for paternity leave. He played an active role at home, cooking dinner most nights, running errands, and shopping for his children's clothes. He also planned to join the Parent-Teacher Association.

The only son of a New York City cop, McIntyre earned numerous citations in his fourteen years with the Port Authority.

OFFICER WALTER McNEIL
Holland Tunnel

Officer Walter McNeil, fifty-three, a police officer and hazardous materials specialist, was called to the World Trade Center just after the first plane hit. He phoned his family to tell them where he was going and said he'd call again later. He was last seen setting up a command post before the second plane hit and was heard telling a coworker to be careful.

McNeil was born in New York City. After graduating from high school, he became a first sergeant in the U.S. Army and served in Vietnam. The decorated veteran left the Army in 1976. He then served in the Army Reserve during Desert Storm. He was recognized for his military service by the New Jersey 369th Veterans' Association and the Port Authority, and in 1991 he was presented with a flag that had flown over the Holland Tunnel's plaza. He was honorably discharged in 1996.

McNeil started his career with the Port Authority thirty-one years ago. He was a facilities operations agent before he became a cop in 1979. A veteran of the 1993 bombing, he had planned to retire in August 2002. He was typically seen outside the Holland Tunnel in Jersey City, where he directed traffic and inspected vehicles for hazardous materials. The area he patrolled became known as "McNeil's Corner" to his coworkers. The twenty-five-year service plaque that was awarded him in 1995 depicted the Twin Towers.

McNeil volunteered at a Jersey City battered women's shelter called Hope House. He was also a member of the New Jersey State Policemen's Benevolent Association Local 116, the Port Authority Police Benevolent Association, and the Port Authority Service Club.

McNeil lived with Sonia Rodriguez and their son, Walter, Jr., in Middle Smithfield Township, Pennsylvania. He also had a grown daughter, Kim, from a previous marriage.

SUPERINTENDENT OF POLICE FRED MORRONE
World Trade Center

Fred Morrone, superintendent of police, was not in his World Trade Center office on September 11 but in a New Jersey office. But after the first plane hit, he got into a car and drove to the Twin Towers. He was last seen near the forty-fifth floor of One World Trade Center, the first building that was hit. Port Authority employees evacuating their offices on the sixty-sixth and sixty-seventh floors said they passed Morrone as he was heading up, offering encouragement and help to everyone he encountered.

Superintendent Morrone was sixty-three years old. He was born in Brooklyn, raised in Rocky Hill, New Jersey, and earned a bachelor's degree in Political Science and a master's in Public Administration. His first law enforcement job was with the Franklin Township (New Jersey) Police Department. After that, he became a New Jersey State Trooper. One of his colleagues said he was a tough investigator and would never give up on a case. After Morrone was promoted to lieutenant colonel, he was in charge of the intelligence services and casino gaming sections. One of his last cases as a state trooper was the 1993 bombing of the World Trade Center, where he and three dozen other troopers were assigned to help the FBI. He retired from the state troopers in 1993.

Three years later, Morrone joined the Port Authority. He is credited with starting many programs such as the Port Authority Police Academy's residential training program, the International School of Airport and Seaport Security, bike patrols at the airports, a scuba team, a Commercial Vehicle Inspection Unit, an Airborne Services Unit, and a Motorcycle Unit. He also toughened training standards for recruits.

Morrone was a member of the terrorism subcommittee of the International Association of Chiefs of Police and the vice president of the International Association of Airport and Seaport Police. He was on the board of directors for the New Jersey Special Olympics and on Seton Hall University's Board of Advisors for the New Jersey State Police Graduate Studies Program.

A Lakewood, New Jersey, resident, Superintendent Morrone is survived by his wife, Linda, their three children, Fred, Alyssa, and Gregory, and two grandchildren.

OFFICER JOSEPH NAVAS
ESU, Journal Square (New Jersey) PATH Station

Joseph Navas, forty-four, enjoyed his high-risk, four-days on, two-days off job with the Port Authority. A twenty-year veteran officer, he had been with the Port Authority's ESU for seven years. He trained for specialized jobs in rescue diving, confined space rappelling, and chemical and biological counterterrorism. He worked out of the Journal Square PATH station in New Jersey.

Port Authority Officer Eric Bulger said he watched Navas lead other ESU officers into the North Tower: "It was like the Marines coming to the rescue," he told *Newsday*. Navas's last transmission was from the basement.

Karen, his wife of fifteen years, said he was a true family man. He enjoyed playing with his three children, Jessica, twelve, Joseph, nine, and Justin, three. He coached Joseph's Little League team as well as an ice hockey team. When he was off during the week, he drove the kids to school and sometimes had lunch with them.

Navas, the son of a retired maintenance supervisor for the Port Authority, seldom talked about his job. It was through the newspaper that his family learned about his involvement in a May 1999 incident in which he was part of an operation to prevent a man from jumping off a George Washington Bridge support tower. Navas dangled out of a door and was able to grab the man after he leaped onto another rescuer standing on a ledge below. At the time, Navas said, "You want to save people, but you also want to get home to your family."

OFFICER JAMES NELSON
Port Authority Police Academy, Jersey City (New Jersey)

"When I go out of this world, I want to know I made a difference," Officer James Nelson, forty, told his wife, Roseanne, as reported in *The Star-Ledger*. He refused to leave while others were inside the Twin Towers, a coworker later told his family. He was evacuating people from the twenty-seventh floor of one of the Twin Towers when it collapsed.

Officer Nelson was the youngest of three children. He grew up in Centereach, New York. He received a full fencing scholarship to St. John's

University in Queens and graduated with a bachelor's degree in Criminal Justice in 1983. He later attended Seton Hall University in South Orange, New Jersey, as a graduate student.

He enrolled in the Port Authority Police Academy in 1984. During the 1993 World Trade Center bombing, he was involved in the rescue operation. "He thought he was going to work crowd control," his wife told *Newsday*. "But they sent him inside to help out with the rescue operation. He was glad he could help." Officer Nelson taught at the Port Authority Police Academy in Jersey City and was there on the morning of September 11.

His family always came first, though. He volunteered to coach his daughter Anne's soccer team and was looking forward to doing the same for his other daughter, Caitlin, when she was old enough to play.

OFFICER ALFONSE NIEDERMEYER III
Commercial Vehicle Inspection Unit, Tech Center

Officer Alfonse Niedermeyer, a sixteen-year veteran of the Port Authority, knew about disasters. He was the recipient of a special citation for his role in rescuing passengers from US Air flight 405 when it skidded off a runway at LaGuardia Airport. His former coworker, retired Port Authority Officer Robert Fischer, called him "a born rescuer," reported the *New York Times*.

Officer Niedermeyer, forty, the son of a retired Port Authority operations supervisor, went to school in Bayside, Queens. He graduated from the University of Dayton, Ohio, in 1983 and in 2000 earned an M.A.E. from Seton Hall University in New Jersey.

On September 11, Niedermeyer had just gotten back from a two-week vacation and was back to his job with the Commercial Vehicle Inspection Unit. He rushed to the South Tower to assist with the rescue effort.

He and his wife, Nancy, lived in Manasquan, New Jersey, with their son, A.J.

OFFICER JAMES PARHAM
Port Authority Police Academy, Jersey City (New Jersey)

Officer James Parham received a promotion from police officer to Port Authority academy instructor shortly before he disappeared on September 11. The certified fitness instructor taught defensive tactics and other subjects at the academy. He would have celebrated his thirty-third birthday on September 13.

Parham was born in Brooklyn. His younger brother, Kevin, remembers him as a prankster. Parham graduated from New Utrecht High School in Brooklyn and attended Central Texas College in Killeen, Texas. He worked for the Texas Department of Corrections and the Federal Bureau of Prisons before joining the Port Authority.

A former U.S. Marine, Parham is survived by his wife, Mutsuko, and his daughter, three-year-old Resa.

OFFICER DOMINICK PEZZULO
Port Authority Bus Terminal

Officer Dominick Pezzulo, thirty-six, commandeered a city bus to get to the World Trade Center disaster. He and four other PA officers, Sergeant John McLoughlin and Officers Will Jimeno, Antonio Rodrigues, and Christopher Amoroso, had just collected rescue gear from a security closet and were heading toward a freight elevator when the South Tower was hit by the second plane. The men were trapped by the debris from the collapsed concourse. After Pezzulo freed himself from the debris, he freed McLoughlin, who was badly injured. He had just started moving the concrete that was trapping Jimeno when the South Tower collapsed. Officers Jimeno and Sergeant McLoughlin were the only men rescued out of the group of five.

Before joining the Port Authority, Pezzulo taught shop at Herbert Lehman High School in the Bronx and fixed airplanes for TWA. He had only been with the Port Authority about eighteen months. A resident of the Bronx, he leaves behind his wife, Jeanette, and two children, Dominick, Jr., seven, and Gianni, four.

OFFICER BRUCE REYNOLDS
George Washington Bridge

Officer Bruce Reynolds, forty-one, joined the Port Authority Police in June 1986. His partner of fifteen years, George Hickmann, told *The Star-Ledger* that Reynolds "was a good cop. . . . If you could exemplify the qualities you'd want in a police officer, he was it."

Reynolds grew up in the Inwood section of Manhattan. As a teenager, he had a keen interest in the neighborhood garden and spent hours tending the spectacular array of roses, evergreens, mums, and violets. He studied advertising and communications at the Fashion Institute of Technology. He then became a ranger in the city parks. After he joined the Port Authority in 1986, he was stationed at the bus terminal on 42nd Street. It was there he got to know Officer Michael Barry who later worked with him at the George Washington Bridge. A formidable team when it came to drug arrests, the two of them were together for thirteen years. Barry had the task of filing the missing person report for Reynolds.

On September 11, Officer Reynolds was sent to the Twin Towers from his post at the George Washington Bridge. Though he had respiratory problems, he went into the South Tower to help with the rescue effort.

On the day of his funeral, the upper deck of the George Washington Bridge was closed in both directions for about five minutes as the hearse drove slowly to New Jersey. When the caravan of two motorcycles and ten cruisers stopped at the Bridge Plaza South command post, a bagpiper played and the officers saluted.

Reynolds married his wife, Marian, who was from County Donegal in Ireland, in 1993. They enjoyed frequent trips to Donegal, where Reynolds was well respected by his in-laws. He enjoyed living in Knowlton, New Jersey, where he could pursue his interests of gardening and fishing. He is survived by Marian and their children, Brianna, four, and Michael, one.

OFFICER ANTONIO RODRIGUES
Port Authority Bus Terminal

Officer Antonio Rodrigues, thirty-five, was in the basement of the World Trade Center picking up oxygen tanks before the towers collapsed on September 11. He was working at the Port Authority Bus Terminal near Times Square and was with fourteen other officers who commandeered a commuter bus to get to the World Trade Center.

Rodrigues grew up in a coastal town in Portugal. At the age of eleven or twelve—before he emigrated with his family to the United States—he had several exhibits of the landscapes he painted. He was trained as an aeronautical engineer but became a police officer because he liked working with people. Before he became a Port Authority police officer, he was a transit worker with the NYPD.

At his memorial service, Deputy Mayor Anthony Coles said that Rodrigues "met the worst of humanity with the best of what America had to offer." Rodrigues leaves behind his wife, Cristina, and their two children, Sara, seven, and Adam, four.

OFFICER RICHARD RODRIGUEZ
Port Authority Police Academy, Jersey City (New Jersey)

Officer Richard Rodriguez, thirty-one, was hired by the Port Authority Police Department in April 1993. A drummer in the Port Authority Emerald Society Pipes and Drums, he went to the Twin Towers on September 11 with Captain Kathy Mazza. Neither one returned.

Rodriguez was born in Perth Amboy, New Jersey. He graduated from Perth Amboy Vocational Technical High School and attended Middlesex County Community College in New Jersey. Though he studied technical drafting at school, he found an interest in public service while volunteering with the first-aid squad in Perth Amboy. He told people he knew he'd won the lottery when he was offered a position with the Port Authority eight years ago.

His first assignment at the Port Authority was in the tactical response bureau, where he trained for special duty to protect the U.S. President at Newark International Airport. Three years ago, he became an instructor at the Police Academy, where he taught patrol operations, motor vehicle stops, water rescue, emergency vehicle operation, and radio procedures. He also coordinated the installation of and training on mobile video cameras.

Officer Rodriguez is survived by his wife, Cindy.

POLICE CHIEF JAMES ROMITO
World Trade Center

"I have to save people," Port Authority Police Chief James Romito told his fiancée, Mary, during their last phone conversation, as reported by *The Star-Ledger*. He went up to the twenty-seventh floor of the North Tower and was supervising rescue workers who were trying to find survivors. He sent some officers outside for first-aid supplies. As the floors above them began to cave in, he ordered personnel to retreat. A colleague said that Chief Romito turned back from a clear stairwell to go back for a group of firefighters. He was found burned under the rubble with colleagues Officers James Parham and Stephen Huczko, Lieutenant Robert Cirri, and Captain Kathy Mazza, along with a woman they tried to rescue.

Romito was born in the Bronx. The son of a corrections officer, he graduated from Adelphi University, Garden City, New York, in 1978. He received an M.A.E. in 1998 from Seton Hall University in South Orange, New Jersey, and taught in the school's master's degree law enforcement program.

Chief Romito, fifty-one, was most recently the commander of the Port Authority headquarters support team and oversaw emergency operations. Prior to this command, he was chief of the Field Aviation Section for two years and was responsible for Port Authority police operations at JFK, LaGuardia, and Newark Airports. An inspector at the time of the 1996 crash of TWA Flight 800, he helped federal and local authorities coordinate information. He received a commendation for valor for his work in the 1993 World Trade Center bombing.

Earlier in the 1990s, when he was assigned to the Port Authority Bus Terminal, he started "Operation Alternative." Now considered a national model, the program offered safe housing, medical care, and social services to the homeless who made their home at the terminal. Operation Alternative resulted in a dramatic drop in crime. It's been praised by both law enforcement and advocacy groups for the homeless.

Chief Romito was in charge of a Port Authority Bus Terminal community policing plan. He was also a member of various associations, including the International Association of Ports and Harbors, the International Association of Chiefs of Police, and the American Association of Airport Executives.

Romito lost his son, Robert, in a car accident in early 2001. He is survived by his daughter, Ellen.

OFFICER JOHN SKALA
Lincoln Tunnel

Officer John Skala, known as "Yash" to his friends, enjoyed making people laugh and being with his friends. Well known for his humor and hospitality, his annual Christmas party was open to everyone.

Skala was called to the World Trade Center on September 11 and was lost when the buildings collapsed.

Born in Passaic, New Jersey, Skala graduated from Clifton High School in Clifton, New Jersey. He attended Metro Technological Institute in Fairfield, New Jersey, and the New Jersey Institute of Technology in Newark.

The thirty-one-year-old Clifton resident was an eight-year veteran of the Port Authority. He was the recipient of two Meritorious Duty Medals for exemplary police actions. A hard worker, he was also a paramedic for the Clifton/Passaic Ambulance Corps as well as a volunteer for the New Jersey Special Olympics and the Juvenile Diabetes Foundation. Skala was a member of the New Jersey Honor Legion, a police organization whose membership is limited to those who have performed heroic acts.

OFFICER WALWYN STUART
World Trade Center PATH Station

Officer Walwyn Stuart was at his PATH station post in the World Trade Center on September 11. After the attack began, he got a trainload of people to return to New Jersey, then evacuated the station. He then went into the North Tower to participate in the rescue effort. His wife, Thelma, called his office when she learned about the attacks and was told that he was safe. She never saw him again.

At the memorial service on October 18, 2001, his wife talked about how loving he was and of the life they'd been building in Valley Stream, New York.

Officer Stuart was the youngest of six children growing up in Brooklyn. He enjoyed playing baseball and chess. He attended the State University of New York–Stony Brook for two years before joining the NYPD, working out of the 88th Precinct in Brooklyn and earning commendations during his two years there. For the next year and a half, he worked undercover in the Narcotics Division of the Organized Crime Control Bureau. After being promoted to detective, he continued to work undercover. He joined the Port Authority Police Department when he learned that his wife was pregnant. His daughter, Amanda, celebrated her first birthday on September 28, 2001.

OFFICER KENNETH TIETJEN
33rd Street PATH Station

Kenneth Tietjen, thirty-one, was at the 33rd Street PATH station on September 11. When he got word of the attack, he commandeered a taxi, then got into an emergency vehicle and went to the World Trade Center. He evacuated people, some of whom were badly burned, from the North Tower. He then took the last respirator before running into the South Tower, which collapsed moments later.

Tietjen volunteered for the Belford Engine Company when he was eighteen. A Port Authority police officer for nine years, he received a commendation for bravery in 2001 when he tackled a man who'd stabbed the sergeant he was working with. In 1996 he received a special commendation when he subdued a man who'd stabbed a police officer after ramming a patrol car in the Holland Tunnel. When he perished, he had almost completed his training to become a member of the ESU.

He was engaged to be married.

OFFICER NATHANIEL WEBB
Holland Tunnel

Officer Nathaniel Webb, fifty-seven, was last seen at roll call on September 11. He was one of three Port Authority officers assigned to the Holland Tunnel who were killed that day. A Port Authority officer for twenty-eight years, Webb was considered a generous and righteous man by his friends and colleagues. He was the recipient of a Meritorious Active Duty Award and a Police Group Citation.

Devoted to family, Officer Webb visited his housebound mother several times a week. He was dedicated to his two daughters, Camille, twenty-three, and Valerie, twelve. At the March 11, 2002, ceremony to dedicate the "Tribute in Light," Valerie was chosen to illuminate the two banks of forty-four spotlights that were in honor of those who'd lost their lives.

OFFICER MICHAEL WHOLEY
World Trade Center PATH Station

Officer Michael Wholey, thirty-four, was hired by the Port Authority Police Department in April 1993. He was assigned to the World Trade Center PATH station as an escort officer.

Wholey grew up in New City, New York, with his three sisters and one brother. He earned a bachelor's degree in political science at the State University of New York at Albany and was a service department assistant manager before he joined the Port Authority.

A fisherman and golfer, Wholey, a Westwood, New Jersey, resident, enjoyed spending time with his wife, Jennifer, and their children, Meagan, eight, Erin, five, and Patrick, four.

K-9 SIRIUS
World Trade Center

On September 11, Officer Dave Lim and his four-and-a-half-year-old yellow Labrador retriever, Sirius, were in the Port Authority's basement office of the South Tower. The ninety-pound canine was getting ready for his job: searching trucks that entered the World Trade Center for explosives. Their day was starting out just like any other when they heard an explosion above them.

Officer Lim did not know what happened, but it sounded as if a bomb had gone off. "One [bomb] must have gotten by us," he told Sirius as he put him in his kennel.

Lim ran over to the North Tower. As he ran up the stairway, he told the people who were coming down that "down is good." When he reached the forty-fourth floor, he watched the second plane hit from the windows in the sky lobby. He started back down, searching from floor to floor, until he reached Chinatown's Ladder 6 rescue of Joanne Harris, who would later be known as the Guardian Angel of Ladder 6. Just then, the building collapsed and he and the others ended up at about the fifth level.

Smelling jet fuel, they went up to what was now the top of the North Tower, the sixth floor. As they made their way across the debris with the aid of ropes, they could hear the ammunition that was in storage being detonated by the fire.

Lim tried to find a way to the South Tower basement to rescue Sirius but the firemen and officers who were securing the scene and setting up rescue operations would not let him search because it was too dangerous.

Officer Lim had joined the United States Police Canine Association only a few months before the attack and had participated in certification trials.

Of K-9 Sirius, Officer Lim told me: "This dog had everything. Good-looking, great disposition, and a great explosive detector too."

On April 24, 2002, more than two hundred people and K-9 Units gathered at Liberty State Park in Jersey City, New Jersey, to honor K-9 Sirius. The tribute included the playing of bagpipes, a twenty-one-gun salute, and a procession of K-9 teams.

A twenty-one-year veteran of the Port Authority Police, Officer Lim now has a new partner, K-9 Sprig, a black Labrador retriever who has also been trained to detect explosives. They are assigned to the Holland and Lincoln Tunnels.

Inscribed on the east wall of the National Law Enforcement Officers Memorial in Washington, D.C., is a brief phrase by Tacitus that epitomizes the sacrifices made by the fallen heroes at the World Trade Center on September 11: "In valor there is hope."

Christopher Amoroso

Maurice Barry

Liam Callahan

Robert Cirri

Clinton Davis

Donald Foreman

Gregg Froehner

Thomas Gorman

Uhuru Houston

George Howard

Stephen Huczko

Anthony Infante, Jr.

Paul William Jurgens

Robert Kaulfers

Paul Laszczynski

David Lemagne

John Lennon

John Levi

James F. Lynch

Kathy Mazza

Donald McIntyre

Walter McNeil

Fred Morrone

Joseph Navas

James Nelson

Alfonse Niedermeyer III

James Parham

Dominick Pezzulo

Bruce Reynolds

Antonio Rodrigues

Richard Rodriguez

James Romito

John Skala

Walwyn Stuart

Kenneth Tietjen

Nathaniel Webb

Michael Wholey

K-9 Sirius

✷ Bibliography ✷

Abadjian, Nick, et al. "Police Rescue Unit 10 Loses Three, Missing Five." *SE Queens Press*, 21–27 September 2001. http://www.queenspress.com/archives/coverstories/2001/issue38/coverstory.htm.

"Alaska Department of Public Safety." www.dps.state.ak.us/.

Alaska State Troopers. "History of the Alaska State Troopers." www.dps.state.ak.us/ast/trooperhistory/index.htm.

——. "Trooper to Receive 'Top Cop' Award." Press release, 9 August 1999.

Amos, Deborah. "Police Chase Psychology: Trying to Stop a Deadly Practice." ABCNEWS.com, 13 July 2000. www.abcnews.go.com/onair/CloserLook/wnt00713_CL_policechase_feature.html.

Anna Maria College, Mortell Institute for Public Safety. www.annamaria.edu/other/Mortell_Institute/.

Anthony, Stavros. *Nights of Fire: Civil Unrest April 30–May 25, 1992 Las Vegas, Nevada.* Las Vegas Metropolitan Police Department, 1993.

Arizona Daily Star, 19 May 1991–31 March 2001.

Asbury Park (New Jersey) *Press,* 31 October 2001.

"Atlas' Special Dedication. Police Service Dogs Killed in Action. Valor page." Eden & Ney Associates. www.policek9.com/Valor/atlas/body_atlas.html.

"Basic Facts About Schizophrenia." http://health.yahoo.com/health/diseases_and_conditions/disease_feed_data/schizophrenia.

Boca Raton (Florida) *News,* 3 February–5 February 2000.

Boling, Rick. "A Cop's Best Friend," *Animals* 131, no. 4 (July–August 1998): 33.

Bonholtzer, Craig and Suzanne. "Electronic Newsgathering: The Unfriendly Skies." *Aviation Today,* June 2000. www.aviationtoday.com/reports/rotorwing/previous/0600/06electronic.htm.

Bucher, Paul. Letter to Chuck Whitlock, Waukesha County Office of District Attorney, 16 April 2001.

Chicago (Illinois) *Tribune,* 31 October 1998.

Chu, Dan. "Recycled as Cyclists, Seattle's Posse of Bike-Riding Crime Fighters Put Their Mettle to the Pedal." *People Weekly* 28, no. 19, 9 November 1987: 53.

City of Tacoma Police Department. Award of Merit to Daniell Griswold.

———. Award of Merit to Mark Feddersen.

———. Award of Merit to Gary Lock.

Coast Star (New Jersey), 27 September 2001.

Columbian (Clark County: Washington), 19 October 1997–1 July 1998.

"Con Games: Personal Stories Paul Ragonese." http://home.earthlink.net/~pdpictures/ragonese.html.

Corcoran, Joseph J. "DEA Congressional Testimony Before the House Judiciary Subcommittee on Crime." U.S. Department of Justice, Drug Enforcement Administration, 8 August 2000. www.dea.gov/pubs/cngrtest/ct080800.htm.

Daily News (New York), 15 September 2001–24 March 2002.

Dale, Steve. "To the Rescue: Canine Heroes Work Tirelessly in the Wake of Terror." *Dog World,* December 2001, 20–22.

"David P. Lemagne: In Memory of a Hero!" University Hospital Emergency Medical Service (EMS). http://www.uh-ems.org/news/dplmemorial.htm.

"DEA Factsheet." U.S. Department of Justice, Drug Enforcement Administration, October 2000. www.dea.gov/pubs/factsheet/fact1000.htm.

"Domestic Violence Against Women and Girls." *Innocenti Digest* 6 May 2000. Preliminary edition.

Eden, R. S. "Point of View—Administration of the K-9 Unit." www.policek9.com/Trainers_Digest/k9admin/body_k9admin.html.

"18th District Sergeant Receives TOP COP Award." Chicago Police Department, 4 November 1999. http://w6.ci.chi.il.us/cp/AboutCAPS/SuccessStories/Dist18.99.11.html

Eisenberg, Clyde, and Cynthia Fitzpatrick. "Police Practice: An Alternative to Police Pursuits." *FBI Law Enforcement Bulletin,* August 1996. www.fbi.gov/publications/leb/1996/aug964.txt.

Evans, Albert S. "A Cruise on the Barbary Coast." In *A La California: Sketch of Life in the Golden State.* San Francisco: A. L. Bancroft, 1873. www.sfmuseum.org/hist6/evans/html.

"Fact Sheet." *Commonwealth Fund 1998 Survey of Women's Health,* May 1999. www.cmwf.org/programs/women/ksc_whsurvey99_fact4_332.asp.

Fairbanks (Alaska) *Daily News-Miner,* 9 September 1998–13 August 1999.

"Federal Animal Partners Gain Protection." *Insight on the News* 16, no. 31, 21 August 2000: 35.

"The Fire: The Oakland/Berkeley Hills Fire Response." *Wildland Firefighter Information.* www.firewise.org/pubs/theOaklandBerkeleyHillsFire/response.

Franks, Steve. "Recommendation for Commendation." Las Vegas Metropolitan Police Department, 5 June 1992.

"Galena Alaska Resource Guide, City of Galena, Alaska Facts and Information." www.pe.net/~rksnow/akcountygalena.htm.

Gaudiano, Nicole. "Bridge Deck Closed in Tribute to 9/11 Victim." NorthJersey. com, 17 March 2002. www.portauthoritypolicememorial.org/Reynolds_ additional_information.htm.

"The Guardians of the Night." California Peace Officers' Memorial. www.camemorial.org/k-9.htm.

Hanson, Steven J., Sr. "My Brother, the Hero." *The Copperhead.* Arizona Air National Guard, Phoenix, July 1997.

Herman, Michele, et al. "Police on Bicycles." In *The Electronic Bicycle Blueprint.* www.transalt.org/blueprint/chapter16/chapter16c.html.

Hess, Russ. "One Got By Us." United States Police Canine Association. www.uspcak9.com/html/wtc.shtml.

"History of SWAT." *LA SWAT GEAR.* www.laswatgear.com/swat_history.htm.

"In Memory: P. O. Stephen Driscoll." NYPD Emerald Society Pipes & Drums. http://nypdpipesanddrums.com/html/driscoll.html.

International Police Mountain Bike Association. "The Results are In!" www.ipmba.org/newsletter-0106-survey.htm.

———. "Frequently Asked Questions." www.ipmba.org/factsheet.htm.

Jersey Journal (New Jersey), 4 October 2001.

"Joseph Vigiano, Emergency Services Unit, Truck 2, Manhattan, 'Now He's Protecting Heaven.' " *The Gold Shield,* December 2001. www.nycdetectives.org/ vigiano.html.

The Journal News (New York), 23 October 2001.

"K-9's Mourners Say Final 'Good Dog.' Friday, March 31, 2000. Memorials to Fallen K-9s 2000, K-9 Cero." www.members.dandy.net/~lulu//memorial2.html.

Kraska, Peter B. "SWAT in the Commonwealth: Trends and Issues in Paramilitary Policing." *Kentucky Justice and Safety Research Bulletin,* June 1999. www.len. eku.edu/Kjsrb/June99.html.

Lake Country (Wisconsin) *Reporter,* 8 March 1988–22 June 1993.

Lamb, Ed. "Meritorious Achievement." Interoffice memorandum to G. C. Smith, Assistant Chief of Police, Uniform Services Division, City of Shreveport, 15 May 2000.

"Las Vegas Cop Gambles and Wins: IACP/*PARADE* Honors Survivor of Fierce Gunfight with Armed Robber." *Law Enforcement News,* 30 November 2000. www.lib.jjay.cuny.edu/len/2000/11.30/p&p.html.

Las Vegas (Nevada) *Review-Journal,* 17 July–31 October 2000.

Las Vegas (Nevada) *Sun,* 30 April 1997–16 March 2000.

"Las Vegas Police Officer Named 2000 Police Officer of the Year." IACP Awards and Campaigns. www.theiacp.org/awards/awards/poloff/2000poloffyr.htm.

Leonhart, Michele M. "DEA Congressional Testimony Before the House Judiciary Subcommittee on Crime." U.S. Department of Justice, Drug Enforcement Administration, 6 July 2000. www.dea.gov/pubs/cngrtest/ct070600_02.htm.

Los Angeles Times, 5 August 1989–1 November 1991.

Maltin, Leonard, ed. *Leonard Maltin's 2001 Movie and Video Guide.* New York: New American Library, 2000.

"Manuel Tarango Jr." *America's Most Wanted*, 19 August 2000. www.amw.com/site/thisweek/tarangojrmanuel20000819.htm.

Marshall, Donnie R. "DEA Congressional Testimony Before the Senate Judiciary Committee." U.S. Department of Justice, Drug Enforcement Administration, 6 July 2000. www.dea.gov/pubs/cngrtest/ct070600_01.htm.

"Mayor Michael R. Bloomberg, Governor George E. Pataki and Former Mayor Rudolph W. Giuliani Dedicate the 'Tribute in Light,'" Press release 052–02, www.nyc.gov.

"Medal of Valor." Las Vegas Metropolitan Police Department. www.lvmpd.com/information/infaward_medal_valor.htm.

"Methamphetamine." U.S. Department of Justice, Drug Enforcement Administration. www.dea/gov/concern/meth.htm.

Miami (Florida) *Herald*, 31 October–1 November 2000.

Milwaukee (Wisconsin) *Journal*, Waukesha County edition, 3 March 1988–5 May 1994.

Milwaukee (Wisconsin) *Sentinel*, 4 March 1988–17 June 1993.

National Association of Police Organizations. "Member of Clark County Sheriff's Office Recognized with Prestigious National Award: Honorable Mention Award Winner, Fifth Annual TOP COPS Awards." Press release, 1 October 1998.

———. "1997 TOP COPS Award Winners: Pennsylvania, Pittsburgh Police Department, Police Officer John Joseph Wilbur." www.napo.org/napo5c.htm.

"National Association of Police Organizations Top Cops: Arizona, Pima County Sheriff's Department." www.crime.com/info/top_cops/pop_topcops_ az.html.

"National Association of Police Organizations Top Cops: Nevada, Las Vegas Metropolitan Police Department." www.crime.com/info/top_cops/pop_topcops_nv_winner.html.

National Law Enforcement Officers Memorial Fund. "In the Line of Duty: Police Pursuits Prove Deadly," 7 October 1997. www.nleomf.com/News/Lineof Duty/pursuitsOct97.htm.

————. "Police Facts and Figures." www.nleomf.com/FactsFigures/.

————. "Year by Year Deaths." www.nleomf.com/FactsFigures/yeardeaths.html.

"News Articles." www.roadspike.com/news.htm.

Newsday (New York), 12 September 2001–5 May 2002.

New York Post, 16 September–24 December 2001.

New York Times, 29 April 1999–3 May 2002.

North American Police Work Dog Association. "K-9 Cero." K-9 Valor Pages. www.napwda.com/valor/.

————. "K-9 Sevo." K-9 Valor Pages. www.napwda.com/valor/.

"The Oakland Firestorm and a History of Fire in the East Bay." University of California at Berkeley. www5.ced.Berkeley.edu:8005/aegis/home/projects/eastbay/shist/htm.

Oakland Police Department. "John Grubensky." Press release, 20 October 1991.

O'Connor, Tom. "Megalinks in Criminal Justice: Police Structure and Organization." North Carolina Wesleyan College. www.faculty.ncwc.edu/toconnor/polstruct.htm.

O'Neill, Patrick. "Garner Woman Mourns Brother Lost in World Trade Center Disaster." *NC Catholic,* 7 October 2001. http://raldioc.org/nccatholic/10072001/garner_ez.htm.

"On Your Bike: Technology and the Police (American Survey)." *The Economist* 329, no. 7831, 2 October 1993: A28.

Oregonian, 18 October 1997–5 May 1998.

O'Shea, Michael. " 'If He Hadn't Believed Me, I Would Be Dead.' " *PARADE,* 31 October 1999, 10, 12.

Palm Beach (Florida) *Post,* 4 February 2000.

Parenti, Christian. "War on Crime." *San Francisco Bay Guardian,* 18 November 1998. www.sfbg.com/News/33/07Features/cops/html.

Parker, Donald R. "The Oakland-Berkeley Hills Fire: An Overview." Museum of the City of San Francisco, January 1992. www.sfmuseum.org/oakfire/overview.html

Pasenelli, Burdena G. Letter to Sheriff Garry E. Lucas, Clark County Sheriff's Office, 20 January 1998.

Petracca, Mark J. "The Pedal-Pushing Patrol." *Women's Sports and Fitness* 18, no. 7, October 1996: 23.

Pittsburgh (Pennsylvania) *Post-Gazette,* 3 July 1996–3 August 2001.

Pittsburgh (Pennsylvania) *Tribune-Review,* 27 June 1996–10 October 1997.

Plichta, Stacy B., and Marilyn Falik. "Prevalence of Domestic Violence." *Women's Health Issues* 11, no. 3, May/June 2001: 244–58. National Council on Child Abuse and Family Violence. http:/nccafv.org/.

Pocono (Pennsylvania) *Record*, 17 September–5 November 2001.

"Police Officer Michael T. Wholey." Port Authority Police Memorial, Additional Information and Press Clippings. http://www.portauthoritymemorial.org/wholey_additional_information.htm.

"Police Officer Nathaniel Webb." Port Authority Police Memorial, Additional Information and Press Clippings. http://www.portauthoritymemorial.org/webb_additional_information.htm.

Portland (Maine) *Press Herald*, 18 September 1999–26 August 2000.

Presentation Remarks, Introduction Speech and Valor Award Speech. Idaho State Police.

Proctor, Pam. "He Said, 'Follow Me.'" *PARADE*, 17 October 1993, 22.

"Quick Reflexes, Agile Minds Fight Clark County Crime." *656 Square: Clark County*, January 1998: 10–11.

Ragonese, Paul, and Berry Stainback. *The Soul of a Cop*. New York: St. Martin's Press, 1991.

Rasmussen, Eric. "Legacies of Courage." NurseWeek.com, 25 February 2002. www.nurseweek.com/news/features/02–020courage_print.html.

The Record (New Jersey), 26 May 1999–1 December 2001.

"Remarks by Robert S. Mueller III, Director, Federal Bureau of Investigation, at the Funeral Mass of FBI Special Agent Leonard W. Hatton, Ridgefield Park, New Jersey September 29, 2001." FBI, Major Speeches. http://www.fbi/gov.pressrel/speeches/funeral.htm.

"Remembering Sirius: A K-9 Memorial Service." http://our.homewithgod/mkcathy/sirius2.html.

Riley, Brian A. "Unit Letter of Recognition," Memorandum to James Anglemier, 21 March 1986.

Salem (Oregon) *Statesman-Journal*, 12 February–30 June 1988.

Schacht, James. Letter to Lt. Thomas C. Strickland, Tacoma Police Department, 19 October 1999.

Scott, Chief Andrew J., III. "Police Officer of the Year–2000: Officer Paul Holland." Boca Raton Police Services Department.

"Sgt. Rory Tuggle." *The Training Wheel: The Training Journal of the Las Vegas Metropolitan Police Department*, January-February 1994: 3.

Shreveport (Louisiana) *Times*, 15 April–2 November 2000.

Smith, Dennis. *Report from Ground Zero: The Story of the Rescue Efforts at the World Trade Center*. New York: Viking, 2002.

Spokane (Washington) *Spokesman-Review*, 8 December 1999–21 November 2000.

Star-Ledger, The (New Jersey), 29 November 1999–14 February 2002.

State of Oregon v Kelly Ray Kaighin. Marion County Circuit Court, Case No. 86-C-20372. 28 June 1988.

State of Washington v Ronald Jay Bianchi. Statement of Defendant on Plea of Guilty. Clark County Superior Court, No. 97-1-01674-6. 4 May 1998.

State of Wisconsin v Alfredo H. Camacho. Criminal Complaint. Waukesha County Circuit Court, Criminal-Traffic Division. Subscribed and sworn on 4 March 1988.

State of Wisconsin v Alfredo H. Camacho. Supreme Court. Review of a decision of the Court of Appeals. Reversed. No. 91-0770-CR. Filed 16 Jun 1993.

Staten Island (New York) *Advance,* 1 October 2001–23 October 2001.

Sun-Sentinel South Florida, 3–4 February 2000.

"Synopsis of Events: Award Nomination for Exceptional Kansas Law Enforcement Performance During 2000." Kansas Highway Patrol, 9 January 2001.

Topeka (Kansas) *Capital-Journal,* 25 September 1998–15 June 1999.

"U.S. Fire Administration Combats Nation's Arson Problem." *EmergencyNet NEWS Service-ENN DAILY REPORT* 2-126, 5 May 1996. www.emergency.com/arsonrpt.htm.

"U.S. Secret Service Employee Missing After Attacks on World Trade Center." U.S. Secret Service Press Release Pub. 09–01, 21 September 2001.

"United We Stand." New York State Unified Court System. www.courts.state.ny.us/united.pdf.

USA Today, 12 December 2001.

Van Auken, William. "3 Missing in Rubble: Court Officers Lost in Mission at WTC." *The Chief Leader,* 5 October 2001, 1.

Velasquez, Steven. "Bye Dad . . . Port Authority Police Officer Robert Cirri Gave His Life for Others." South Amboy Fire, 15 November 2001. http://SouthAmboyfire.org/events/wtc/cirri/cirri/htm.

Waukesha County (Wisconsin) *Freeman,* 3 March 1988–17 June 1993.

"Welcome to the USPCA." United States Police Canine Association. www.uspcak9.com/html./home.shtml.

Werner, Robby. "Expect Casualties in the War on Crime." Columns and Opinion by Robby Werner, 3 March 2000. www.robbywerner.com/diallo.htm.

Worcester (Massachusetts) *Telegram and Gazette,* 2 February 1994–29 January 1995.

★ Captions and Credits for Photographs ★

John Grubensky, page 1
Courtesy Oakland Police Department

Paul Ragonese, page 9
Courtesy Paul Ragonese

Alexander Petigna and Howard Dickinson, page 17
Courtesy Alexander Petigna and Howard Dickinson and the Kansas Highway Patrol

Barry Croy, page 25
Courtesy Barry Croy and the White House Public Relations Office

Dennis Devitte, page 31
Courtesy Martin LePire Photography

Richard Carmona, M.D., page 37
Courtesy Richard Carmona and NAPO

David Foster, page 43
Courtesy David Foster

Glen McGary and James Sweatt, page 49
Courtesy Portland Police Department

Robert J. Mortell, page 57
Courtesy Paxton Police Department and Chief John L. Hebert, Sutton Police Department

Terry Lawson, page 67
Courtesy Terry Lawson

Daniell Griswold, Mark Feddersen, and Gary Lock, page 79
Courtesy Tacoma Police Department and Daniell Griswold, Mark Feddersen, and Gary Lock

William R. Niemi and K-9 Cero, page 89
Courtesy William R. Niemi and Ashtabula County Sheriff's Department

K-9 Sevo, page 91
Courtesy Scott Gilchrist

William Sterling Johnson and K-9 Atlas, page 94
Courtesy William Sterling Johnson and Robert Eden, Eden & Ney Associates, Inc.

Hilton Henry and Stephen Kehoe, page 97
Courtesy Los Angeles Police Department and Hilton Henry and Stephen Kehoe

William J. Hanson, page 109
Courtesy of Tucson Police Department and William J. Hanson

Rory Tuggle and Andrew Ramos, page 115
Courtesy Rory Tuggle and Andrew Ramos and Las Vegas Metropolitan Police Department

Wayne Longo and Fred Swanson, page 121
Courtesy Wayne Longo and Fred Swanson and the Idaho State Police

Craig Hogman, page 129
Courtesy Craig Hogman

Richard A. Bach, page 137
Courtesy Richard A. Bach and the Waukesha County Sheriff's Department

James Anglemier and Larry Roberts, page 143
Courtesy James Anglemier and the Salem Police Department

John Joseph Wilbur, page 149
Courtesy John Wilbur and The White House Public Relations Office

Paul Holland, page 155
Courtesy Paul Holland and the Boca Raton Police Services Department

Michael Presley, page 161
Courtesy Shreveport Police Department and Michael Presley

Peter Reynolds, page 167
Courtesy Peter Reynolds and the Miami Police Department

James McMullin, page 173
Courtesy James McMullin and NAPO

Mark Cota and Dennis O'Mahony, page 179
Courtesy Mark Cota

Leonard Hatton, page 212
Courtesy Federal Bureau of Investigation

John Coughlin, page 212
Courtesy New York City Police Department

Michael Curtin, page 212
Courtesy New York City Police Department

John D'Allara, page 212
Courtesy New York City Police Department

Vincent Danz, page 212
Courtesy New York City Police Department

Jerome Dominguez, page 212
Courtesy New York City Police Department

Stephen Driscoll, page 212
Courtesy New York City Police Department

Mark Ellis, page 212
Courtesy New York City Police Department

Robert Fazio, page 212
Courtesy New York City Police Department

Rodney Gillis, page 212
Courtesy New York City Police Department

Ronald Kloepfer, page 212
Courtesy New York City Police Department

Thomas Langone, page 212
Courtesy New York City Police Department

James Leahy, page 212
Courtesy New York City Police Department

Brian McDonnell, page 212
Courtesy New York City Police Department

John Perry, page 212
Courtesy New York City Police Department

Glen Pettit, page 212
Courtesy New York City Police Department

Claude Richards, page 212
Courtesy New York City Police Department

Timothy Roy, page 212
Courtesy New York City Police Department

Moira Smith, page 212
Courtesy New York City Police Department

Ramon Suarez, page 212
Courtesy New York City Police Department

Paul Talty, page 213
Courtesy New York City Police Department

Santos Valentin, page 213
Courtesy New York City Police Department

Joseph Vigiano, page 213
Courtesy New York City Police Department

Walter Weaver, page 213
Courtesy New York City Police Department

Thomas Jurgens, page 213
Courtesy Joan Jurgens

William Harry Thompson, page 213
Courtesy Rashaan Thompson and the New York State Office of Court Administration

Mitchel Wallace, page 213
Courtesy Colleen Brescia and the New York State Office of Court Administration

Christopher Amoroso, page 241
Family photo courtesy of the Port Authority PBA Inc.

Maurice Barry, page 241
Family photo courtesy of the Port Authority PBA Inc.

Liam Callahan, page 241
Family photo courtesy of the Port Authority PBA Inc.

Robert Cirri, page 241
Family photo courtesy of the Port Authority PBA Inc.

Clinton Davis, page 241
Family photo courtesy of the Port Authority PBA Inc.

Donald Foreman, page 241
Family photo courtesy of the Port Authority PBA Inc.

Gregg Froehner, page 241
Family photo courtesy of the Port Authority PBA Inc.

Thomas Gorman, page 241
Family photo courtesy of the Port Authority PBA Inc.

Uhuru Houston, page 241
Family photo courtesy of the Port Authority PBA Inc.

George Howard, page 241
Family photo courtesy of the Port Authority PBA Inc.

Stephen Huczko, page 241
Family photo courtesy of the Port Authority PBA Inc.

Anthony Infante, Jr., page 241
Family photo courtesy of the Port Authority PBA Inc.

Paul William Jurgens, page 241
Family photo courtesy of the Port Authority PBA Inc.

Robert Kaulfers, page 241
Family photo courtesy of the Port Authority PBA Inc.

Paul Laszczynski, page 241
Family photo courtesy of the Port Authority PBA Inc.

David Lemagne, page 241
Family photo courtesy of the Port Authority PBA Inc.

John Lennon, page 241
Family photo courtesy of the Port Authority PBA Inc.

John Levi, page 241
Family photo courtesy of the Port Authority PBA Inc.

James F. Lynch, page 241
Family photo courtesy of the Port Authority PBA Inc.

Kathy Mazza, page 241
Family photo courtesy of the Port Authority PBA Inc.

Donald McIntyre, page 242
Family photo courtesy of the Port Authority PBA Inc.

Walter McNeil, page 242
Family photo courtesy of the Port Authority PBA Inc.

Fred Morrone, page 242
Family photo courtesy of the Port Authority PBA Inc.

Joseph Navas, page 242
Family photo courtesy of the Port Authority PBA Inc.

James Nelson, page 242
Family photo courtesy of the Port Authority PBA Inc.

Alfonse Niedermeyer III, page 242
Family photo courtesy of the Port Authority PBA Inc.

James Parham, page 242
Family photo courtesy of the Port Authority PBA Inc.

Dominick Pezzulo, page 242
Family photo courtesy of the Port Authority PBA Inc.

Bruce Reynolds, page 242
Family photo courtesy of the Port Authority PBA Inc.

Antonio Rodrigues, page 242
Family photo courtesy of the Port Authority PBA Inc.

Richard Rodriguez, page 242
Family photo courtesy of the Port Authority PBA Inc.

James Romito, page 242
Family photo courtesy of the Port Authority PBA Inc.

John Skala, page 242
Family photo courtesy of the Port Authority PBA Inc.

Walwyn Stuart, page 242
Family photo courtesy of the Port Authority PBA Inc.

Kenneth Tietjen, page 242
Family photo courtesy of the Port Authority PBA Inc.

Nathaniel Webb, page 242
Family photo courtesy of the Port Authority PBA Inc.

Michael Wholey, page 242
Family photo courtesy of the Port Authority PBA Inc.

K-9 Sirius, page 242
Courtesy David Lim

✷ Index ✷